Feeding
Baby
Green

Feeding Baby Green

The Earth-Friendly Program for
Healthy, Safe Nutrition During Pregnancy,
Childhood, and Beyond

Alan Greene, M.D.

ORIGINAL ILLUSTRATIONS BY RICHARD SHEPPARD

JOSSEY-BASS
A Wiley Imprint
www.josseybass.com

Published by Jossey-Bass
A Wiley Imprint
989 Market Street, San Francisco, CA 94103-1741—www.josseybass.com

Jossey-Bass books and products are available through most bookstores. To contact Jossey-Bass directly call our Customer Care Department within the U.S. at 800-956-7739, outside the U.S. at 317-572-3986, or fax 317-572-4002.

Jossey-Bass also publishes its books in a variety of electronic formats. Some content that appears in print may not be available in electronic books.

Library of Congress Cataloging-in-Publication Data
Greene, Alan R., date.
  Feeding baby green : the earth-friendly program for healthy, safe nutrition during pregnancy, childhood, and beyond / Alan Greene.
    p. cm.
  Includes bibliographical references and index.
  ISBN 978-0-470-42524-4
  1. Infants—Nutrition—Environmental aspects. 2. Pregnancy—Nutritional aspects. 3. Pregnancy—Environmental aspects. 4. Sustainable living. 5. Green movement. I. Title.
  RJ216.G747 2009
  618.92—dc22   2009025873

Printed in the United States of America
FIRST EDITION
PB Printing   10 9 8 7 6 5 4 3 2

Contents

PART 4
From Babies to Toddlers (and Beyond)

Foreword

Frances Moore Lappé

WHEN I WAS carrying Anna thirty-five years ago, I'd already written *Diet for a Small Planet* and, fortunately, knew a lot about healthy eating for both of us. But so much more is known today and Dr. Greene brings it together in this book. He lays out essential truths and the new knowledge in a compelling way—backed by science and endorsed by personal experience. It is no wonder that Anna, now carrying her first baby, has found so much joy in reading and applying the wisdom Dr. Greene shares in *Feeding Baby Green.*

August 2009

Anna Lappé

ON HALLOWEEN NIGHT, as we heard trick-or-treaters squealing through our Brooklyn streets, we watched as a light-blue plus sign formed on our home pregnancy test. My first thought: "We're pregnant?!" was quickly followed by the realization that life as I knew it was going to change, permanently—and I was excited.

I predicted the usual things: an expanding waistline, achy hips, sleepless nights, and hormonal surges that would get me crying at public service announcements. Then I took my first bite of food, and I realized eating would be fundamentally transformed, too.

Crunching into that first bowl of cereal, I had the distinct feeling I was not only feeding myself, I was feeding my baby too. Quickly what I thought might be hard—giving up those glasses of Syrah or the Dragon Rolls at my neighborhood sushi joint—was surprisingly easy. Just as I wouldn't put Bordeaux in a baby bottle, I simply didn't have the taste for wine any longer. And raw fish? No thanks.

Hungry for a deeper understanding about what to eat while I was pregnant to ensure a healthy me and a healthy baby, I voraciously read pregnancy books. To say the nutrition information in many of them was sparse is putting it mildly. Most of the core lessons can be summed up in a few words: don't eat anything that might harbor food-borne illnesses. Deli meats, unpasteurized cheeses, raw fish, and raw meat are all off the list. Eat lots of healthy fruits and vegetables and drink lots of water.

Some books go beyond these bare mentions to add specific ideas about how to get enough protein, iron, and other key nutrients, but I was still hungry for more. I wanted to know about the connection between what I eat as a pregnant mom and what my baby experiences. I wanted to know about how to engender healthy eating habits in my child. I wanted to understand what to do *after* nine months.

This book was what I was looking for.

I first met Dr. Alan Greene in the summer of 2008 in Modena, Italy, at the International Forum of Organic Agricultural Movements. It was a fitting first meeting: Dr. Greene is a powerful advocate for organic foods as a way of keeping ourselves healthy and ensuring that our environment stays that way.

In this book, Dr. Greene combines his knowledge about the benefits of organic agriculture and his wisdom as a pediatrician to provide us pregnant moms and our partners with unique insights into the food life of babies *in utero* and during their first few years. His nonjudgmental approach to dietary and nutrition insights is refreshing. Putting away the "you-shoulds" and scare tactics, Dr. Greene has created a unique prenatal and postnatal guidebook to healthy eating for you and your baby. In the process, he dispels that tired myth I've been battling for years that kids just don't want to eat healthy foods. Tell that to the teens I've met farming in Red Hook, Brooklyn, who can't get enough of their arugula or the elementary school students in Berkeley who raise their own produce and scramble for seconds of kale.

I'm about halfway through my pregnancy, at that sweet point when I have just started to feel her little kicks, stretches, and dance jigs. (She's moving like mad right now; maybe she knows I'm talking about her.) In just a few short months, I'll meet my daughter.

Thanks to this book, instead of feeling that her birth—with the breast-feeding, bottles, and meals to come—is the *beginning* of my feeding her, I see it as the continuation of the nutrition and food lessons she's learning every day—and at every meal—through me. Now, instead of dreading her possible food finickiness, I am looking forward to exploring my daughter's taste buds and food delights, with the insights and tips this book has given me. I'm excited to share with her the love of diverse, nutritious, and green food my mother taught me, and that Dr. Greene celebrates here.

Midway through reading this book, I walked down to our neighborhood farmers market. It's January in Oakland, California, and the strawberry season has just begun. As someone who has lived in New York City for the past decade, fresh organic strawberries in January seemed like an apparition. (When I pried the farmer in amazement about the growing season, he answered matter-of-factly, "January to August." *January to August?!*) I selected one of the picture-perfect green baskets and popped a large juicy berry into my mouth. As the fruit's flavors burst onto my tongue, I appreciated it in a way I never have, thinking to myself (to her, really): *Bambina, this is what a strawberry tastes like.* And she loved it.

August 2009

Acknowledgments

"ITADAKIMASU." MY CHILDREN taught me this Japanese expression, said before eating, after some of them returned home from a school exchange program in Japan. Their hosts explained that it meant something like, "Respectful thanks to everyone and everything who brought this food to us."

We've incorporated this little ritual into our family meals for the last four years. We share deep thanks for good food and to those who work in the fields, who grind our grain, who keep shop, who cook, and who clean: all those who bring us good food—from the soil to the plate.

As each meal depends on many hands, so does each book.

Respectful thanks to my wife, Cheryl, for her role as inspiration, first reader, and creator of many of our best recipes.

Respectful thanks to my incomparable editor, Alan Rinzler, to his capable and talented wife, Cheryl Rinzler, and to my marvelous new colleague, Naomi Lucks, without whom this book would not have been completed until sometime next decade. Respectful thanks to my wise and winning literary agent, Vicky Bijur, and to the great crew at Jossey-Bass and John Wiley & Sons, including Jennifer Wenzel and Mike Onorato in marketing, editorial assistant Nana Twumasi, production editor Carol Hartland, copyeditor Donna Cohn, pager Beverly Butterfield, proofreader Joanne Farness, collator Sophia Ho, copywriter Karen Warner, publisher Paul Foster, and Debra Hunter, CEO. Thanks also for the helpful suggestions and criticisms of early readers Wendi Gosliner, M.P.H, R.D.; Amy Block Joy, Ph.D.; and Khanh-Van Le-Bucklin, M.D., and to Chef Suzy Farnsworth, who provided valuable feedback on the recipes.

Of course this book rests on the expertise of research scientists, nutritionists, pediatricians, and parents too many to name. I'm especially thankful for my own parents, who continue to teach me, and to my sisters and their families, with whom I've shared many of my life's most important meals.

Many thanks to the new breed of healthy-organic chefs who have influenced our lives and provided wonderful meals for our family. Special thanks to Jesse Cool, to Donna Prizgintas, to Akasha Richmond, to Ann Cooper, to Erin (and Ford) Andrews, and to Domenica Catelli for recipe consultation.

Thanks to all the people who submitted their personal stories to share. We didn't have room to use most of them, but we were inspired by your journeys with food.

A special thank you to the new breed of baby-food makers, who work tirelessly to provide an option for parents who cannot always make their own baby food, and many of whom shared their recipes with us because they want to empower parents in any way possible.

The chefs, baby-food makers, grocers, and farmers are part of a larger organic and natural food community that is changing my life and influencing the way we all eat. I will forever be grateful.

Thanks to my colleagues at Healthy Child Healthy World, the Environmental Working Group, the Society for Participatory Medicine, Ideasphere, SNAP!, the Center for Information Therapy, Lucille Packard Children's Hospital, and the Organic Center for your ongoing work on behalf of a healthier tomorrow.

I'm grateful for the entire DrGreene.com family (and especially Cheryl, Beverly Richardson, Lori Gonzales, Beth Ziesenis, Khanh-Van Le-Bucklin, M.D., Liat Snyder, M.D., Teri Smith, Brittany Richardson, Heather Cunningham, Sharlyn Richardson, Cindy Paiva, Claire Greene, Kevin Greene, and Jon Lebkowsky) for keeping us moving forward while I was in "book mode."

Thanks to Shelley Reichenbach for supporting us during this crazy time and for test cooking many of the recipes.

Thanks to my amazing kids, Garrett, Kevin, Claire, and Austin, who bore the brunt of so many precious hours spent with Dad tucked away in the scribble den writing, so that together we could share this book with you.

And respectful thanks to you, reader, for the part you play in feeding our next generation well.

Itadakimasu!

To friend and mentor

JULIUS RICHMOND, M.D.
(1916–2008)

U.S. Surgeon General

Founding Director, Head Start

*Chair, National Academy of Science's Forum
on the Future of Children and Families*

Champion of Children

Feeding
Baby
Green

Introduction:
TODAY'S GREENER WORLD

THE ENVIRONMENTAL MOVEMENT, which has become part of the mainstream conversation since former vice president Al Gore's popular book and film, *An Inconvenient Truth,* taught us that the health of our planet and the health of our species are tightly linked.

I'm grateful that the first book in the "Baby Green" series, *Raising Baby Green,* is playing a part in the Green Baby Movement, which is helping to raise consciousness about the connection between the health of the planet and the health of our children.

Parents today have an unprecedented awareness and eagerness about the necessity of providing safe, wholesome, nutritious foods for their children. At the same time, most Americans haven't yet learned about the lasting influence of those first months of nutrition, starting before the baby is born. They haven't yet started to make the changes we need for our children's sakes—the very changes you will learn in *Feeding Baby Green.* This revolutionary thirty-four-month program of nutritional training will guide you as you teach your baby to enjoy the perfect amount of a wide variety of healthy, nutritious foods—starting *before birth*—and during each of the crucial formative stages of your child's life. This simple program makes it easy to understand the why, when, what, and how of feeding your child, and puts you in charge—customizing the food you provide to satisfy the unique tastes and needs of your child and your family.

We stand at the crossroads of two divergent paths: one toward the principles of *Raising Baby Green* and caring for our planet, the other toward blindly ravaging our planet while unintentionally poisoning our children. Ironically, paying attention to the environment *is* paying attention to ourselves and our children.

Why We Can't Wait

Headlines confirm that most of America's eating habits during these last few decades don't work for our kids. We've trained them to eat too much and to eat the wrong foods. We're on a conveyor belt toward a preference for overprocessed, oversweetened, oversalted, empty calories, with unhealthy additives blended in.

When children use their own money to buy food, what do they choose?[1] They are most likely to buy (in this order) candy, chewing gum, soft drinks, ice cream, salty snacks, fast food, or cookies. Our culture has taught children to make unhealthy food choices, and we are already seeing the health consequences.

The problem of childhood obesity has drawn the attention of the press and policymakers, and for good reason. In the United States today, we are experiencing a true epidemic of childhood obesity. The 2007 Institute of Medicine progress report on childhood obesity asserts that frank obesity has increased more than fourfold since 1971 in school-age children. One out of three children in the United States is already overweight or obese.[2]

This has serious present and future health implications. When I started in pediatrics, not that long ago, high blood pressure, abnormal cholesterol, abnormal triglycerides, abnormal blood sugar, and waist size over thirty-eight inches were considered problems of middle age. It was very uncommon to see them in children. In a major recent study, two-thirds of today's high school students already had at least one of these problems![3] Even worse, type 2 diabetes, which recently was a problem of the elderly and the middle-aged that was so rare in teens that it was called adult-onset diabetes, has now overtaken type 1 diabetes (previously called juvenile diabetes) and is more common in some groups by age ten.[4]

At the same time that America's next generation is awash in excess calories, many children are suffering from suboptimal intakes of critical named nutrients, including fiber, calcium, iron, magnesium, zinc, folate, vitamin A, vitamin C, vitamin D, vitamin E, and omega-3 fatty acids, including DHA.[5]

Why Feeding Baby Green Means Taking a Stand

Many parents are overwhelmed by economic forces and time constraints that conspire to make it easier for them to settle for feeding their kids the less-than-optimal diet that most American kids eat. When both parents work, and children are busy with their own interesting lives, it can seem difficult to gather around the family table for a balanced meal in the way my parents' generation took for granted.

Worse, when parents choose food they face "assistance" from aggressive fast-food advertising campaigns, readily available convenience foods, and well-intentioned but overindulgent grandparents and other caregivers. It's no wonder that by eighteen to twenty-four months old, most children in the United States eat no servings of whole grains on a typical day. A third eat no fruit on a typical day. For those who do, the variety is limited to a few familiar fruits that will not provide the range of nutrients needed. By contrast, 91 percent of kids consume high-sugar desserts or sweetened beverages on a given day. For those who eat vegetables, French fries are far and away the number one choice.[6]

Parents want a change. In a major marketing survey:

- 95 percent of mothers believe there is a real obesity epidemic in the United States.

- 86 percent say, "Establishing good eating habits is among the most important lessons I can teach my child."

- 70 percent say that they don't have the *time* to feed their families the healthiest options.

How important is it to get kids to eat fruits and vegetables?

- 28 percent say important

- 67 percent say *extremely* important

But 80 percent of parents report that they are unable to feed their children healthy foods because they are inconvenient, or unavailable in their communities, or their children don't like the taste.[7]

That's about to change.

It's time for a fun, intuitive, delicious, radical change in the way most Americans feed their babies. We now understand much more about how long-term food preferences develop over time, and about how food choices affect both health and behavior. Now you will have the tools to create good eating habits by teaching your child to enjoy the taste of healthy food in the womb and immediately after birth, and you will have effective strategies for overcoming the challenges to eating well that they'll be faced with every day. Taken together, this knowledge will give you the ability to teach your baby to eat well for life.

Welcome to the delicious revolution!

1

How Nutritional Intelligence Benefits Your Family

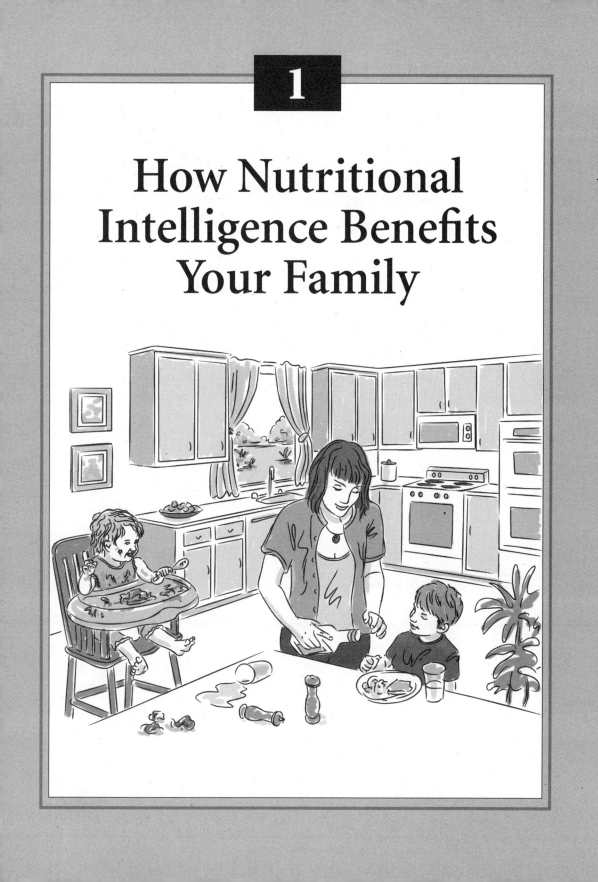

1

The Journey Toward
Feeding Baby Green

To get an idea of how *Feeding Baby Green* may help your family, imagine your child a few years down the road, eating lunch at school. Most of her friends have snagged French fries or chips to complement their meals. Instead, your daughter reaches for a salad and a yogurt.

Without you there to remind her, without her deliberating, she's made a healthy food choice because that's what she's learned to love.

Or imagine your young son at a local restaurant, ordering Brussels sprouts, or a fresh egg dish with mango salsa. He's *excited* to try the new flavors, *wants* to eat fresh, wholesome food.

For many parents, these scenarios seem almost unbelievable. Brussels sprouts? And no French fries? But these examples come from my own family, when my daughter, Claire, was in high school and our youngest, Austin, was a middle schooler. More than one chef has come to the table and complimented them on their adventurous palates and excellent taste. Other parents are even more likely to comment.

Parents today assume that children just won't enjoy certain foods for one reason or another (taste, genetic predisposition, because they are kids, and so on). They feel that they have to provide them with kids' meals, or endure food battles, or trick them by disguising the food so they'll eat it.

Feeding Baby Green will show you how to start creating an enjoyment of healthy foods even before birth. Their comfort foods can be healthy foods. Your kids won't need to settle for junk food. You won't have to resort to subterfuge, hiding healthy foods in comfort foods, if you want kids to eat fruits and vegetables. You won't need a team of medical or scientific experts or your own Ph.D. in nutrition to be able to feed your baby correctly. What you will need is an awareness of how food preferences develop over time, and a plan for how to use this knowledge to give your baby the best start. Knowing how it all works can empower you to be your own expert when it comes to feeding your child.

By starting early—even before birth—not only can you teach them to love appropriate amounts of healthful foods, but you can also help set the trajectories of their

- Health

- Intelligence

- Weight and metabolism

- Allergies and immune system

After you finish *Feeding Baby Green* you'll understand the simple plan to give your children the amazing gift of nutrition that will last a lifetime. *Feeding Baby Green* will create the blueprint for the generation that revolutionizes the way kids eat—a delicious revolution.

What Is "Baby Food"?

"Baby food" is a myth. A useful myth, perhaps, but it's worth pulling back the curtain to reveal that baby food was an invention of twentieth-century food corporations. The modern idea that babies should get entirely different fruits and different vegetables and different seasonings than what the rest of the family is eating is about as modern as the Gerber baby.[1]

When my father was born, "baby food" was rare. By the time I was a baby, in the late 1950s, a particular style of jarred baby food had become a shared rite of passage. In just one generation we had a change in how we feed babies that was so dramatic and so pervasive that it now seems like it has always been this way.

The fact is, babies don't need to eat baby food, particularly factory-made baby food from a little jar. Throughout the long, successful history of our species, babies have done remarkably well without it. We have always had food for babies, of course, but what we think of as baby food is a recent shared myth, made tangible as commercial products.

Before baby food, before kids' meals at fast-food restaurants, before infant formula, indeed in every century but part of the last, most young babies were breastfed, either by their mothers or a wet nurse. Later, after some teeth had come in, these babies began to eat much of what their parents ate—though the texture was changed to accommodate their young and growing mouths. And what these babies ate varied with the season of the year, depending on what was available locally.

When store-bought baby food was introduced, this innovation was embraced by parents and pediatricians alike because it offered a convenient, modern way to feed a baby. It seemed sterile, scientific, safe, and clean. And commercial baby food held out the gleaming promise of providing all the important fruits and vegetables all year round. The baby-food aisle in the supermarket had a shiny sameness—far removed from the earthy biologic rhythms of the farm, or of the breast.

"You can't, with ordinary home equipment, prepare vegetables as safe, as rich in natural food values, as reliably uniform as ready-to-serve Gerber products!" declared an early baby-food ad in *Ladies' Home Journal*.[2] The idea was that good baby food was scientific, uniform, measurable, twice-boiled, and perfectly smooth—and that you couldn't do it yourself no matter how hard you tried.

This way of thinking undermines people's confidence in being able to do something as basic as feeding their own baby. The task seems difficult, complicated, and exhausting. And the work entailed wouldn't just be bad for you alone. Another ad warned: "For Baby's Sake, Stay Out of the Kitchen! It isn't fair to baby—really—to spend long hours in the kitchen . . . For baby's sake and for your own—learn what doctors tell young mothers just like you." People who know better than you do say that it's better for food preparation not to intrude on your time with your baby. I've got a contrasting view.

It's important for a baby to see a real, yellow banana. To touch its skin. To smell its (to us) faint aroma. To see Mom peel the banana and playfully feed a chunk to Dad (or vice versa). To see Dad mash some with a fork and take a bite, perhaps with a dash of cinnamon, if you want to get fancy. For Mom to feed a bite of this not-uniform mash to the baby and to see her baby's grin.

Maybe it's a sweet potato. Let your baby see and feel its dark skin first. Then steam it (or microwave it for five minutes, if you like). See together how bright orange it is inside! Mash with the same fork. Maybe a little sprinkle of nutmeg or ginger. Or cinnamon. Or just serve plain—grins either way. And the simple leftovers will last several days in the fridge, or a month or more in the freezer.

Or maybe a steamed carrot . . .

Bringing real food into your family's life can be fun and energizing. It can take minutes, not hours, minutes that are well spent. It can provide better nutrition than what you would get from a pre-cooked food in a jar or a plastic tub. It can connect and draw people together. It can silently teach deep lessons about life and love and health.

You will probably end up choosing a combination of ways to feed your baby: many as simple as a mashed avocado, some that are more complicated recipes made at home, and some from among the better fresh or frozen ready-made baby foods you can buy (especially for when you are on the go).

But the fundamental difference with the ads above is that it's all your choice, your creativity, your control. And food is fun. It's messy. It's real. It's not supposed to be a chemistry experiment, concocted in beakers and flasks, but one of life's most frequent pleasures. A pleasure to be enjoyed and savored. A pleasure with the power to connect. Its place is near the center of a family's life, not as a distraction to be pushed to the outer margins.

Commercial baby food entered the scene as part of the larger processed, preserved, convenience food movement. It separated parents from their children. It trained babies to become ideal consumers of the low-quality foods you see many children and teens eating today. And much baby food found in today's supermarkets is still stuck in this twentieth-century industrial nutrition mind-set.

Gwen Greene holding baby Alan. Taken in Atlanta, Georgia, in 1959.

My Own Journey Toward
Feeding Baby Green

My parents were married in 1957—the same year that margarine sales first exceeded butter sales in the United States, General Foods introduced Tang breakfast drink as a scientific improvement over fresh-squeezed orange juice, and Kentucky Fried Chicken began selling chicken in buckets as a substitute for cooking dinner at home. In just a few months, the artificial sweetener Sweet'n Low would be introduced, along with the first diet cola.[3] A non-dairy coffee creamer wouldn't be far behind.

As I was preparing to enter this world, Pizza Hut first opened its doors, destined to become the world's largest pizza restaurant chain (and the world's largest user of cheese).[4] Domino's Pizza would be founded soon afterwards. General Mills introduced Cocoa Puffs cereal for kids, containing 43 percent sugar. Kellogg quickly followed with Cocoa Krispies, delivering 45.9 percent sugar.[5]

One Baby's Story

I was born in 1959, the same year that Enfamil launched its first infant formula and McDonald's opened its one hundredth restaurant.[6] That was also the same year that Hormel & Co. proudly sold its one billionth can of Spam (announcing that "94 percent of Americans" now enjoy Spam, but not mentioning that the processed meat product only contained 6 to 8 percent ham).[7]

The nation glowed with the optimism of science. In earlier decades, breast milk substitutes had been called artificial foods; now they were percentage formulas—science's improvements on breast milk. The great majority of mothers bought into this myth (literally) and chose these formulas for their babies over their own milk. These babies were now being raised on the steady, uniform taste of an infant formula, not the subtle, shifting rainbow of flavors found in breast milk.

For the first three months of my life, my mother had breastfed me exclusively. She was told by my doctor that it would be time to wean to formula at three months. She did start me on the bottle then, but she couldn't bring herself to stop nursing for another couple of months. I last nursed at five months old. At six months, my doctor told my mother it was time to wean from the bottle to a cup, using whole milk straight from the carton. No more formula, no more sterilizing the glass bottles.

My first bite of solids was the bland taste of processed white rice flour: boxed instant rice cereal, marketed as the best first food for babies. Along with other babies of my generation, I soon graduated to the salty, sugary, starchy tastes of overcooked jarred fruits and vegetables. My parents went along because, as experts and ads proclaimed, "They're the finest vegetables Baby can eat—and Baby deserves the best!"[8]

A shopping list survives from my early childhood. It was for the first day of a trip to visit my grandmother in Atlanta at my first birthday. It's striking to me that the only item we shared as a family was the milk. All of the vegetables and all of the fruit were entirely different.

It doesn't surprise me that just a few years later my favorite foods were canned fruit cocktail (in heavy syrup), pizza, SpaghettiOs, Wonder Bread, cheeseburgers, French fries, Twinkies, Ho Hos, and Hostess pies. My sisters' favorites were canned B&M baked beans and ultra-smooth instant mashed potatoes made from potato buds (which taste eerily similar to the instant white rice cereal of our first foods).

Monday A.M.
Apr. 25, '60

Dearest Mother,

We have reservations on Delta's flight 729 on Wednesday, April 27, arriving there at 7:10 PM EST. Hope you can meet us all right. We'll look for you at the usual place —— the baggage pick-up stand outside the terminal there.

It would be a tremendous help if you could buy some baby food in advance and have some on hand for at least the day after we arrive. See the following if you can:

- 2   JARS   GERBER'S   STRAINED EGG YOLKS
- 2   "   "   JUNIOR PEACHES
- 2   JARS   "   STRAINED VEAL OR LAMB
- 1   "   "   STRAINED PEAS

The first page of a shopping list that Gwen Greene sent to her mother in preparation for a family visit to Atlanta, Georgia, in 1960.

Alan Greene eating animal crackers, 1961.

My First Nutrition Decisions: Connections to the Past

During my preschool years, the food industry was industrious. Frito-Lay, Inc., was founded when I was two, introducing snack foods that would fill the lunchboxes of children across America. McDonald's one *billionth* hamburger was served by Ray Croc on television in 1963.

Cool Whip, an artificial substitute for whipped cream, was introduced when I was in first grade, and within only three months it was outselling all other whipped topping products. The Pillsbury Doughboy (Poppin' Fresh) was born that same year, a friendly, giggling marketing reminder that busy parents can save time by choosing tasty processed food products. Pillsbury crescent rolls made many visits to our family table during those years.[9]

My elementary school's food didn't have colors. We had a stainless steel cafeteria line with steam trays and a lunch lady. It's all steel and grey-green-brown-beige in my memory, warm and smooth and uniform.

I remember sliding the celery-green school lunch trays with their compartments to separate the entrée, two sides, and a dessert. The vegetables were overcooked and soggy, and often had a stringy texture that made them seem inedible to a kid (and yucky even now). It didn't matter much what was on the menu (except the longed-for pizza day, once a month).

More often than not, my sisters and I brought our own lunches with us to school. My mom prepared a fresh sandwich, and sent us packing with a small bag of chips, a piece of fruit, and packaged dessert.

There Was Something About That Sandwich, Though . . .

When I look back over my entire food childhood through the haze of memory, a few wonderful flavors stand out. We had a small garden in the back yard as I was growing up. I remember playing in the dirt with my father and planting seeds with a trowel. I remember pulling weeds every now and then, drenched with sweat, gnats buzzing about in the humid summers of the Washington, D.C., area. I remember laughing and chasing my sisters through the backyard sprinklers afterwards to cool off. And getting stitches in my knee from an enthusiastic run at a Slip 'n Slide.

And the lettuce! Before the summer we first had lettuce in our garden, I would only eat iceberg lettuce in Mom's sandwiches, and then only as a barely tolerated, barely tasted obstacle to the good stuff—a particular favorite was sliced turkey or meatloaf with lettuce, tomato, mustard, mayonnaise, and pickle.

But the lettuce I picked in our garden actually tasted different. It tasted really good to me. It made sandwiches better. It still brings a tear to my eye when I think of the sandwiches my mom made—and when she makes one for me now, as she did recently for my father and me to take to a baseball game, it transports me back to the summers of my childhood.

Another essential sandwich ingredient was . . . the tomatoes! We grew them from seeds, poking each one into the dark soil and splashing them with water. We

Alan Greene in middle school, Bethesda, Maryland, around 1974.

Greene kids ready to "work" in the garden of their Bethesda, Maryland, home in 1968. Standing: Alan Greene. From left to right in wheelbarrow: neighbor Linda Zell, Laura Greene, Lisa Greene.

marveled as the plants grew, the tomatoes appeared, and began to change from green to red. We learned the difference between the "mostly red" of almost ripe, and the "vivid red" of a firm, ripe tomato ready to explode with flavor.

In the lunchroom, I always held on to Mom's sandwiches with the home-grown, hard-earned lettuce and tomato, but I admit to sometimes trading my fruit with friends to try to score some extra sugar or salt. I'd also look for ways to finagle more opportunities for sugary, salty snacks after school.

But What Are They Putting in My Food?

I loved my mom's sandwiches, but my preference for the processed foods I was weaned on still ran deep. The Quarter Pounder, introduced in 1971, became my number one sandwich choice.[10] Pop Rocks were my favorite treat, and I loved M&M's. When Red Dye No. 2 was banned in 1976 because it could cause cancer and red M&M's disappeared for more than a decade, I grieved—but I took notice. I also paid attention when cyclamate, a very popular artificial sweeter, was banned because it was then thought to cause cancer. It's the first time I can remember ever thinking about the various unknown ingredients in my food.

I had also noticed when the pesticide DDT was banned because it was killing birds. I had been moved by Rachel Carson's *Silent Spring*, the

---

Feeding Baby Green Report

The DES Story

I certainly didn't connect my growing worry over food additives with a news story about the prescription drug diethylstilbestrol (DES). In an attempt to prevent miscarriages, this synthetic hormone had been given to up to ten million pregnant women in the United States since well before I was born. The hormone had been shown not to prevent miscarriages in 1952, but continued to be prescribed for that purpose anyway. How could a little dose of hormones hurt? And what does that have to do with the food I was eating as a kid?

We learned of the side effects of DES when it was too late: DES daughters were less fertile; the women who took it had an increase in breast cancer; and the grandsons of women who took DES were twenty times more likely to be born with hypospadius (where the opening of the penis isn't at the tip, but somewhere along the shaft). Doctors stopped prescribing DES to pregnant women in 1971 because it was found to cause vaginal cancer in DES daughters as young as eight years old.[11]

Giving DES to pregnant women was a tragic mistake.

I didn't suspect at all, and even today most people don't know, that DES was also given to our cattle. By the mid-1950s, about two-thirds of U.S. beef cattle were given DES. Hundreds of millions of Americans were getting small amounts of DES every day—without adequate safety testing. And when DES was stopped for pregnant women, it continued to be used in our cattle for the rest of the decade.[12]

I loved burgers. I was probably getting DES quite often.

definitive environmental awareness book of the 1960s. Like many of his generation, my father had been raised on a farm. Like so many in my generation, I was raised in the suburbs. At the time, we called it "progress." Part of this progress involved a veritable explosion of new chemicals in our environment. Many of them were in our foods or used in food production, and many had never been tested for health or safety. I knew of only three that had been banned, but it was enough to set me wondering if we really knew what we were doing.

As a student, I started asking questions about chemicals in our food and environment. I wrote papers, even running for student council president in the ninth grade on a platform that included better food in our cafeteria. But back then, we just didn't have the information that we do now to be able to make connections about our food and our health. Food industry giants were creating more and more synthetic ingredients for our dinner tables, but regulations did not require the companies to list ingredients on the label. I guess they thought we didn't need to know, and that if we did, we wouldn't make wise (or profitable) decisions with the information. After all, the companies said the synthetic ingredients were as good (or better!) than the all-natural originals, just as they told us partially hydrogenated margarines and trans-fat artificial creamers were the perfect substitutes for butter and cream.

Even though I knew about DDT and Red Dye No. 2, my unconscious cravings never listened. By high school, the pretense of my eating fruit and vegetables at school had disappeared. Hot dogs or cheeseburgers on white buns, slices of pepperoni or cheese pizza, fries, and soda were the typical lunch fare, occasionally punctuated with spaghetti or meat loaf. I continued to eat pretty well at home and on the weekends, but when left to make my own choices, I went back to the processed flavors and textures of my infant and toddler years.

I headed off to college at Princeton in 1977. For the first time, I made all of my own food choices twenty-four hours a day, seven days a week.

Where I got into trouble was the Commons, a large gothic hall with a seemingly limitless supply of the food I craved the most. The food wasn't great, but I could satisfy my yearnings. I can't remember even once choosing any vegetables or fruits or whole grains there. But I loved the meats and pizza and sandwiches and potatoes—and oh! the berry pies—does that count as fruit?

Just like many kids today, I chose unhealthful foods that affected my body systems and my weight. Not until my last two years as an undergraduate at Princeton did I learn to appreciate real foods over processed. This was the result of getting a part-time job in a kitchen. In my junior year, I joined Charter Club, one of Princeton's eating clubs, and worked in the kitchen to help foot the bill. I learned from Chef Steve what went into creating a balanced, varied monthly meal plan. I was involved in everything at Charter, from the meal planning to the dish scrubbing.

Like watching the tomatoes ripening with my father, being involved in creating the meals increased my appreciation of the end product as well as my understanding of the process. I began to prefer the taste of real food,

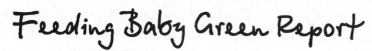

Feeding Baby Green Report

And Then, as 1980 Rolled Around . . .

Four other things happened while I was in college to further deplete the average American diet:

1. Coca-Cola began replacing half of the sugar in Coke with high fructose corn syrup, because sugar had gotten so expensive. This new ingredient would quickly become a major source of kids' calories.

2. The FDA approved aspartame (NutraSweet), another chemical ingredient that would be consumed in large quantities by millions.

3. McDonald's launched Chicken McNuggets, and they were an overnight smash hit.

4. The USDA, under President Ronald Reagan, declared that ketchup could be counted as a vegetable in school lunches.

Meanwhile, I decided to go to medical school.

thoughtfully prepared. It brought to mind the dinners my mother prepared, and, of course, those wonderful sandwiches. I was finally making a connection with other food memories from my childhood.

Medical Training and Firsthand Experience

I studied medicine at the University of California, San Francisco, which featured excellent nutrition teaching. Nevertheless, nutrition was a tiny part of my medical studies, and soon a tiny part of my life. The pace of training often led to vending machine meals or mediocre hospital cafeteria fare when we had the luxury of time.

My first son, Garrett, was born while I was in medical school. My first glimpse of him was a profound moment, but in those early days as a new dad, I had no idea of the scope of the new territory I was to discover with him and the three others to come. I delighted in teaching my son Garrett how to throw a ball, make animal noises, and recite the alphabet. As a doctor in training, I especially loved teaching him about his body parts ("Where is your sternum?" "Point to your appendix."). While I was an intern, I taught him to read, to add, and to brush his own teeth. But when Garrett was young, I didn't understand that teaching him about great food was one of the best lessons I could have provided.

Garrett learned his lessons about food from what we fed him. In 1986, we did what most other parents were doing. We introduced one food at a time, one taste at a time. We fed him so much of a single jarred vegetable that his skin literally turned a bit orange.

Thankfully, the baby-food companies had stopped adding so much extra salt to their foods for the youngest babies in 1977, but the brand we used continued to add it to the jars he began to eat from soon afterwards.[13]

My son also learned from what he saw us buy and eat. As a busy medical student, intern, and then resident, I regressed to eating a typical rushed American diet—with more convenience foods, snack foods, fast foods, and junk foods than I wished, and not enough fruit and even fewer vegetables. My habits were reflected in Garrett's food preferences.

I was more interested in nutrition than many of my colleagues in med school. I went out of my way to pursue extra learning in the subject. Still, I knew too little. And what I did know was often pushed aside by habit and a busy schedule. And Garrett was eating the way I was by the time he was two.

Alan Greene holding his first child, Garrett, moments after birth. Taken at the University of California, San Francisco, Medical Center Hospital in 1986.

When I Decided to Take Charge

Over the years my family grew. After Garrett, along came Kevin (the easy-to-please omnivore), then Claire (who really loves vegetables—and good chocolate), and finally, the adventurous Austin. With each child I knew more about nutrition and health and learned more about life from each of them. After I finished my training, my own diet had gotten healthier, and so had the family's.

In March 1996, something happened that radically accelerated changes in my personal food trajectory. Cheryl was nursing Austin. She and I were enjoying working together, both in parenting together as well as on our pioneering physician Web site, DrGreene.com (with Cheryl, the heart and soul of the site, handling the design, and me answering the questions). Life was good—no, great!

. . . until Cheryl discovered a lump in her breast. A chill went down our spines. Since many lumps prove to be benign, we hoped for the best. But the results of Cheryl's biopsy hit us like a truck.

From left to right: Claire, John, Gwen, Alan, Garrett, Austin, and Kevin Greene (Cheryl behind the camera). Taken in our backyard in 2006. On the menu: a selection of barbecued veggie burgers, barbecued chicken breast sandwiches, or barbecued hamburgers accompanied by salad, grilled summer vegetables, fresh corn on the cob, and watermelon. Every bite organic!

Cheryl had cancer. Stage III, high-risk, inflammatory breast cancer. The prognosis was grim. She was diagnosed in March, and not expected to live to see the New Year.

I helped Cheryl navigate through the best treatment options. Over the next year, she had four surgeries, thirty-eight radiation treatments, and ten harrowing months of intensive chemotherapy, followed by another eighteen months of experimental therapy.

Against all odds, Cheryl survived her cancer, and today, years later, is an ever more vibrant, giving woman. She is still the heart and soul of DrGreene.com. We're grateful every day for the opportunities we've had since 1996. Her cancer has changed us forever.

But that first night in March 1996 when we heard the diagnosis we had no idea what the future held. Her doctors told us in no uncertain terms that she must stop nursing. With tears in her eyes, she turned to me and asked,

"What do we feed our baby?"

As a pediatrician, I'd been asked that question by parents many times, but when Cheryl posed the question that night, it took on a new urgency. It started me on a path toward understanding the central role that nutrition plays in everyone's life, from potential mothers to preschoolers and beyond.

How This Book Developed

This book grew from my search for answers to that profound question, a search that began the same year that Dolly the sheep became the first mammal cloned from an adult animal, and that genetically modified foods first entered the market. When my last son was born, no one was eating genetically modified food; today more than 30 percent of our cropland is already planted with genetically modified crops, and most Americans eat genetically modified foods every day.

Our personal changes began right away, but my understanding of the importance of the food that we provide for our babies took much longer to develop into the strong, science-based system that you'll find in this book. As recently as 2000 I worked with Gerber to educate parents about the staging of foods according to what were then accepted guidelines of starting only one new food at a time, separated by several days, and of delaying certain foods such as egg whites, peanuts, or fish beyond the first birthday—or longer. I no longer agree with those out-of-date guidelines, but you may happen upon them in a Web search some day and you need to know that for me, this has been a long journey.

What Was in the Baby Food Jar?

As soon as Austin could eat solid food, jarred organic baby food was his standard fare, though we emphasized a variety of flavors and made some of our own. In February 1996, while Austin was still eating baby food, Marion Burros wrote a fascinating column in the *New York Times:*

THIS is not a trick question:
If you had a choice between feeding your baby a jar of mashed bananas that contained 80 to 90 percent bananas and one that contained 50 percent bananas, which would you choose?

And this is not a trick answer:
The vast majority of parents in this country choose the jar with 50 percent bananas, the rest sugar and modified food starch. That is what is sold by the Gerber Products Company, which controls about 70 percent of the baby-food market.[14]

Salt, sugar, modified food starch, and other thickeners were common ingredients in jarred baby or toddler food in those days, not so long ago. They were probably very common when you were a baby.

Our taste buds naturally steer us toward sweet and salty foods. These baby and toddler foods exploited the landscape of the tongue, and created artificial, pumped-up flavors that babies come to prefer, while saving the food manufacturers and marketers millions of dollars by replacing fruits and vegetables with inexpensive fillers.

But what made babies and toddlers smile has had lasting consequences for you and for me, and for a whole generation. It has programmed us to feel deeply that extra sugar, extra starch, extra salt are what we need. It has programmed us to accept processed, diluted, nutritionally depleted foods.

Some prepared foods were already available without the additives. Beech-Nut hadn't used any added salt since 1977 or starch since 1986, and since 1991 had reserved sugar for baby-food desserts. Earth's Best organic baby food and Growing Healthy frozen baby food, both barely blips on the baby-food radar in those years, didn't use any of those ingredients at all. That's part of why we preferred Earth's Best for Austin.

At the time, the Center for Science in the Public Interest, which publishes a valuable resource called the *Nutrition Action Health Letter,* compared 3.5-ounce jars of Beech-Nut Banana (without fillers) with Gerber's best-selling baby food, Bananas With Tapioca (Gerber's name for their modified food starch). Beech-Nut provided 244 milligrams of potassium, versus only 145 milligrams in Gerber, 1.5 grams of fiber versus only 0.7 grams, 68.5 International Units (IU) of vitamin A versus only 20 IU in Gerber, 0.9 grams of protein versus 0.5 grams, and 0.29 milligrams of iron versus 0.1 milligrams.[15] Most American babies were getting about half as much nutrition per bite. And learning to love it.

What was called tapioca on the label, by the way, was not natural tapioca, but a starch modified with chemicals such as acetic anhydride, propylene oxide, epichlorohydrin, sodium trimetaphosphate, and adipic-acetic mixed anhydride. And what was often called "a small amount of sugar" on baby-food labels could be as much as four-and-a-half teaspoons in a six-ounce jar.[16]

In June 1996, shortly after the publicity in the *New York Times* and the pressure from the Center for Science in the Public Interest, Gerber announced that they would be removing all of these additives from most of their foods for the youngest babies.

But this book isn't about how to feed your child high-quality jarred baby food. It's about real kids eating real food in the real world. Using your creativity and making your own good choices—and helping your children make their own good choices—is a pleasure to be enjoyed and savored . . . a pleasure with the power to connect us to each other, as a human family, and to the earth, where we live and grow.

The good news is that there are excellent solutions for feeding our babies that fit the busy lives of twenty-first-century parents, and still set kids on a road to great real food and great health. *Feeding Baby Green* is a revolutionary new program designed to provide children the food that is good for them even before they are born, while teaching them to enjoy healthy amounts of wonderful foods throughout their lives. *Feeding Baby Green* is not intended to be a diet or program you follow for a few years, until your child goes away to college: it's a fun and healthy way of eating and living that lasts a lifetime—for you *and* your children, and your children's kids too!

Ready? Let's get started.

What You Need to Know About Nutritional Intelligence Before You Begin

The *Feeding Baby Green* program in this book provides a practical thirty-four-month roadmap for giving your child the best start possible and for establishing a foundation for enjoying a lifetime of healthy eating habits. The program carries you from conception (and even before) through the first two years of life, with a glimpse into the future. Ultimately, you will teach your child not just to eat a healthy diet but *to enjoy* great food for a lifetime.

As parents, we have a deep, instinctual desire to feed our children well. But in today's world, that quiet voice of wisdom is often obscured by a dizzying array of options, the clamor of products marketed to parents, inherited processed-food habits, and the ever-increasing pace of life. *Feeding Baby Green* cuts through this clutter with a clear, intuitive path, rooted both in human history and in cutting-edge science. It's a choice that parents and kids will love—and will be very glad they have made.

This is a program of what I call *nutritional intelligence.* It's a powerful gift for your child. The late-twentieth-century way of feeding babies inadvertently trained children to enjoy the flavors and textures of processed foods, preparing them for classic kids' meal fare of French fries, cheese-burgers, chicken nuggets, and grilled cheese. *Feeding Baby Green* gives you what you need to train your baby's palate to appreciate the delights of the more complex flavors of healthy, unprocessed foods.

The Eight Essential Steps for Teaching Nutritional Intelligence

These eight simple steps to teaching nutritional intelligence will help you lay a strong foundation for building a healthy and delicious future for your child.

1. *Take Charge!* You are your child's first teacher, and the primary agent of change in the way she approaches what she eats. It's not an over-statement to say that unless you take steps to prevent it, your child's food style will likely become a blend of the way you eat and the pre-dominant American kids' food culture—weighted strongly toward the latter. The prevailing current is strong; but by making conscious choices now, you can make a lasting difference in your child's health and his enjoyment of food.

2. *Use Windows of Opportunity.* Every child has his or her own unique developmental progress. Yet the stages of early development—from birth through about the end of the second year—provide special opportunities for you to make a deeper impact on future choices more easily than it will be later on. Learn to advance your child's food devel-opment in coordination with other unique stages of development that you see happening in your baby. Being out of sync often leads to food battles or refusing healthy food. Working together is one of life's joys.

3. *Engage All the Senses.* Use your baby's senses, even before birth, to help teach her to love great food, to create a deep sense of familiarity and joy about these healthy foods, and to help forge the comfort foods of her future. Enlist food's many flavors, aromas, and textures, and even its appearance and the language you use to talk about food. As you learn to conduct the orchestra of her senses at each developmental stage, with just the right amount of repetition and novelty, healthy food will become a shared joy.

4. *Choose the Right Amount.* The amount of food your child eats—before birth and after—not only affects growth now but can change hunger, metabolism, and health far into the future. Learn how to tell how much and what to feed your child at every age, and how to help her learn how much is just right for her.

5. *Choose the Right Variety.* Repetition is critical to acquiring tastes for new flavors, but so is novelty. A balanced diet is just that: a wide variety of colors and types of foods that meet all of your child's nutritional needs. You'll learn to select foods that provide abundant nutrition, while creating a framework for nurturing an adventurous eater.

6. *Customize Needs for Every Body.* Learn to use foods to help address your family's specific health issues, including ADHD, allergies, asthma, cancer, diabetes, ear infections, and eczema. Learn to adapt the *Feeding Baby Green* program if you or your child has the "bitter taste" gene, and to fit your food preferences, schedule, beliefs, or culture.

7. *Exercise!* Exercise really is good for every body—yours and your child's. It's closely linked to how a body desires and uses food every day. Working in tandem with good nutrition, it's the best start you can give your baby. If fitness has been part of your life up to now, it can still be part of your life during pregnancy and early motherhood. It's never too early to begin modeling the joys of exercise for your baby, and to find ways to play together that encourage her to run, twirl, dance, catch and throw, and jump for joy!

8. *Reap the Benefits of Green.* Making connections—with where food comes from, with how it is prepared, and with others who share the food—is a powerful way to instill love for real food. The basics are simple: Eat seasonally. Eat locally. Grow something together. And choose organic. Avoiding extra hormones and toxic synthetic chemicals in our food and food containers is good for the environment and great for your baby.

As we move chronologically through the thirty-four months of the program, each chapter will address these keys. Now let's consider each of these basic steps in more detail.

Step 1. Take Charge!

What and how much your child likes to eat is not simply the result of happenstance. It's not random. It's not just predetermined by genetics. As a parent, you have tremendous influence over what your child will come to enjoy, and how much. Take charge early!

Taste acquisition comes through a complex interplay of our genetic predispositions and our experience. Whatever your baby's genetics, you can provide an array of experiences to help her learn to love healthy amounts of wholesome foods that will work for her. And it will feel instinctive and right precisely because it fits with your drive to nurture and to give your baby the best, and with your child's developmental drive to learn from you about the world at each stage.

Central to the idea of "taking charge" is first and foremost *taking charge of your own eating habits.* This one decision will make all the difference to you and your child.

Although the mechanisms are different before birth and after the baby is born, what parents eat and how much they eat influences not only the foods their baby will like and how much their baby will eat, but helps to set their baby's metabolism and weight gain trajectory.

I understand that changing your own eating habits can be hard. Even when people change the way they eat for a brief time—because they are suddenly worried about a health problem, or want to lose weight—they often snap back to their previous eating patterns. The deep grooves of many of these habits extend back to your own childhood. It often takes a major disruptive event such as being diagnosed with a disease—or having a child—to make a permanent change.

Having a baby may be your best opportunity to make changes that you—both parents, not only Mom—would like to make in your diet, either permanently or even just for those months when you have the biggest influence on your children. Having a new baby can provide an extra dimension and degree of motivation, and can even have an impact on your own nutritional intelligence.

One more note: Some parents confuse "taking charge" with dictating or micromanaging every bite their child eats. Nothing could be further from the true intention of this step! In fact, this kind of taking charge is ineffective, and can be counterproductive and even harmful. Instead, act from your confidence in yourself as your child's wise guide. In this book you will gain an understanding of what constitutes a healthy, balanced, green diet, and how your role as her "nutritional trainer" can help your child learn these lessons for herself and make good food choices on her own. If you do your best to maintain your high expectations, set firm boundaries (and gently pull her back when she inevitably steps over them!), and keep your warm, loving, positive attitude, you will be taking charge of your child's nutritional training in the best way possible.

Step 2. Use Windows of Opportunity

Food frustrations and battles often occur when we are not in sync with our kids' natural developmental urges and rhythms. With this program, you'll learn how to use your child's normal drives at each stage to help her learn great eating habits.

The ebb and flow of development creates transient eddies of opportunity, when learning and strengthening certain healthy habits is easy and fun.

This program is rooted in an understanding of the unfolding story of your child's development. Development is often partitioned into four closely interlinked lines: gross motor, fine motor, cognitive, and social-language.

I propose that there is also a fifth line of development: the development of eating habits and of flavor and texture preferences that comes with its own set of milestones. I call this "Nutritional Intelligence." There are many ways to describe or divide development, but I believe learning to be intelligent about what we eat is important enough to merit special attention, because eating is so central to overall health and behavior.

Just as there can be gross or fine motor or language delays that affect children's lives, I believe we have created an environment that fosters developmental delays in learning to like vegetables or whole grains. You and your child are part of the solution.

It's important to consider what else is going on in a child's development in order to teach him healthy eating habits. As children change in their physical and mental abilities, what motivates them also changes. As they grow, their interests, behaviors, and skills are inextricably linked to the cutting edge of their development.

The *Feeding Baby Green* program is organized chronologically around eight key windows of opportunity. You may have heard that there are language windows in early childhood, when it is easiest for children to learn to distinguish and say subtle sounds in different languages. They may be able to learn later, but earlier it's almost effortless.

This almost effortless learning can also happen with food! (When I say almost effortless learning, I mean for your baby—the teaching will require awareness and some work from you.) Learning the food of our culture is much like learning the language of our culture.

Even learning to love core foods we are designed to thrive on, such as fruits and vegetables, happens best during certain windows. Here's one:

Why will an eight-month-old put almost anything in the mouth to sample, even a rock, while a fourteen-month-old toddler will reject the flavor of a ripe peach? Because toddlers are built not to like or trust new fruits or vegetables indiscriminately! Historically, parents would not want their new walker to toddle out of their view to pick an unfamiliar berry or munch on a leaf of a random plant. The results of this experimentation might be disastrous! Toddlers are *supposed to be* picky eaters.

But six months earlier in their development, they are designed to sample a wide variety of foods. They are built to learn to enjoy foods their parents have let them experience repeatedly. It's a time for protected learning of the healthiest foods available to the family.

Today, though, most kids get only a few processed flavors during that crucial window just before toddling, when they are curious about everything they encounter. During that window they grow used to the taste and texture of peaches from a jar, but find the taste and texture of fresh peaches an unpleasant surprise when it is introduced later, during the toddler stage. If they are introduced to the flavor and then the texture of fresh peaches at key moments in their early development, most children will come to love peaches.

In this book, soon-to-be parents as well as those with small children will learn about the very best foods with which to nourish and nurture their children at each stage. It's important to note, though, that these stages do not correspond exactly to ages, but to stages of development. When it comes to feeding options, it's more important to pay attention to your baby than to the calendar.

I would not recommend starting solids, for instance, on a certain pre-ordained date. Different babies develop at different rates. Instead, this book offers general time frames, and specific developmental clues about when to move from one emphasis to the next. By learning to see these subtle and not-so-subtle cues, you'll become an expert on his mental, physical, and emotional development when it comes to food.

The earlier you start this program, the easier it is. But you can always jump to the chapter that corresponds to your baby's level of development.

Step 3. Engage All the Senses

It's important to engage all of the senses—taste, touch, smell, sight, and hearing—when training your baby's taste buds. Foods—with their bright colors, lovely aromas, and many flavors and textures—are perfect vehicles for engagement. And the language you and your baby use about food is an all-important component of continued enjoyment.

Engage with Flavor Infants have the ability to experience the basic tastes of life—sweet, sour, salty, bitter, and umami (or "delicious flavor" in Japanese, the taste found in such foods as mushrooms and cheese)—long before they are born. Four of the taste buds have been known for thousands of years. In 2002, umami was recognized as the fifth core taste. More recently, scientists have identified a series of receptors in the throat that also contribute to flavor, including one for heat (both temperature and capsaicin) and cool (both temperature and menthol). That's why peppers taste hot and mint tastes cool.

These basic types of taste buds are like the primary colors of taste—the millions of flavors we can taste are composed of some combination of these five. Pure flavors, like sweet and salt, are uncommon in nature and can be unnaturally powerful. Pure sugar, for instance, when fed to babies as sugar water, acts like a potent narcotic. Food companies have learned that by adding sweetness or saltiness to their products they can make them almost addictive.

For babies, and even for older children, all of their taste sensations appear to be stronger than ours—we slowly lose our sense of taste as we age. But because strong bitter tastes can overwhelm the others, their bitter sensation can protect youngsters from poisons and spoiled foods—or from vegetables like chard and broccoli, unless we train them early that these are safe and good.

The taste buds we are born with are just a blueprint for taste: our early taste experiences can be critical in determining our food preferences later in life. That's because one of the keys to acquiring new food preferences is *repeated, relaxed exposure to certain combinations of flavors at the right times*. It often takes fifteen or more exposures to a flavor before a child develops a taste for it. Don't give up too soon!

And don't be afraid to use the herbs and spices you love. These are a kind of cultural language—cumin and coriander, thyme and tarragon, turmeric and cardamom, tamarind and cloves—whose flavors and aromas can bring visceral feelings of memory and delight. Across the globe, people naturally feed their children the food of their own culture—spicy Mexican mole or Indian vindaloo, Thai papaya salad or Sichuan hot and sour soup, Polish braised cabbage or collard greens and black-eyed peas from the American South, baba ghanoush and hummus from the Middle East, hearty Mediterranean fish stews with fennel and garlic and saffron, Greek egg-lemon soup and tart feta cheese . . . And in the United States, Americans continue to enjoy the foods of their cultural heritage.

For many Americans, raised on bland foods themselves—even those with parents and grandparents who were born in other countries—the idea that babies and children might enjoy these "daring" foods can be a revelation. During the last half of the twentieth century, American baby food was bland and essentially spice-free—the first foods flavored only with sugar and salt. In contrast, most cultures have successfully used spices to welcome babies to the flavors of their society. Like the rolling sound of a perfectly pronounced French "r," spices are a language of food best learned before the first birthday. During the right moments, they are easy to learn to love. Missing this window may lead to later unpleasant struggles or to years of enjoying only bland flavors such as white bread and white flour macaroni and cheese.

Engage with Aroma Our sense of smell plays a subtle but powerful role in acquiring new food preferences. Try this: pinch your nose shut, close your eyes, and try to distinguish between a chunk of apple and a chunk of raw potato.

To most people, the two taste almost identical. Open your nose, though, and the familiar aroma of the apple—so subtle you may not even notice it—infuses the apple chunk with the cool, crisp taste that makes you say, "Apple!"

Now imagine a selection of food smells. Perhaps fresh-baked bread or a bubbling Italian sauce with garlic. A slice of lemon. A sprig of mint. Brewing coffee. Your body and mind begin to respond before the food ever touches your lips. A welcome aroma can awaken your appetite and make you long for a particular food.

Now think about this: You baby's sense of smell is far keener than your own. We'll explore ways to enlist aromas to entice your baby with wholesome foods.

Engage with Sight The sense of sight is surprisingly strong in developing kids' food preferences. The appearance and color of the foods, the look of the foods they see others eating, scenes of shopping and food preparation, and food in the media. They're watching.

And of course, this all changes along a developmental arc. For instance, color vision appears right around the same time that babies begin to sit with support—and this can be a game-changing event. Babies' fascination with bright colors provides a new opportunity to reinforce or introduce a love for colorful vegetables and fruits.

Engage with Sounds and Language How we talk about food to our kids and in front of our kids makes a difference. Children are listening, even before they are born, and are rapidly learning what sounds and tones of voice mean.

We now know that how we talk when kids are exposed to certain foods can influence how much they like them. Begging, coaxing, and making airplane noises are out. Naming foods is in. All other things being equal, they will be drawn to items whose names they recognize. Later, adding adjectives before a food name could actually make food taste better.

The sounds foods make when we eat them or cook them are also important. The snap of a fresh carrot, the crunch of celery, bubbling soup, sizzling stir-fries . . . these sounds all play a part in our enjoyment.

Engage with Touch Texture training is another important aspect of nutritional intelligence. In the second half of the twentieth century, pureed foods have been made overly smooth. Thus kids today may love pasta with tomato sauce but not fresh tomatoes—or even a chunkier sauce made of fresh tomatoes and other vegetables. They will eat spongy white bread but not hearty whole grains.

Right from your baby's first bite of solid food, *Feeding Baby Green* will guide you along the texture path, incorporating some soft lumps of real food, ground a bit but not completely blenderized, to give your child the experiences needed to acquire a broad palate for great food.

You will discover how to work in sync with your child's developing tastes to make better nutrition choices easy, fun, and practical. At each stage you'll learn what flavor combinations to focus on, when to persist and when to quit, and how to make the most of the flavors they already love. We'll also consider the order in which you introduce tastes and textures.

Along the way, it's important for babies and toddlers to handle real food. This will become especially important when they begin the stage of holding finger foods; but even before then, the sense of touch can connect them to what they will later eat.

For kids who will be eating some mashed avocado, for instance, an avocado can be a great item to hold and explore: to feel the weight of it, the bumpy green skin, the smooth dip where the pit was removed. Or the leathery orange peel of a small tangerine, and later its nose-tingling aroma and unique flavor. Lemons are among my favorite toys for babies: they can roll them around like balls, and later watch as your drop slices into a big glass jug of water on the kitchen counter.

Step 4. Choose the Right Amount

Deciding what and how much to feed yourself and your baby should be fun, easy, and natural. General guidelines for how much of which foods to eat at each stage will make it simple for you to provide the optimal ingredients for your child to thrive.

You'll learn at what stage to feed on demand, and when to move to a schedule as a family. And you'll learn how to encourage and train babies' inborn skill of knowing just when to stop eating (rather than quash that ability, as we inadvertently did to an entire generation).

When it comes to their health and to weight, what kids drink is sometimes as important as what they eat. Learning to love healthy amounts of healthy beverages is also a part of *Feeding Baby Green* all along the way.

To help fill in the gaps, you'll also get the straight scoop on supplements: preconception, prenatal, nursing, infant, and toddler—what to look for, what to avoid, what matters, and what doesn't.

Step 5. Choose the Right Variety

While you train your baby's taste buds for the future, you will also be giving her the very best right now. During this critical thirty-four-month period, every ounce of tissue in your growing child's body will be assembled from food: what Mom eats, what parents provide, and what they allow.

Choosing the right variety and balance of different foods gives optimum fuel for today, as well as ideal building blocks for the growing body. It delivers the tools needed for the body to prevent and repair damage.

Later, I'll provide a list of twenty-one different families of food that humans have eaten for thousands of years (see the "Experience Biodiversity in Your Own Kitchen" in Chapter Four and also the checklist at the back of the book). By teaching your child to enjoy something from each of these families, you will be ensuring a lifetime of abundant variety of the many healthful nutrients food has to offer. At each stage you'll also get general guidelines for balancing this variety—how much of baby's diet should consist of meat, grain, fruit, or vegetable.

Most of the real food concerns that parents express to me in person and online come down to questions about variety. Their children like only a small selection of foods. *Feeding Baby Green* will teach you to foster a delight in variety, to help prevent extended "food jags" (demanding the same food day in and day out) that are common in so many children, and how to deftly deal with food jags when they inevitably occur. You'll also find in *Feeding Baby Green* tasty sample recipes to give you ideas of the kinds of things to eat to make the biggest difference. These include meals for parents to eat before the baby is born and afterwards, as well as meals that you can all share as a family when your toddler is able to handle a fork and spoon. The recipes have been tested by a professional chef, Suzy Farnsworth, who lives in Menlo Park, California, where she was able to purchase the necessary ingredients for all the dishes for under $200.

Step 6. Customize Needs for Every Body

The choices you will make as you follow the suggestions in *Feeding Baby Green* will work best if they really fit the needs of your family and your child.

The *Feeding Baby Green* program can work well whether you are a vegetarian or an omnivore. You can adjust it to fit particular foods you want to be sure to include in your family's diet, or foods you want to be sure to avoid. You can adapt it to those born with a gene that makes certain vegetables taste more bitter. And you can adjust it to help prevent specific health problems that may run in your family.

Eating to Prevent Problems This section in each chapter will focus on prevention. Eating the right foods in the right amounts at the right time can help prevent both diseases and allergies. Did you know that following a Mediterranean diet during pregnancy has been linked to substantially lower asthma risk for babies? You'll learn more in Chapter Three about this diet high in plant foods (fruits, vegetables, wholegrain breads and cereals, legumes, and nuts), moderate amounts of dairy products and eggs, and very little red meat. The diet is also high in olive oil and fish.

Allergies are an increasing concern for many families. You'll learn how the timing of starting different foods for your baby relates to developing allergies and eczema. When is the safest time to start strawberries for a baby? Yogurt? Peanuts?

Some of the most common problems new parents encounter involve sleep issues. We'll discuss the changing, two-way relationship between food and sleep. How do sleep habits affect eating? How do eating habits enhance or disrupt sleep—theirs and yours?

Eating as a Message to Your Genes Not too long ago, scientists used to think that DNA was a big but simple molecule, not too different from others. The seemingly random string of A, C, G, and T components wasn't believed important. Then, in the 1950s, James Watson and Francis Crick deciphered the double-helical structure of DNA and how pairs of these four components formed a code, a language that is central to describing who we are. This is so recent in the span of human history that

James Watson is still alive as I write this paragraph. Yet this understanding of DNA has revolutionized our understanding of biology, of genetics, and of life itself.

In the twenty-first century, a revolution has begun in how we understand food. The science of nutrigenomics teaches us that what we eat is also a language, a code. What and how and when we eat is one of the most direct ways we can turn on and off specific genes. How do we "program" our bodies? Through the molecular language of how we eat.

Each bite we eat triggers a complex, orchestrated array of metabolic processes. Eating good food in the right amounts and at the right times turns out to be a powerful lever—far beyond anything we had ever thought.

As one example, something as simple as which oil you choose to dress your salad can send a radically different message to your genes. Oils rich in omega-3 fatty acids, for instance, such as walnut oil or flaxseed oil, send a message to a receptor called PPAR-alpha, which in turn flips switches, turning on genes to improve fat burning and to reduce inflammation. Primarily choosing a "vegetable oil" such as the corn oil or cottonseed oil found in many commercial salad dressings can have the opposite effect, decreasing fat burning and increasing inflammation—not what most of us need in today's environment.

If we are carried by the tide of typical American food choices, we send our bodies confusing, contradictory, or harmful messages. With just a little thought, though, we can enjoy the optimal settings that good food can provide. The simple program I lay out in this book takes this emerging science into account.

Eating to Fit Your Lifestyle This book will provide guidance not only for parents who'd like to make all of their own baby food in only an hour a week, but also for parents who choose to buy only premade baby foods—as well as those parents who choose to do a bit of both.

This should not be time-consuming, but a practical alternative to the fast-food status quo. The program allows for flexibility to fit your own food preferences and eating style. It will give you the tools you need to help your baby learn to like the foods that you choose from your own heritage, whatever it is. The program is also flexible enough to fit different budgets, different family structures, and different schedules.

Step 7. Exercise!

Today, good nutrition combined with a moderate level of exercise is generally advised for every healthy woman before, during, and after pregnancy.[1] This is great news for active women who want to keep active, and important information for women who tend to a more sedentary lifestyle. Any mom will tell you: the better your fitness level, the better you will feel about yourself and your changing body, the more quickly you will recover from delivery, and the more joy and energy you will have to give your family.

And it's not just moms who need exercise. Your child's growing body is built to move! Exercise really does build strong bones, healthy hearts, and (along with healthy eating) helps children avoid obesity and obesity-related illness such as type 2 diabetes. According to the American Heart Association, the benefits of exercise for children are many: controlling weight, reducing blood pressure, raising HDL ("good" cholesterol), reducing the risk of diabetes and some forms of cancer, and improving psychological well-being and self-esteem.[2]

Step 8. Reap the Benefits of Green

The final key to revolutionizing the way our children eat is to connect the dots about where food comes from, its nutritional and organic purity, and its impact on sustaining the future of our environment. Food doesn't magically appear in take-out containers through a window in your car. Learning—firsthand, if possible—about where food comes from, and how it grows, can change your child's relationship to food.

Learning that sharing food is part of being a family is also important for solidifying and maintaining the gains you make in the first thirty-four months. The goal isn't to have a two-year-old who eats a diet that reads like a greasy kids' meal menu, but one who enjoys smaller portions of whatever healthy and tasty food the rest of the family is eating.

And all of this connects the dots back to the environment. It leads to nurturing and protecting our soil, our water, and our air. It's one of the greenest things we can do. That's why teaching children to enjoy healthy amounts of real, wholesome food is *Feeding Baby Green.*

Over the last fifty years, conventional agricultural techniques have resulted in depleted soil and bland produce. In addition, the animal foods we eat and drink have been raised increasingly on refined grains rather than rich pastureland.

In one recent analysis of more than one hundred studies comparing the nutrient levels of organic versus conventional crops, items of organic produce—foods grown *without* the use of chemical fertilizers, toxic synthetic pesticides, antibiotics, cloning, or genetically modified seed but *with* a reliance on cultivating healthy, living soil to produce healthy plants—averaged 25 percent more healthful nutrients per serving. The health of soil, the health of plants, the health of animals, and the health of people are all linked.[3]

Whether you choose organic or conventionally grown food, you tend to get more nutrients if the food was recently harvested or flash frozen quickly after harvest. You also tend to get more flavor—the two are closely connected. It's best to shop fresh, local, and in season during the thirty-four months of *Feeding Baby Green* and afterward.

Besides possibly providing fresher foods with fewer chemicals, local food choices can help to reduce or eliminate the carbon footprint created by trucking, shipping, and airfreight to deliver nonlocal food from medium range or often even huge distances (China, Chile, Africa). Eating local foods also saves precious resources and decreases the production of transportation-related emissions and other toxins.

As we maximize the variety of beneficial nutrients we feed our children, we also want to minimize their intake of the mixtures of artificial sweeteners, high fructose corn syrup, trans fats, coal-based artificial colors,

Feeding Baby Green Tip

The Recipes: Dairy and Sweeteners

In our recipes we always prefer to use organic produce, dairy, and meat products when possible. We also prefer to use the natural sweetness of fruits and vegetables. I don't like introducing added sweeteners in the first two years. And remember: NO HONEY IN THE FIRST YEAR.

You can choose between nonfat, low-fat, and whole milk (or substitute soymilk), according to these guidelines:

- **Babies:** Fat is important for brain growth. Before the first birthday, the dairy your baby gets should be whole. Because so many American kids get so much fat in their diets, the latest AHA recommendations are two-percent milk from age one to two and nonfat thereafter. The American Academy of Pediatrics still says whole milk to age two. Generally, nonfat or one-percent milk is not appropriate before the second birthday.[4]

- **During pregnancy:** Using low-fat or nonfat milk can be an important way to get your calorie totals in line. I'd rather see you use heart-healthy fats like olive oil and omega-3s than extra-saturated fats like milk fat.

chemical preservatives, and toxic synthetic pesticides that are regularly used in commercially produced food. Mixtures of these chemicals often have a combined effect on growing bodies that is greater than the effect of each ingredient in isolation.

A 2008 analysis has shown that by choosing organic produce across the board you can slash pesticide exposure from food by about 97 percent.[5] You can also greatly reduce pesticide exposure just by choosing domestic produce in season. The common lists of most contaminated fruits and vegetables seen in the media take into account the amount of pesticides, but not their toxicity. A 2008 Organic Center analysis of USDA data on pesticide amounts cross-referenced with EPA data on pesticide toxicity provides a different shopper's guide—depending on whether the produce is from the United States or is imported.[6] Many foods raised in foreign countries have more pesticides than those produced in the United States, whether organic or not. You'll learn more about this in Chapter Three, Early Pregnancy and Before.

Let's Get Started

The thirty-four-month *Feeding Baby Green* program provides key answers for parents seeking healthier, stronger babies, including how to

- Obtain peak brain development

- Set optimum metabolism

- Achieve ideal weight

- Make food battles unnecessary

- Prevent allergies and asthma

- Teach your children to love healthy food forever

After all, just knowing the best foods would not be very helpful if you didn't also learn how to teach children to love these healthy foods in healthy amounts.

How can pregnant moms transform their own eating habits to help their babies' favorite foods become the ones that are best for them? And how can parents help create a lasting love for vegetables, fruits, and whole grains in their children by the second birthday? How do they prevent their children's food drives from being tricked by empty calories, added fats, sweetened drinks, and other nonnutritive kid-friendly foods? Throughout the program you'll learn the stage-specific keys to how to do all of this and more.

My wife, Cheryl, and I have included a number of recipes in this book that are drawn from foods that have become favorites in our own home, even now, when our youngest is a teenager. All of the recipes, no matter what chapter they are in, can be used in the following ways: during pregnancy and nursing, to eat as a family by pureeing portions for your baby, to use as dips for finger foods, and to share as an entire family as soon as your baby is eating food in the same consistency that you are.

Cheryl and I recognize that parents have busy lives (we do!). Planning ahead can help immeasurably, and doesn't take a lot of extra time. Simply make extra food for babies and toddlers and freeze what you can't use within twenty-four hours. I like Fresh Baby's BPA and phthalate-free trays (www.FreshBaby.com) with snap-on lids, which let you freeze your homemade baby food in one-ounce cubes.

But just planning ahead isn't enough for all situations. If you're traveling, or simply pressed for time, there are now some wonderful organic baby food companies that make fresh and frozen foods. Many of them offer flavors that are great examples of the principles you'll learn in this book. We're so impressed that we've included a few of their recipes scattered throughout this book.

❧

As we noted in the beginning of our first book, *Raising Baby Green,* having a baby changes *everything:* your priorities, your awareness, the way you think about your responsibilities. I hope it will also affect the way you think about the food you eat, and how you choose to teach your child about food and its connection to her own body and the world we live in. I hope you and your family continue to enjoy the many benefits of living green in the years to come, just as my family has.

Your personal journey to *Feeding Baby Green* begins on the very next page. Let's join together in the delicious revolution.

Bon appétit!

2

Pregnancy

Early Pregnancy and Before
(FIRST TEN WEEKS)

When I'm in the delivery room and see a new baby being born, I often notice one of the parents taking a quick peek to count that there are five fingers on each hand and five toes on each foot. Each time, I marvel afresh that every finger and every toe, and everything in between—everything that parents see when they look at their baby—has been transformed and reshaped from the food eaten by Mom (and to a tiny but significant extent, Dad), either during pregnancy or beforehand.

Simply put, babies are built from food.

Babies Are Built from Food

When a brand-new baby opens her eyes and, for the first time, settles her gaze on her parents with a spark of recognition, something very complex has taken place. The light in the room has focused through a tiny living lens to project an image on the canvas of tightly packed nerve cells in the back of her eyes. The postage-stamp of tissue that we call the retina contains miraculous little rods or "black-and-white" receptors that photograph the ever-changing patterns of light and darkness before her eyes. They trans-form images from across the room into coherent neural signals that race along the optic nerve, through the optic chiasm, separating and rejoin-ing until they reach the occipital lobe of her brain, a processing system of daunting speed, power, and complexity.

Before long, the rods will be joined by more than five million cones to analyze the different wavelengths of light that we call color. Underlying this is a complex network of intermediary cells (bipolar cells, horizontal cells, and amacrine cells) that functions much like a powerful computer to interpret the wealth of data generated by the proportionately differ-ent stimuli to the cones and then upload it rapidly to the server in the occipital lobe.

Then, as quick as her next glance, the patterns change, and her eye is able to generate another picture of the world around her.

When your daughter sees your eyes, the image will be combined with data from other sources—the sound of voices she has been listening to in the womb for months, and your own faint scent. Transmitting and pro-cessing each input is a marvel in itself, and each is then compared to her store of previous experience and to deep and ancient instinctual patterns etched by genes into her unconscious mind. Then various glands secrete a tiny liquid orchestra of hormones that will help sway her choice to focus on your eyes.

And all of this intricate, invisible complexity in her first glance has been built out of food.

The realization that babies are built from food is both liberating and inspiring. With a new baby, you have the ability to "get in on the ground floor" when you invest in your child by making healthy food choices.

During pregnancy, and in the months before, each healthy food choice has a bigger payoff than at any other time of life. Even a little change in the right direction can have big rewards. It can help you become even better soil in which your child grows.

As we'll see, a mother's body is designed—with its special cravings and aversions, with its changing sense of taste and smell—to help choose the best foods for her baby. And her baby is designed to make the best use of those foods, to learn from her mother about what foods to eat, how much to eat, and how to use those calories. It starts even before she is born.

Before Pregnancy

Why not be as healthy before you get pregnant as you want to be during pregnancy? If you are trying to conceive, I suggest preparing your body in the following ways:

1. Take a prenatal vitamin every day for at least three months before getting pregnant.
2. Do what you can to eat a variety of healthy, real foods: vegetables, fruits, whole grains, beans and nuts, and good sources of protein and calcium.
3. Aim to be at a healthy weight for you.
4. Get at least thirty minutes of moderate or strenuous physical activity every day.
5. Stop smoking. Call 1-800-NO-BUTTS for help.
6. Only drink alcohol in moderation, and not inadvertently when you might conceive.
7. Avoid toxic exposures, including chemicals or solvents at home or at work. Talk with your health care provider about any medicines or supplements you might be taking now.

Much of what baby needs for the first fifty-six days of rapid and incredible development actually comes from what the mother has eaten in the previous three months. That's why the Center for Disease Control (CDC) urges women to get plenty of folic acid if they might become pregnant.

Dad's diet may also help babies even before conception! And taking a multivitamin in the three months before pregnancy may be as important for Dad as it is for Mom (though he shouldn't take the same prenatal vitamins—they contain far too much iron for men).[1]

Researchers have found that men who take in enough folic acid before fertilization may help their offspring be less susceptible to cancer, according to a study published in the February 2001 issue of the journal *Fertility and Sterility*.[2] For years, women have been encouraged to get enough folic acid to help prevent birth defects. Now it appears that folic acid can also lead to strong, healthy sperm that can produce healthier kids.

This breakthrough suggests that other factors in the father's life not yet looked at may also play a role in the strength and vitality of his sperm and the subsequent health of his children.

My previous list of seven suggestions for hopeful parents is for both men and women. The most recent research suggests that prospective dads should get at least 700 micrograms of folate daily, from food, supplements, or a combination thereof.[3] Fruits, vegetables, and nuts are rich in other nutrients that may also be helpful; conversely, tobacco, pesticides, and other toxins may damage sperm. Most studies focus on the three months before conception because it takes about three months for sperm to reach maturity.

What parents eat before pregnancy may have an even bigger effect than we once thought. Researchers at the universities of Oxford and Exeter had mothers keep a food diary before and during early pregnancy. Mothers who skipped breakfast or who ate low-fat or low-calorie diets before conceiving were more likely to have a girl. Mothers who ate more calories and more nutrients, such as calcium, potassium, and vitamins C, E, and B_{12} were more likely to have boys. So were those who regularly consumed cereal for breakfast (often fortified with vitamins and minerals). The effect was small—the odds of having a boy went from about 45 percent in one group to about 56 percent in the other.[4]

This is only one study, and it may not prove true, but it is consistent with the tendency of some animals to vary the proportion of genders depending on environmental conditions. The idea here would be that having human men in the tribe is riskier than having women. Men, on average, require more calories and more protein, but are more vulnerable and have a shorter average lifespan. During times of plenty (signaled by more calories and more nutrients in the mother's diet), it may be worth the risk

Feeding Baby Green Tip

Hydration Solutions

During pregnancy, it is especially important to ensure that your body has the fluids it needs to support all the changes necessary to support you and your baby—but it's not always easy to remember! Here are two solutions that make staying hydrated simple and fun.

The Family Water Jug

We always have a large "lemonade jar" with a spigot sitting on our kitchen countertop. Most days we fill it with ice and add some fruit, vegetables, or herbs, then fill with water. Every time we walk into the kitchen we're reminded that we need to drink more water!

Our favorite add-ins are:

- Fresh spearmint (it grows wild in our garden—to get maximum flavor, gently squeeze and crush the spearmint before adding it to the jar)
- Cucumber slices
- Lemon slices

Don't retire the jug when you bring your baby home! You'll need to stay hydrated while nursing, especially at the beginning. And your family will always enjoy this refreshing hydration choice.

Mocktails

Colorful and delicious "mocktails" are perfect when your sensitive tummy is screaming "No!" to food—they keep you hydrated, and help you keep up your weight. During the first few months of her pregnancy, sometimes these were the only calories my wife, Cheryl, felt like consuming—and they helped get her through some very rough times.

They're also a great alternative to cocktails, wine, and beer, especially if you are at a party or out to dinner with friends. Ask the bartender (or your partner) to mix up one of these combinations—but go light, because they can be loaded with calories.

Here are a few of our favorite combinations:

- Sparkling water, tart cherry juice, twist of lemon
- Sparkling water, cranberry juice, slice of lime
- Soda water with acai juice, pineapple juice, spear of pineapple
- Soda water, grapefruit juice, stalk of celery or a green olive

to have a higher proportion of men to help the tribe expand and grow. During lean times, it may make more sense to depend on the sturdier bet of having a higher proportion of female offspring to nurture the tribe and see it through this time of famine.

Beyond this, a mother's prepregnancy weight—her own metabolic set points—can influence a child's later metabolism and weight gain. With all of these things, it's never too late to make positive changes, but the earlier we start, the bigger the benefit.

Your Baby's Development

The centerpiece of your child's development in early pregnancy is an utter and complete transformation. Your baby began as a single fertilized egg, too small to see, and then divided into two identical cells, which each divided again.

By day 56 after conception (which corresponds to about seventy days after the last menstrual period, or what we call ten weeks pregnant), dizzyingly fast growth and transformation has resulted in a tiny, well-formed human fetus. Your little one now has elbows and knees, eyelids and nipples, and hair follicles on the chin and upper lip. A working diaphragm separates the tiny lungs in the chest from the intestines in the belly. Working kidneys now allow your baby to help produce part of his own water-filled world. As we'll see in the next chapter, your little ten-week-old gourmet now has working taste buds. And on those baby feet with teensy separate toes are a brand-new set of footprints the world has never seen before.

This is one of the most complicated building projects ever completed, on a time schedule that boggles the mind. Proportionally, it outmatches the building of the Pyramids or a modern skyscraper. Dozens of experts couldn't possibly coordinate and manage this phenomenal cascade of events.

And yet this wonder of the world has happened successfully again and again throughout history, with everyday parents. This was your own story, before memory, inside your own mother. And it was hers before you.

By the end of this time, your baby has already made it through life's most precarious stage—more babies are miscarried before day 56, often without parents ever knowing they were pregnant, than are carried full term. You have already ferried your baby safely across the period of greatest changes and most critical growth.

At the end of this elegant frenzy of growth, your baby is about an inch-and-a-half long, from stem to stern, but weighs only about one five-hundredth of a pound. This doesn't take a lot of calories. What it does take is protection.

Mother's Changes, Sickness, Aversions, and Cravings

As baby is beginning to develop, many mothers experience a combination of fatigue, a turning up of the volume of their bitter-sensing taste buds, a heightened sense of smell, and perhaps morning sickness.

Food aversions are common at this time, especially to foods that spoil easily or that naturally contain toxins. Sometimes this is called the "elevated disgust sensitivity" of the first trimester. One study found that pregnant women are more likely to react negatively to just the odors of

Feeding Baby Green Report

Ginger

An analysis of six randomized, double-blind, controlled trials published in 2005 confirmed what many mothers have known for a long time: ginger can significantly reduce both nausea and vomiting in early pregnancy, safely and without side effects.[5]

It doesn't take much: an inch of ginger root, sliced a few times and steeped in a cup of hot water, can make a soothing tea. Or you might try mashing some sweet potatoes with a bit of grated ginger and orange juice. Or simply grate a bit of ginger over rice.

Enjoy inhaling the aroma of ginger on your fingertips! Ginger will be a great flavor to teach your baby to love. It's delicious, and packed with anti-inflammatory, anticancer, immune-enhancing phytochemicals.

rum, cigarettes, and coffee. I suspect that these are all different ways to accomplish the same thing: to protect your baby during this most vulnerable period.[6]

What about those famous pregnancy cravings, such as pickles and ice cream? For some women cravings are not much of an issue; for others they are intense and specific. My wife, Cheryl, had an intense relationship with tuna fish sandwiches. The most popular cravings vary from culture to culture. In India, sour foods top the list.[7] Probably the most common cravings in the United States are for fruit, fruit juices, dairy, ice cream, chocolate, and other sweets or desserts—but almost anything could be on the list. I have known women who craved salted tomatoes and milk, cough drops in spaghetti sauce, and even elementary school paste.

Scientists disagree as to the reasons for these cravings. Some think that they are just psychological. Others believe they are an unimportant side effect of hormone fluctuations and don't signal anything about the mother's or baby's needs. Still others try to link each craving directly to a specific nutrient need.

I take a different view. In medical school, I learned about an interesting phenomenon called referred pain—where pain is felt in a part of the body other than its source. The first example I learned about was pain felt on the left arm when the problem was in the heart. The same nerve can detect problems in both places; if there is an irritation somewhere along that neural pathway, the brain guesses the source of the problem and assigns where you feel the pain. In phantom pain, it can even assign the pain to a limb that is no longer there.

I believe pregnancy cravings are an example of something I call *referred craving*. The cravings are a true sign that the body is yearning for certain nutrients—but they may or may not be present in the food you crave. Yes, cravings for calcium-rich foods like milk or ice cream may suggest a real need for calcium. Vegetarian women may crave meat to get B_{12} or iron. Cheryl's craving for tuna may have been linked to a desire for the brain-healthy omega-3 fat DHA.

But a craving for ice chips may be related to a mineral not in the ice at all. The brain takes the craving and assigns it to some item on the same "desire pathway." You may not need that item at all; it may even be harmful. (I'm not convinced the chemical alum often used in paste is safe during pregnancy.)

Feeding Baby Green Recipe

Cinnamon-Apple Oatmeal

If morning sickness is a problem for you, you may be able to decrease it by not letting your stomach get too empty or too full. A small meal before you go to bed, or first thing in the morning, may be just what you need. This comforting bowl of oatmeal is a good source of folate, the seeds are rich sources of minerals (including magnesium, selenium, calcium, iron, and zinc), and the apples do more than flavor the oatmeal. In 2003, a new set of healthful polyphenols were found in apples (and organic apples have been found to have higher levels of these polyphenols and other phytonutrients).[8] Made with milk, this meal provides even more calcium.

1 sweet apple (any variety other than Red Delicious), cut in quarters, de-seeded, and sliced

1 teaspoon walnut oil (or other high-quality vegetable oil)

½ teaspoon ground cinnamon, divided

1 cup old-fashioned rolled oats

2 cups water

¾ cup raisins

1 tablespoon sesame seeds

1 tablespoon sunflower seeds

1. In a large saucepan, over medium heat, sauté the apples in oil until caramelized (toasty brown on one side)—this will bring out their natural sweetness. Remove from heat, toss with a ¼ teaspoon of the cinnamon, and set aside.
2. In a saucepan, combine the oats, ¼ teaspoon of cinnamon, and water or milk and cook over medium-low heat until the liquid has been absorbed and oatmeal is done to your taste, about 5 to 10 minutes (or follow package directions).
3. Stir in the raisins and the apples. Spoon into four bowls, sprinkle seeds on top, and serve.

Serves 4

NUTRITION FACTS (AMOUNT PER SERVING)

Calories: 294	Sodium: 8mg	Sugars: 21.66g
Total Fat: 5.51g	Total Carbs: 55.77g	Protein: 8.34g
Cholesterol: —	Dietary Fiber: 6.46g	

Feeding Baby Green Tip

Ten Things Every Pregnant Woman Should Avoid

1. *Cigarette smoke:* Cigarette fumes have an immediate effect on fetal blood flow. Whether you smoke, or you are around second- or third-hand smoke, the nicotine and carbon monoxide in the fumes are harmful to your baby and known to cause complications in pregnancy. If you smoke, STOP.

2. *Marijuana:* Marijuana smoking during pregnancy may affect your baby's nervous system during development in adverse ways. If you smoke marijuana, STOP.

3. *Alcohol:* No level of alcohol has been proven to be safe for an unborn child. If you drink alcohol, STOP.

4. *Caffeine:* Caffeine jolts your baby, just as it does you. Keep caffeine to less than 150 milligrams per day (about one eight-ounce cup of brewed coffee) at most, and perhaps avoid it all together. Remember, even decaf (use water-processed decaf only) has some residual caffeine.

5. *Unnecessary medications:* Most things that pass through your bloodstream pass through your baby's bloodstream. If a medication is not necessary or the benefits do not clearly outweigh the risks (according to your health care provider), don't take it.

6. *Mercury and PCBs* (polychlorinated biphenyls, found in contaminated sport fish, old appliances and fluorescent lights, and contaminated sites) can harm you and your baby. Stay away! [9]

7. *Raw or partially cooked eggs, meat, poultry, or fish:* Make sure to cook these thoroughly to avoid the risk of getting infections such as Salmonella or E. coli. AVOID SUSHI.

8. *Soft cheeses:* Listeria, a bacteria found in unpasteurized soft cheeses such as Brie, Camembert, feta, and blue cheese. Listeria can flourish at refrigerator temperatures, so leftovers and meats that require refrigeration should be heated to steaming hot before you eat them.

9. *Smelly fumes:* This is the time to choose safe, nontoxic cleaning products in the home, and get someone else to pump your gas.

10. *Toxic ingredients:* Beware of toxic synthetic pesticides or other toxic chemicals in plastic containers or in what you eat, drink, or put on your body (see *Raising Baby Green* for more details).

I suggest neither obeying every craving nor automatically rejecting them as irrelevant. Pay attention to your cravings and take a moment to ask yourself what your body or your baby may *really* be hungry for. If the craving is for something safe, you may want to just go for it. If it's for something risky, such as too much swordfish (which contains DHA but also too much mercury), you might want to think of another way to get DHA, such as grilled wild salmon.

The Essential Steps for Teaching Nutritional Intelligence

The beginning of your pregnancy is a great time to start making any necessary changes in how you approach your health. Let's look at these early steps to unlocking a delicious future for your child during early pregnancy.

Take Charge!

Simply becoming aware that your baby is depending on you to make wise choices for her, and that the actions you take to benefit your baby have real power, increases your odds of making a real change in your habits. More women are able to stop smoking during pregnancy, for instance, than during any other comparable period in life.

Nonetheless, I know that eating habits are deeply ingrained and can be very hard to change. Understanding the lasting value of positive changes now will help give you the motivation you need to make those choices. Pregnancy may be the easiest time in your life to give up bad eating habits—take advantage of it!

How we eat will have an impact on our children at every stage, but during pregnancy this may be more important than at any other time. In a very real sense, moms are eating for two (or more, with twins or triplets). Your child won't be exposed to unhealthy food except through you. And your child won't get key nutrients unless you've gotten what's necessary from your diet during pregnancy or before.

Use Windows of Opportunity

Because there are so many variables that influence a child's health over the years, it can be very difficult to measure the role that parents' food plays. A 2008 study of pregnant and nursing animals, though, was able to keep everything identical in their lives but the food.[10] The lasting benefits of good food were staggering.

In one part of the study, half of the animal mothers had only a balanced selection of healthy food during pregnancy and nursing. The other half of the mothers had some healthy food, plus free access to high-fat, high-sugar, high-salt treats such as candy, cheese, chocolate, cookies, crackers, doughnuts, muffins, and potato chips. They ate a lot of the junk food.

Once these baby animals were weaned, they all had free access to both the healthy food and the junk food (and as much as we want to protect our own children, they may well have free access to junk food and to peers eating junk food at some point in their childhood too). The offspring in the study were followed all the way through adolescence to adulthood.

When these offspring became young adults, those whose mothers had the healthy diet during pregnancy and nursing were significantly more likely to have normal weight, normal blood sugar, normal insulin, normal triglycerides, and normal cholesterol than the other children—*even though all the offspring were offered the same diets after weaning.* Or put the other way: those whose mothers enjoyed lots of junk food were significantly more likely to be fat, and to already have abnormal levels of blood sugar, insulin, triglycerides, and cholesterol by the end of adolescence. The difference was even more pronounced in female offspring than in males.

Part of the effect could be explained by the mother's diet measurably turning on or off at least ten different genes that change metabolism, appetite, weight, and health. In addition, part of the effect could be explained by variations in the offspring's food preferences, depending on what their mother had eaten, and differences in the amount that felt right for the offspring to eat. But the key point is this: mothers' healthy diet, just during the very early stages, programmed offspring for health.[11]

Pregnancy is perhaps the easiest time to give your child the lasting gifts of great food. Throughout much of this book you'll be hearing more about taste, taste, taste—but in the earliest stages of development, other windows of opportunity take center stage.

Feeding Baby Green Recipe

One Smoothie, Your Way

This is a great recipe for getting nutrition when you don't feel hungry!

½ cup plain, nonfat yogurt

1½ cups (12 ounces) 1 percent milk
or soymilk

1 teaspoon vanilla

1 banana (or 1 frozen peeled banana)

Agave nectar (optional)

1. Combine yogurt and ½ cup of the milk, pour into ice cube trays, and freeze overnight.
2. Put frozen yogurt-milk cubes into blender. Add vanilla, the rest of the milk, and the banana.
3. Blend until smoothie consistency. Taste for sweetness. If not sweet enough, sweeten with a dash of agave nectar.

Variations:

Ginger Smoothie: To soothe nausea, or for a great ginger flavor any time, add 1 teaspoon (or more or less, to taste) grated fresh ginger.

Blueberry-Acai Smoothie: Omit the banana and add 1½ cups frozen blueberries and ½ cup (about 3½ ounces) frozen acai pulp. *Note:* You can use any frozen fruit to make this smoothie—blackberries, raspberries, strawberries, and mangoes are all great choices. Acai is a superfruit that is loaded with antioxidants, so I often try to use it for one of the fruits.

Serves: 2 (12 oz. servings)

NUTRITION FACTS (AMOUNT PER SERVING)

(Will vary slightly depending on the fruit used)

Calories: 245	Sodium: 123mg	Sugars: 29.08g
Total Fat: 1.96g	Total Carbs: 40.66g	Protein: 10.48g
Cholesterol: 9mg	Dietary Fiber: 2.93g	

Engage All the Senses

During these first ten weeks, your baby isn't paying much attention to the outside world. This isn't the time to engage her eyes or to teach the language of food. Her little eyes are closed and her ear canals contain tiny ear plugs to further muffle outside noise. She can't learn texture, because everything she swallows is a clear liquid. But let's take a moment first to celebrate the sense of smell.

The sense of smell is probably the first to develop (we'll talk about the sense of taste in the next chapter), and is easily the most intense before babies are born. It's not until after birth that sight and sound become more important ways to enjoy and navigate the world. In the early, quiet darkness of the womb, however, the nose is the first entertainment and the earliest teacher.

But what is there to smell?

Feeding Baby Green Report

Peppermint

The unique flavor of fresh peppermint and the even gentler spearmint is wonderful and unmistakable. An added bonus for women in their first trimester of pregnancy is mint's effect on nausea.

For some women, even the smell of fresh mint leaves is enough to decrease nausea and soothe the tummy. Others enjoy hot or iced tea made from peppermint leaves. I don't recommend taking concentrated peppermint oil during pregnancy, but a gentle mint tea can be healthful, refreshing, and delicious.[12] Or you might try mint leaves on a fruit salad. Pound for pound, peppermint has more nutrients than most fruits, vegetables, or grains—and two tablespoons of this flavorful gem is only about one calorie.

Inhale some freshly bruised mint leaves. It's a treat for you, and a great smell to share with your baby.

By about eight weeks of pregnancy your baby is able to smell the salty, liquid aroma of your amniotic fluid. This is a unique and changing aroma. When given the opportunity shortly after birth, babies are able to recognize the smell of their own amniotic fluid, and prefer it to that of others. They develop a deep fondness for familiar pleasant smells. It can influence their choices.

But the smell of this amniotic fluid is always changing, strongly influenced by your external and internal environment. The same volatile molecules that awaken the odor receptors in your nose tend to slip across the placenta so you can share the experience with your child.

Beyond this, the foods you taste often make their way into the amniotic soup. Yes, they will later stimulate your baby's taste buds, but first they will allow you to begin sharing the aroma of good food. Smell and taste are inextricably linked. It's not too soon to notice the smells around you and know that you are sharing them with your baby.

If you smell something that bothers you, your baby may be reacting in a similar way. Babies have been seen on ultrasound to react with disgust to the smell of cigarette smoke. You may want to move away from unpleasant aromas if you can, or to avoid eating the source if it is food.

However, if you come across healthy food that smells delicious to you, pause and take a deep breath. You're inviting your baby to sample something you love. You may also want to arrange an encounter with that healthy, pleasant aroma again, so that it begins to become familiar to your child.

Choose the Right Amount

The amount of food you eat during pregnancy is important. Besides providing energy to fuel the changes in your own body and the growth of your baby, you are also signaling to your baby about how plentiful food is right now in the outside world. In this way you are helping to program how much your child will want to eat, and how he will use the calories he does eat.

Wouldn't you love to feel full after eating just the right amount? Wouldn't you love to store just the right amount of fat? These are gifts you can begin to give your child now—and continue to give during the developmental stages that follow.

Eating too many calories during pregnancy says "these are times of plenty" and sets a pattern of overconsumption. It seems to whisper to children to eat lots, just like Mom. The baby learns to use the calories for growth, but to keep eating and store lots of fat because Mom must think that there will be lean times later.

Conversely, eating too few calories during pregnancy tends to signal that food is scarce. This also predisposes kids to eat too much and to store too much as fat. Looking for food becomes a higher priority for them. They use the minimum amount they can for lean body growth, but are hungry for more so that they can store more fat.

You're aiming for a happy medium—more than you ate before, but not a whole lot more. You want to signal that we live in a time of reliable food supply, but not an excess. Your choices whisper that they will have plenty available for their growth needs, but this is not the time to try to store excess fat.

Calories   The total number of calories you should be getting each day depends on how active you are, your height, your prepregnancy weight, and how far along you are in your pregnancy (calorie needs are lower in the first trimester than later in pregnancy—early on they may go up little, if at all).

I suggest using the tool at www.mypyramid.gov (MyPyramid Plan for Moms) to learn the average number of calories you need per day. It might be as few as 1,800 calories in the first trimester for a woman who is five feet tall, 100 pounds, and not very active, or as many as 3,000 calories for a five foot, ten inch woman who weighs 200 pounds and who is very, very active. This tool can be very useful; but if you have a medical condition such as diabetes, celiac disease, or kidney disease, be sure to ask your health care provider how this might affect your food choices.

Even if you don't have a medical condition, your individual calorie needs may be more or less than the average reported by the online tool.

It's nice to have a ballpark idea of calorie numbers, but please don't obsess about them. It's better to follow weight gain (usually two to four pounds *total* during the first trimester—gaining about a pound per month, more or less), and to aim for eating a healthy variety of whole foods.

But don't obsess about weight either—some very healthy pregnancies will produce either more or less than the average weight gain in the first trimester. Use your weight gain as one kind of feedback and as a starting point for conversations with your healthcare provider.

Feeding Baby Green Report

Weight Gain During Pregnancy

The right type of pregnancy weight gain benefits both you and your baby. Happily, the right type of weight gain is also the kind that turns out to be easiest to shed, according to research published in the November 2003 *American Journal of Obstetrics & Gynecology.*[13]

Clearly, the amount of weight you gain is important. But not all weight gain is the same. During pregnancy, you add both lean body mass (protein and water weight) and fat. It's normal and healthy to add some of both. It turns out, though, that the added lean body mass is the weight that has been shown to benefit you *and* your baby the most, and to disappear easily after pregnancy. In this study, gains in lean body mass literally vanished after delivery, having no effect on post-pregnancy weight.

Gaining weight too quickly, or because of sedentary habits, leads to packing on the extra weight as fat storage. But gradual weight gain accompanied by moderate, weight-bearing exercise throughout pregnancy can help pack the extra weight on as lean body mass—a great gift to yourself and your baby.

And pregnant women usually need more to drink—a total of about three liters of water a day, when the temperature is comfortable. This includes water by itself and the water in other beverages, as well as the moisture in food. (See "Hydration Solutions," earlier in this chapter.)

Supplements I agree with the USDA's recommendation that pregnant women take a prenatal vitamin and mineral supplement every day *in addition to* eating healthy amounts of healthy foods. I also recommend this for women who are trying to get pregnant, or who might get pregnant within the next three months. The CDC recommends that every woman of childbearing age take a supplement containing 400 micrograms of folic acid every day.

I suggest choosing a brand of supplements that is "clean"—that is, made without artificial colors, flavors, or preservatives, and manufactured in a reputable facility with rigorous quality testing. Look for beta carotene instead of preformed vitamin A (too much vitamin A can be harmful to your baby). Folate needs increase to at least 600 micrograms a day during pregnancy. Avoid products boasting more than about 200 percent of various nutrients: beyond a certain point, more is not better.

It's important for most pregnant women to get at least 1,000 milligrams a day of calcium, whether or not they are vegans. If you are not getting that amount between your diet and your prenatal vitamin, I suggest taking additional calcium, balanced with magnesium and vitamin D. For comparison, a glass of milk contains about 300 milligrams of calcium.

Many pregnant women do not get enough DHA and other omega-3 fats from what they eat. If you are not, I suggest also taking an omega-3 supplement containing DHA. Fish oil can be a great source, but be sure it is purified or microdistilled to avoid mercury or other toxins. And again, it should not contain too much vitamin A. If you don't like capsules or fish oil, you can get vegetarian DHA as a pleasant-tasting powder.

If you are taking more than one supplement, I suggest choosing those that are designed to go together, in order to avoid inadvertently getting more of some nutrients than you want.

Although I am a fan of herbal and botanical supplements in some situations, many of these have not been adequately tested for safety for unborn babies. Natural doesn't necessarily mean safe. The USDA suggests avoiding these during pregnancy, unless your health care provider knows that they are safe.

It's wise to alert your health care provider about any supplements (or over-the-counter remedies) that you are considering taking during pregnancy or breastfeeding.

Choose the Right Variety

I'm often asked by worried mothers-to-be what to do if they just don't feel like eating in early pregnancy. How can they get the nutrition their baby needs? During the period of elevated disgust sensitivity, I encourage moms to eat the healthy foods that seem palatable to them at this point, and to relax. The time will come later for more food and more variety—and your body will help you do it.

For most pregnant women, it's wise to try to eat some vegetables every day. Over the course of the week, it's a good idea to roughly balance between dark green vegetables (such as broccoli and spinach), red-orange vegetables (such as carrots, red peppers, tomatoes, and sweet potatoes), and other vegetables (such as cucumbers, cauliflower, and green beans)—with a slight edge toward the dark green vegetables. But if you can't look a salad in the eye right now, don't despair—there will be plenty of time later in pregnancy.

Getting some fruit each day is also good, as well as some whole grains. Having legumes (such as beans or dried peas) at least a few times a week is also valuable. Look for additional sources of protein and calcium, which could be more beans and broccoli or may include milk and meat.

Folic Acid Folic acid needs go up immediately by 50 percent to at least 600 micrograms a day. I typically recommend 800 micrograms a day. For high-risk pregnancies (such as moms with diabetes, epilepsy, or obesity), I often suggest even more.

Folic acid is mostly found in leafy green veggies (foliage), as well as in legumes, oranges, and orange juice. It is now fortified in lots of foods, but I believe that your body and the baby's will benefit even more from foods that naturally contain folic acid. These also contain lots of other micronutrients that we are just beginning to learn about—including stilbenes, flavones, anthocyanidins, isoflavones, flavanols, proantho-cyanidins, and other polyphenols. These are nutrients not typically fortified in foods, but are naturally in foods that pregnant women have been eating since antiquity.

Iron Iron intake also needs to go up 50 percent, from 18 milligrams up to 27 milligrams a day. This is needed both for your increased blood volume and for your baby. The baby will be born with about 500 milligrams of iron—all of which comes from your diet.

Iron is found in leafy green vegetables; and for nonvegetarians, meat can be a good source of iron. I recommend choosing grass-fed organic meat during pregnancy. Not only are these cattle getting their green leafy vegetables (with benefits to you), but they also are not pumped up with the synthetic hormones often used to send commercially raised beef cattle into a growth spurt. There is increasing evidence that even the small amounts of these hormones still present when you eat them may not be good for you or for your baby (see "The DES Story" in Chapter One for more on this).

Zinc Zinc, important for a healthy immune system, also needs to go up by almost 50 percent, to 11 milligrams a day. Dried beans are one great source. So are sesame seeds, pumpkin seeds, peas, and some mushrooms.

Vitamin B$_6$ Vitamin B$_6$ needs go up almost 50 percent, to 1.9 milligrams. This is important for creating serotonin and other neurotransmitters, for brain and muscle function, and to help remove heavy metals to which you may have been exposed, such as lead or mercury. Average women in the United States get about 1.4 milligrams per day of vitamin B$_6$ from what they eat. A single baked potato or banana is enough to make up the difference.

Don't discount the lowly potato! For many centuries, Chinese medicine has valued a plant called *Lycium chinense* for its healthful properties in addressing both heart disease and cancer. In recent decades, western scientists isolated the main responsible compounds—called kukoamines—and proved their health effects. The exotic Chinese plant was the only place to find these powerful compounds—until 2005, when a new analytic technique found them at significant levels in potatoes![14]

Potatoes are sometimes looked down upon in nutritional circles. But even these lowliest of vegetables are packed with surprising goodness if properly prepared. However, by simultaneously destroying nutrients and adding fat and calories, deep-frying can turn a healthy food into a junk food. The frying can even create a carcinogen called acrylamide in potatoes.

When baked, steamed, or lightly sautéed, with the skins, common potatoes are low-calorie, high-fiber foods that provide a good source of vitamin B$_6$ (so important in pregnancy) as well as sixty other micronutrients—not to mention the blood-pressure lowering kukoamines, that have been a hidden treasure for millennia. Potatoes could be a good choice to help prevent pregnancy-induced hypertension. Red potatoes also pack antioxidant power comparable to that of broccoli, spinach, or Brussels sprouts. They can be a delicious way to get key nutrients early in pregnancy when other vegetables look unappetizing.[15]

Iodine Iodine needs also go up almost 50 percent during pregnancy, to 220 micrograms. Iodine is important for your and your baby's thyroid glands.

Iodine is present in foods that grow in the sea, or that grow in soil where the sea has been. Most American women get plenty of iodine, now that table salt is iodized. But people who live in areas where the produce is low in iodine, who don't eat much seafood, who don't eat packaged goods with added sodium, or who use salt without added iodine, could become iodine deficient during pregnancy. (It would seem natural that sea salt would contain iodine because it comes from the sea, but it is not a reliable source.)

Customize Needs for Every Body

Everything we've discussed in this chapter, and everything that we will discuss throughout the book, can be customized to fit your unique needs, and the needs of your baby after he is born.

Getting Enough Calcium We discussed earlier the need for most women to get 1,000 milligrams a day of calcium while they are pregnant. The most common way women do that is through milk, yogurt, and cheese. This can be a fine choice, though I also strongly recommend organic dairy during pregnancy, which is produced without the use of artificial hormones, antibiotics, toxic synthetic pesticides, genetic modification, or cloning. Some women with lactose intolerance may choose lactose-free dairy products or to take a lactase supplement. Others may choose goat's milk, perhaps because they are allergic to cow's milk protein or because they just like the taste.

Others may prefer to avoid dairy altogether, and to get their calcium from spinach, sesame seeds, and blackstrap molasses (one cup of cooked spinach has almost as much calcium as one cup of milk, with a fraction of the calories; a quarter cup of sesame seeds has even more than one cup of milk, but also has more calories; two tablespoons of blackstrap molasses has about the same amount of calcium and calories as a cup of milk).

Turnip greens have more calcium than spinach, but more people like spinach than turnip greens. Basil, dill, thyme, oregano, cinnamon, and rosemary all have more calcium per calorie than milk, but it wouldn't be practical to reach 1,000 milligrams every day by counting on these alone. Still, they could be important pieces of a calcium puzzle, perhaps along with a bit from other sources such as broccoli, tofu, oranges, and asparagus.

Others may reach the calcium target with a clean calcium supplement, or by strategically choosing foods and beverages fortified with calcium.

There are many routes to the same goal, depending on your preferences, tastes, beliefs, schedule, and allergies. The key is to find what works for you.

Allergies In the next chapter, we'll consider things you may want to be sure to add to your diet to reduce the risk of specific conditions that run in your family, including various forms of allergies. I'm not going to suggest adding anything tailored to the diet during these first ten weeks or so, but we should discuss the possibility of eliminating or avoiding certain things if allergies run on either side of the family.

Does it make sense for pregnant women to avoid cow's milk and eggs to help reduce the chance that their child will develop eczema (or perhaps asthma, or other allergies)? This has been suggested in the past. But the 2006 Cochrane review of all available evidence has concluded that there is no benefit to avoiding these.[16]

Another series of studies, however, did suggest a significant decrease in eczema among children whose milk-drinking mothers switched to organic milk during pregnancy and nursing—slashing eczema by about a third. The fatty acid profile of the women's breast milk contained higher

Feeding Baby Green Stories

"Cut Out the Fruit Juice, Eat the Fruit!"

When I was pregnant with my first child, I was determined to make every bite count. It had taken me fourteen months to get pregnant, so now it was show time!

I started the day with organic juices and a full breakfast, I learned new recipes for kale and chard, I embraced "good" (and some bad) fats, and tracked my daily grams of protein—even added wild salmon to my decades-long vegetarian diet. Not surprisingly, given such great nutrition, I felt great! So it was with much pride that I'd show up at my midwife appointments—my nausea-free, energetic pregnancy boded well for my goal of a natural home birth.

Toward the end of my first trimester, however, I was surprised when one of the midwives said that I was gaining weight too fast and should cut out the fruit juice and just eat the whole fruit. That way, she said, I'd cut calories, still get vitamins, and add fiber, too. It all makes perfect sense now, but at the time I burst into tears. How dare she call me fat AND criticize my valiant attempt at perfect nutrition?

I still think of that great advice (and chuckle at my response) every time I cut up ANOTHER organic apple for my fruitaholic kids. We rarely drink fruit juice. Our family's favorite beverage? Water.

Susan Comfort
Washington, D.C.

percentages of healthy fats. The evidence is not strong enough to make recommendations based on this one series of studies. Still, given that I suggest choosing organic milk during pregnancy anyway, I think it especially makes sense for those with eczema or allergies in the family.

What about avoiding peanuts? This was also suggested by the American Academy of Pediatrics in the recent past, to help stem the rapid rise of peanut allergies.[17] More careful, long-term research, though, has not found avoiding peanuts to be helpful.[18] And in 2008, the AAP reversed its previous official statements: "At the present time, there is lack of evidence that maternal dietary restrictions during pregnancy play a significant role in the prevention of atopic disease [eczema or allergies] in infants."

However, as we'll see in the next chapter, there is mounting evidence that including certain types of food during can benefit a baby with a family history of eczema, asthma, or allergies.

Reap the Benefits of Green

We began this chapter with a compelling controlled study looking at the long shadow of excessive junk food during pregnancy. Not all of the current obesity epidemic in children can be written off simply as coming from too many calories or not enough exercise during pregnancy or childhood. Environmental exposures can also play a role.

Pollution can make kids fat, according to groundbreaking new research. Researchers measured levels of the pesticide hexachlorobenzene, a known endocrine disruptor chemical, in the umbilical cords of more than four hundred children, who were then followed for more than six years.[19] Those with the highest levels of this environmental pollutant, which gets into food, were twice as likely to be obese by the time they were in school.

This raises a question: Is the pesticide changing the metabolism and triggering obesity? Or is it an innocent bystander, a marker for something else?

You can't really do a randomized study in children—giving half of them the pesticide and half of them organic produce—to find out. But this study has been done in animals, where the only difference between groups was whether they received endocrine disruptor pesticides or not. Animals who were given the pesticides wound up significantly more obese.[20]

We already knew that prenatal exposure to cigarette smoke has a similar effect on later obesity. It appears that environmental pollution—including in our food—is indeed one of the factors contributing to the rise of obesity. *Feeding Baby Green* can be good for you, your child, and for the environment.

Pesticides and Other Unwelcome Guests in Our Food It's smart to decrease exposure to unnecessary toxic, synthetic pesticides during pregnancy, especially during the first trimester. Again, there are a variety of possible strategies for doing this.

Choosing organic produce, which decreases toxic pesticide exposure from food by an average of 97 percent, is one possibility. Some studies suggest that choosing organics has the added advantage of increasing nutrients by an average of 25 percent per serving.[21]

Another way to achieve a similar goal is to choose produce grown locally and in season. The food is less likely to have high amounts of toxic synthetic pesticides and more likely to be picked when it is freshest, ripest, and most nutritious. The odds are even better if you select them from someone that you know at a farmers market or by subscribing to community-supported agriculture (CSA), in which a basket of farm-fresh produce, flowers, fruits, eggs, milk, meats, or other farm products from local growers is delivered to you regularly. Better yet, grow some of your own.

Bananas and citrus fruits, with their peels, tend to contain low levels of pesticides however they are grown. But the outer layer isn't always a reliable guide: imported cantaloupes are still a concern because the pesticides are taken up inside the fruit.

Here's a list of the eight imported fruits and nine imported vegetables at the supermarket that tend to have the highest levels of concerning pesticides: grapes, nectarines, peaches, pears, strawberries, cherries, cantaloupe, and apples; and sweet bell peppers, lettuce, cucumbers, celery, tomatoes, green beans, broccoli, peas, and carrots.[22] (Many grocers note the origin of produce on the shelf tag. If yours doesn't, ask!) Again, one goal, many routes.

Plastics A similar case can be made regarding prenatal exposure to certain ingredients in plastics, such as bisphenyl A (BPA). Most stories of BPA in the news have focused on its presence in baby bottles, but prenatal exposure may be even more important. Parents can reduce BPA exposure by drinking water and other liquids from BPA-free containers, by avoiding foods (especially pastas and soups) in cans lined with a BPA-containing resin, and by avoiding microwaving or cooking food in a BPA-containing plastic (recycling symbol #7). If you are going to decrease or eliminate canned foods for one time in your life, pregnancy is a great time to do it.

∾

While you are trying to conceive, and during the difficult early weeks of pregnancy, you are also filled with new possibilities and hopes for the future. Take advantage of this private time before your pregnancy goes public to establish your healthy green lifestyle.

As you approach the end of your first trimester, you will probably be glad to move on from the exhaustion and nausea that you may have experienced during the first ten weeks of your baby's development. You can look forward to enjoying a wider variety of foods, and introducing your baby to some of your favorites, old and new.

4

Middle and Late Pregnancy
(SECOND AND THIRD TRIMESTERS)

By the second and third trimesters, you and your baby have something to celebrate. The work of creating each organ is largely finished. At this point, babies switch gears—from creating organs to growing, programming, and fine-tuning them. This is the time when the metabolism and immune system are set on course, and when the brain lays down its foundational awareness of the outside world. Babies sleep up to 90 percent of the time, in part to allow for this programming to occur.

While baby sleeps, mother gets in gear. At some point, conveniently, the nausea and fatigue typical of the first trimester give way to the fresh enthusiasm and hunger typical of the second trimester. Your appetites, food preferences, and energy levels change, encouraging you to seek out a wide variety of flavors and nutrients to introduce to your unborn child.

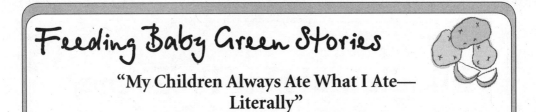

Feeding Baby Green Stories

"My Children Always Ate What I Ate—Literally"

From the time my eldest, Joshua, was born in 1970, I saw no reason for processed baby foods. We didn't have processed food until modern times, so why did we need it now? My children always ate what I ate—literally. Prior to their birth, I ate as much organic whole foods as possible. And being of "hippie" descent, and from a strong Jewish/Italian background, the restrictions of no garlic, no wine, no whatever did not exist.

When it was time for my kids to begin to taste our food, I bought a small food mill and ground up whatever we ate. If we happened to be traveling, I did what Native Americans intuitively and historically did: I first chewed the food and then fed it to my children. This may not be the healthiest, when I look back now, but it is what I did . . . much to the amazement of those around me.

My children were rarely sick and actually begged for me to let them stay home for a "sick day," like other kids in their school.

They now have gardens, go to the farmers market, and cook for their families and others. My children love food, and are willing to pay more money in their budget to buy ingredients that they know are clean, healthy, more nutritious and ultimately simply delicious. And I have two grandchildren who from the age of three months ate everything—broccoli, spinach, oysters, sausage. Everything.

Jesse Cool
Celebrity Chef and Author of *Simply Organic:*
A Cookbook for Sustainable, Seasonal,
and Local Ingredients
Palo Alto, California

The Essential Steps for Teaching Nutritional Intelligence

You've already laid a beautiful green foundation during the first trimester of your pregnancy. Now, during the second and third trimesters, you can continue to take positive action to encourage your baby's health and your own. Here are the key steps to take during these important weeks.

Take Charge!

Sometimes, when mothers get their appetites and energy back, it can be tempting to grab hold of the idea of "eating for two" and interpret it as "I can eat anything and everything I want!" Not so. It's even more important at this time to remember to take charge of your own and your baby's nutrition and eat not only well, but wisely.

Use Windows of Opportunity

During this period, two wonderful windows of opportunity intersect: one in your development, and one in your baby's.

Your baby's attention begins to turn to the outside world, in an effort to learn what she can about her parents and the environment they live in. This will help her bond with you both after birth, and will help her set her metabolic processes and immune system in ways that are appropriate to the current conditions.

Meanwhile, just as your baby is starting to pay attention to what she is eating, your body is changing to encourage you to eat a wider variety of foods. The hormones of pregnancy usually trigger changes in how foods taste to you.[1] And if you really listen to what your body is asking, you may be surprised to discover that it wants food that supplies plenty of nutrition along with good flavor.

You might have experienced food cravings—perhaps especially for chocolate—associated with your period. In part, that's because taste-bud sensitivity tends to fluctuate with the menstrual cycle, perhaps to help prepare the body for pregnancy. The changes after conception, though, appear to be stronger and more consistent.

When moving from not being pregnant into the first trimester, increased sensitivity to bitter tastes may help prevent against eating toxins, spoiled food, or unnecessary medicines during the delicate weeks when new organs are forming.

During the second and third trimesters, however, there can be a decreased sensitivity to bitter tastes—and they can taste more pleasant. Citric acid, found in many fruits, can taste more pleasant as well.

If you never liked broccoli, this doesn't mean that you will suddenly like it more than another nonpregnant woman who has always loved broccoli. But it may mean that broccoli will taste better to you during these trimesters than ever before. And if not broccoli, perhaps a different vegetable.

Some studies have also found a decreased sensitivity to salts in the second and third trimesters. The salts can also taste more pleasant, making it easier to retain the extra fluid that you and your baby need (but, we hope, not too much!).[2] In the past, this was probably quite useful, but today, with so much sodium in so many processed foods, the enhanced desire for salt leads some women astray. Whether pregnant or not, a woman shouldn't get more than 2,300 milligrams a day of sodium—and getting only 1,500 milligrams a day would be better.

These changes in your body can support you as you choose a wide variety of healthy fruits, vegetables, and grains to build your child's body and to teach healthy flavors.

Engage All the Senses

Your baby's senses are all at work as your baby explores the world in your womb—and pays attention to every available clue to the world outside. Hearing and sight may be muted, but taste and smell are heightened in this dim, muffled enclosure.

Engage with Flavor Babies have more taste buds before birth than at any later time. Why might this be? Why go to the trouble of building taste buds that aren't going to last? Perhaps so that babies can form an imprint of Mom's food culture even before birth.

Most parents think that before birth, babies get all of their nutrition through the umbilical cord. They don't realize that babies also drink and digest amniotic fluid, swallowing the equivalent of up to three eight-ounce bottles a day of this nutrient. By birth they are already getting 10 to 20

Feeding Baby Green Recipe

Penne with Broccoli and Sun-Dried Tomatoes

This pasta dish, one of our family favorites, draws from the Mediterranean tradition with a California twist. Soft cheeses, such as feta, are not recommended during pregnancy unless they are pasteurized. Many soft cheeses are *not* pasteurized, so be sure to check the label before buying!

2 ounces (¾ cup) sun-dried tomatoes, julienned

5 cloves garlic, coarsely chopped

¼ cup olive oil

8 ounces penne pasta

4 ounces portabella mushrooms, sliced

3 cups fresh broccoli florets, cut into bite-sized pieces

4 ounces kalamata olives or other black olives

4 ounces pasteurized feta cheese

2 ounces Parmesan cheese (optional)

1. Put the sun-dried tomatoes and chopped garlic in a small bowl and pour the olive oil over them. Let them stand at least 30 minutes before cooking, or overnight, to allow the tomatoes to reconstitute and the oil to become flavored. If you allow the flavors to marry for longer than four hours, put them in the refrigerator.
2. Cook the penne according to package directions in a very large cooking pot.
3. While the pasta is cooking, begin cooking the sauce. Heat a large skillet over medium heat, and add the tomato-garlic-oil mixture to the pan. Sauté for one minute. Add the mushrooms and broccoli, and sauté over medium heat, stirring occasionally, until the broccoli is tender but still crisp—about 5 or 6 minutes. If the mixture appears to be dry, add 1/4 cup of water during the process.
4. When the pasta is al dente, drain the water and pour the penne back into the cooking pot. Add the tomato, garlic, broccoli, and mushrooms to the pasta. Gently stir in the olives and feta cheese. Mix thoroughly.
5. Divide into four servings and sprinkle Parmesan on each serving (if desired).

Serves: 4 (Yield: 6½ cups)

NUTRITION FACTS (AMOUNT PER SERVING)

Calories: 418	Sodium: 1,113mg	Sugars: 8.30g
Total Fat: 24.90g	Total Carbs: 31.70g	Protein: 17.63g
Cholesterol: 53mg	Dietary Fiber: 4.63g	

percent of their protein from what they drink![3] And it's a *flavor-rich* soup. The fluid is flavored by what Mom has been eating and drinking.

The idea that what Mom experiences during pregnancy can have a life-long effect on her baby is ancient. But in the case of food, we have twenty-first-century scientific support.

The classic modern study showing that a baby's first food preferences can be altered by his mother's food choices appeared in June 2001. Researchers at the University of Pennsylvania's Monell Chemical Senses Center worked magic with ten-ounce glasses of carrot juice. Some of the women drank the big glass of juice four days a week for three consecutive weeks during the last trimester of pregnancy—a total of 3.5 liters of carrot juice divided into a dozen servings spread out over twenty-one days. Other women got 3.5 liters of water instead. (Still others had the carrot juice when nursing. See the "Engage with Flavor" section in Chapter Six for the rest of the story.)

The babies were born, grew, and eventually started being fed cereal. After they had been enjoying the cereal for four weeks, and before any other foods had been introduced, the babies were fed cereal mixed with carrots.

Strikingly, those who had experienced carrots through their moms more than six months earlier enjoyed that first serving of carrots significantly more than those whose mothers drank only water, when measured by observers on a nine-point scale.

The authors said, "These very early flavor experiences may provide the foundation for cultural and ethnic differences in cuisine."[4] This idea has been strengthened by later research.[5]

These results make sense. Those who work with animals have long known that offspring typically prefer whatever the mother had been eating. This is a situation where the veterinary literature was far ahead of the human literature. One thing we've learned from animals is that this learning of taste from what Mom eats isn't just a matter of early exposure: there is something distinct about amniotic fluid that is designed to program flavor preferences. After animals have been born and weaned, if you expose them to a new flavor (even one like alcohol, which they would normally shun) *along with a sample of amniotic fluid,* everything changes. Something about the amniotic fluid itself helps imprint the new flavor.[6] Mammals are built to learn from our moms before we are born.

After the landmark carrot study, the research accelerated. The findings have been confirmed using other foods, including peaches.

The phenomenon is so important that it prompted the American Academy of Pediatrics to make a remarkable statement in 2006, which went largely unnoticed. The statement appeared in the first major revision of their official feeding guidelines in a quarter century. It reflected this rapidly growing body of scientific studies that had already been building for more than a decade. They said (emphasis mine):

> Both amniotic fluid and breast milk provide flavor exposure to the fetus and infant. *These exposures influence taste preference and food choices after weaning.* Thus, exposure to healthier foods through maternal food consumption during pregnancy and lactation may improve acceptance of healthy foods after weaning. Because infant responses to taste are different from mature taste, these early exposures may be **critical** in determining food preference later in life.[7]

It's not just fruits, vegetables, and grains that make a difference; the spices that mother eats also flavor the amniotic fluid.[8] Even adults have been able to detect, for example, garlic, cumin, and curry in samples of amniotic fluid after meals containing those spices.

When a child develops a taste for an Indian curry or an Italian sauce, for instance, even before birth, it can help him accept each of the next stages of textures as they come—from purees to soft foods to finger foods to fork foods. Also, once kids like those flavors, parents can more easily introduce new vegetables by flavoring it with the already loved sauce.

Engage with Aroma "The Scent of Gerbil Cuisine" is the curious title of a fascinating research study from the University of Texas at Austin.[9] Pregnant gerbils and their mates were fed a diet of either Purina Laboratory Chow or Pooch dog food. After the gerbil pups were born, they showed

Feeding Baby Green Report
Herbs and Spices

Spices and herbs are more than just tasty additions to flavor our foods: their concentrated flavors mirror the concentrated nutrients within. It's no surprise there are so many health benefits suggested from research into herbs and spices. Here are a few examples:

- **Basil:** Packed with flavonoids and anti-inflammatory oils, basil is also loaded with vitamin K, iron, calcium, and vitamin A. It can help prevent and beat infections.[10]

- **Cinnamon:** Most of the recent scientific excitement has been around its ability to help control blood sugar,[11] but even the smell of cinnamon can improve brain function.[12]

- **Cumin:** Part of the great flavor of Tex-Mex and Latin cuisine, cumin is also used in dishes from India and the Middle East—and for good reason. This curry ingredient contains potent antioxidants to help prevent and repair damage of many kinds.[13]

- **Mustard seeds:** Mustard has been used medicinally since the time of Hippocrates. It helps to prevent damage from chemicals in the environment.[14]

- **Oregano:** Popular in foods from Mexico to the Mediterranean, this herb provides its own unique mix of antioxidant,[15] antibacterial, and antifungal properties.[16]

- **Sage:** The Latin name for this herb, Salvia, means "to be saved." But the most recent science centers around sage's ability to enhance memory and help brain function.[17]

- **Thyme:** This herb has a long history as a natural medicine for infections, especially for respiratory infections and other respiratory problems. Recent research is confirming its value.[18]

- **Turmeric:** This curry spice is a scientific superstar with perhaps more studied benefits than any other herb or spice. It contains the potent anti-inflammatory curcumin, which can be effective in preventing childhood cancers such as leukemia, and protecting the brain—among many other benefits. If you're going to teach love of only one spice, consider the yellow wonder, turmeric.[19]

a strong preference for odors coming from adult male gerbils that had been eating the same chow as their mothers. Cage material used by these males felt more like home, and the pups preferred being with these males to males who had been eating the other diet.

As we'll see in the next chapter, human babies have a sense of smell far stronger than that of adults. They start out navigating the world by smell. Dad's sharing meals and flavors with Mom during this stage of pregnancy, and beyond, may turn out to be another way to help dads and babies bond when they get to see each other face-to-face.

Researchers have found that odors can produce more emotionally distinctive memories than other senses.[20] Marcel Proust famously wrote about this effect almost a hundred years ago, describing how the aroma of a particular cookie, a madeleine, dipped in a particular tea, transported him to the intense joy of his childhood. Now, twenty-first-century neuroimaging provides evidence of the extreme emotional potency of odor memories.[21]

Can human babies remember odors from before they are born? One study gave four-day-old babies a whiff of the distinct, licorice-like aroma of anise.[22] The babies who had been exposed to anise before birth recognized and preferred the aroma. They turned their heads toward it to see what they had smelled. They lingered. Their facial expressions warmed. They began to mouth, wanting a taste.

But the babies who had not been exposed before birth were either neutral to the new aroma or wrinkled their faces in dislike. They quickly lost interest. They turned away. Prenatal experiences can change the way babies experience the world as newborns.

A similar study gave four-day-old formula-fed babies a chance to smell a sample of their formula versus a neutral control odor: they liked the formula. They also smelled a sample of their amniotic fluid versus the neutral odor: they liked the amniotic fluid. Then they were placed between samples of the formula and the amniotic fluid. The babies demonstrated a strong preference for the aroma of their amniotic fluid.[23]

These babies preferred a smell they had learned before birth to one they learned as a newborn. Is this preference for the odor of their amniotic fluid because it was something that was familiar for so long? Or is there something almost magical about amniotic fluid?

I suspect the answer is both. Before birth, taste and smell are the dominant senses, coloring the baby's experience of the world. But amniotic fluid itself triggers heightened acceptance of new tastes and smells. It's the signal that this experience is brought to you by Mom.

When you smell something, there's a good bet that those same molecules make their way across the placenta so that soon your baby smells it too. Their noses can learn aromas from what you smell and from what you eat and drink. Nasty smells can create aversions. Good smells can create pleasant associations. We still have much to learn about how this all works.

Do these prenatally learned aroma preferences last beyond infancy? We don't know yet in human babies, but in animal studies the answer is yes.[24]

What should you do about all of this?

First, you don't need to do anything. That's right. Babies are beautifully designed to get to know the real *you*. They learn about your world from what you eat and drink and from the aromas you smell. This is truly effortless learning and effortless teaching. Your baby is already imprinting on you much in the same way a baby duckling imprints on his mother.

Second, you could do *something*. We sometimes behave a little better when we know that others are watching. We're our best selves. Now that you know that your baby is paying attention to what you eat and drink, you might find yourself naturally choosing healthier options from whatever is available. (If you need some ideas, choose any delicious options from the twenty-one plant families listed in the "Biodiversity Checklist" at the end of the book.)

Third, you might plan ahead to share with your baby the tastes and smells you would love for her to love (and perhaps skip, at least for a few months, the tastes you don't want her to crave).

How often does a baby need to taste something to form a preference? We know from animal studies that injecting a flavor into the amniotic fluid even once can make a lasting difference.[25] Even once may be significant for human babies as well—especially for strong flavors.

I recommend that if there is a flavor or aroma you really want your baby to learn, aim for twelve times during the second and third trimesters. This works out to having the flavor at least about every other week, on average. Or every week for a shorter burst. Or three times a week for a month.

Feeding Baby Green Recipe

Bombay Vegetable Stew

Lentils are much easier to prepare than other dried legumes—they do not need to be pre-soaked and they cook quickly. When done, they should be firm, but not crunchy.

½ cup lentils, dried (or 1 cup canned lentils)

1 tablespoon extra virgin olive oil

1 medium onion, chopped

4 cloves garlic, minced

1 tablespoon minced fresh ginger

3 large carrots, large diced

1 cup cauliflower, broken into small florets

1 (14.5 oz.) can of diced tomatoes

1 teaspoon curry powder

½ cup cooked chickpeas

1 cup green peas

1½ cups of water (if using canned lentils, include the liquid from the can with the water to equal 2 cups total)

Kosher salt, to taste

1. In a large saucepan, cook the dried lentils according to package directions. (For bulk lentils, follow these guidelines: Pick over dried lentils to remove debris, rinse, and drain. Cover with water or broth and boil for 2 to 3 minutes (to aid in digestion). Reduce heat and simmer until tender. Depending on the variety and age of the lentils, cooking time may take anywhere from 10 minutes to 1 hour.) Drain and set aside.

2. In a large saucepan, heat the olive oil over medium heat and sauté the onions and garlic until the onions are tender. Add the ginger and stir.

3. Add the carrots and cauliflower to the onion mixture and continue to cook until the carrots are warm all the way through, but still crisp. Add the tomatoes and curry powder and cook a few minutes more.

4. Add the lentils, chickpeas, green peas, and water. Simmer on low heat for about 20 minutes. Season with salt to taste. Turn off heat if you are not serving immediately to prevent the vegetables from becoming mushy. The flavors will intensify and blend beautifully. Reheat briefly before serving.

Serves 4 (Yield: 8 cups)

NUTRITION FACTS (AMOUNT PER SERVING)

Calories: 233	Sodium: 365mg	Sugars: 7.28g
Total Fat: 4.23g	Total Carbs: 39.56g	Protein: 11.33g
Cholesterol: 0	Dietary Fiber: 12.20g	

Feeding Baby Green Tip

Enjoy Flavor Threads

Variety is the spice of life—and so is spice! Whether it's an Italian blend (olive oil, tomato, basil, oregano) or an Asian sauce (soy, rice wine, ginger) or curry mix (turmeric, coriander, cumin, cinnamon)—or a Greek, Mediterranean, Caribbean, Latin, or any other flavor combination—taste mixtures can be even more powerful than individual flavors.[26] I call these flavor threads, and they are basic to my program of nutritional training.

You can start using them right now to introduce your baby to the flavors you love. Later, when your child enjoys a particular flavor thread, you can use it to give a familiar taste to new foods you want to introduce to your child. (We'll revisit flavor threads throughout this book.)

Using flavor threads: Choose at least one flavor thread that is very, very simple—the easiest one I know (and one of my favorites) is olive oil, chopped garlic, salt, and pepper. You can toss all sorts of cut-up vegetables—onion, peppers, cauliflower, sweet potatoes, whole green beans—in this (or any other) mixture, and cook them as you like (roasted in the oven, or sautéed on the stove, or grilled over a fire) for a wonderful and special flavor.

If you don't have time to cook, warm up a premade sauce or a seasoning packet so you and your baby can just enjoy the smell together. Later, you can use it with leftovers—such as grilled veggies, or pasta, or a piece of chicken—for a simple meal to reinforce the experience.

Engage with Sight As we'll see in later chapters, better sleep leads to better eating, and vice versa—for both moms and babies. Good sleep increases leptin, the hormone that both keeps hunger in check and increases fat burning. Poor sleep can actually lead to becoming overweight. But what does this have to do with the sense of sight?

After babies are born, we know that they sleep better if their environment is very dark all night and light during the day. This rhythm supports the daily rhythm of melatonin, which supports the rhythm of sleep. An overhead light on for even a minute after sunset can disrupt melatonin levels for the rest of the night.

I suspect that starting this pattern of dark nights and light days during the third trimester may help babies to start out with a better sleep rhythm. By week 26 of pregnancy, babies will turn to face a light shining on their mothers' bellies, even though the babies' eyes are still shut tight. By week 28, babies' eyes open and they begin looking around. But what do they see, day after day, in the muted darkness of the womb? The dominant landscape is the pattern of light and dark through Mom's abdominal wall. I suspect this is to help the baby get on your rhythm.

If dim evenings don't fit your lifestyle, perhaps an opaque fabric over your belly will suffice.

Engage with Sounds and Language Dramatic research in recent years shows that babies hear, prefer, and remember specific rhymes overheard multiple times during the last trimester. Earlier in pregnancy, babies' ears are protected by tiny natural earplugs. They are "tuned out" to their parents' voices in a way foreshadowing the teenage years.

Around week 28 of pregnancy, though, these earplugs fall out and babies begin listening intently to the sounds of the outside world. They react if just one syllable changes in a familiar song. Research has confirmed that, for at least a year after they are born, they can remember some sounds they hear repeatedly during these weeks.

In one of my favorite studies, Dr. Anthony DeCasper and colleagues asked sixteen expecting moms to read aloud, twice a day, one of two different rhyming books to their unborn babies *The Cat in the Hat*, or a lesser-known classic, *The King, the Mice, and the Cheese.*

Each baby heard the same story repeatedly for a total of about five hours spread out over about a month and a half.

Three days after the babies were born, they were introduced to recordings of both stories. Fifteen out of sixteen of these newborns chose *the* story their mom had read to them before birth. Remarkable! Of course, they couldn't tune a stereo with their fingers. Newborns simply don't have the fine motor control to accomplish this. But they do have excellent fine motor control with one part of their body—their mouths. These babies had been given special pacifiers that automatically switched which recording was playing based on the infants' sucking speeds.

These babies figured out the connection (an amazing feat in and of itself) and maintained the correct sucking speed to hear the one story that was so special to them.[27]

We know that later in infancy, all other things being equal, babies tend to prefer items they recognize the words for.

How does this relate to food? To me this seems like a great opportunity to introduce foods by sound. Parents may want to come up with simple rhymes to read (and even better to sing) that contain the names of key fruits, vegetables, and whole grains that you want your baby to fall in love with. Here are a few examples:

Broccoli, broccoli, broccoli trees
We want carrots, peas, and green beans, please.

Sweet potato, sweet potato, sweet potato pie
You like sweet potato and so do I.

Apples, bananas, peaches, and pears,
Plums and apricots—somebody cares.

Try creating some of your own.

Choose the Right Amount

The second and third trimester is normally a time when mothers gain weight. This may upset some women who are concerned about their appearance and the major changes going on to their bodies. But, please: this is not the time to go on a weight-loss diet! Part of this weight is the baby, placenta, and amniotic fluid, but part of this added weight comes from healthy changes in your own body to help support your baby's amazing growth now and to prepare for nursing later.

Some moms-to-be enjoy their new womanly body, especially those who were naturally very thin before they got pregnant. Others, who may have always struggled with their weight, may agonize over every pound they gain. But this is not a time either to take advantage of nature by eating as much as possible, or by restricting your diet in hopes of regaining a slim figure soon after delivery. It *is* a time to continue what you've already been doing: eating well for you and your baby.

Which brings us to the main question: How much is the right amount to eat?

You can't rely on how much other women are eating or how much weight they are gaining for your answer. Average total weight gain during

Feeding Baby Green Report
How Much Weight Gain Is Right for You?

Recommended total pregnancy weight gain for healthy women expecting one baby:[28]

Low BMI (<19.8)	28 to 40 pounds
Middle BMI (19.8–26)	25 to 35 pounds
Overweight (26 to 29)	15 to 25 pounds
Obese (>29)	at least 15 pounds

How weight gain might change over time:[29]

13 to 20 weeks	0.3 to 1.5 pounds per week
20 to 30 weeks	0.7 to 1.4 pounds per week
30 to 36 weeks	0.4 to 1.3 pounds per week

pregnancy in the 1940s thru the 1960s was just under twenty pounds. By the 1970s, and into the 1990s, it had jumped—from twenty-six to thirty-one pounds. And to confuse the issue further, in one recent large study of American women, 27 percent were given no advice on how much weight to gain over the course of their pregnancies. Among those who did get advice, many got a generic number, not tailored to their particular situation. This resulted in 14 percent being told to gain less than they really should and 22 percent being told to gain more than they should.[30]

One size does *not* fit all! Here's the bottom line: *how much weight you should gain during pregnancy depends on your weight and height before you get pregnant*—your body mass index, or BMI. If you don't know your BMI, just search for a BMI calculator online and enter your weight and height. It's an important number to know because it points you toward a fairly broad range to aim for. (See table above.) Women expecting twins

Feeding Baby Green Report

How Many Extra Calories Does It Take to Grow a Baby?

You don't need to focus on calories during pregnancy, but you may be interested in the number of extra calories in your diet it takes to grow a baby. (Remember, the number varies widely, depending on your metabolism, daily activity, and a variety of other factors.)

During the second trimester, you'll turn an average of about 180 calories a day into new tissue (for yourself and the baby). You'll also burn an extra 160 calories a day in increased energy needs, for a total of 340 calories a day—about the equivalent of three heaping tablespoons of peanut butter.

During the third trimester the 180 calories a day of new tissue continues, plus 272 calories a day of increased energy needs, for a total of 452 calories a day—still considerably less than the lowest-calorie hot fudge sundae on the Baskin-Robbins menu![31]

should aim for higher ranges: 37 to 54 if normal weight, 31 to 50 for those who are overweight before pregnancy, and 25 to 42 for those who are obese.

Around the beginning of the second trimester is a good time to notice how many pounds you have yet to gain in the remaining twenty-seven weeks or so, and to consider about how much you want to be gaining per week in the second and third trimesters. You might want to recalculate again at the beginning of the third trimester, just to see where you are. Discuss all of this with your health care provider and decide together on the plan that works best for your situation.

Don't be alarmed if your weight gain is a bit higher or lower in any given week. If you gain less than 2 pounds or more than 6.5 pounds in a *month,* it's certainly worth alerting your health care provider to consider why.

Choose the Right Variety

Variety is a key to life. To aim for balance between different types of foods day to day through the second and third trimesters, you might use the USDA food pyramid for pregnancy as a guide. At mypyramid.gov you can enter your due date, age, height, and weight to get a customized food plan for how to balance grains, vegetables, fruits, dairy, meat, and beans during each trimester of your pregnancy.

Or you might choose to follow one of several traditional food pyramids (the Mediterranean Diet Pyramid, the Asian Diet Pyramid, the Latin American Diet Pyramid, the Vegetarian Food Pyramid) hosted by the Oldways food issues think tank (oldwayspt.org). I've worked with them on the Mediterranean Diet Pyramid—a delicious and healthy style of eating that relies on olive oil as the primary fat for grilling vegetables, dressing salads, dipping bread, and so on.

Whatever you choose, be sure that the emphasis is on real foods, and that the different food groups are balanced with each other in one of the many ways that can work well.

And remember to go for variety! One of my goals in this book is to help your unborn child enjoy at least one food from twenty-one different families of plants (see "Experience Biodiversity in Your Own Kitchen"). Each of these families has well over a millennium of history of human consumption. Try to eat one food from each family—that's twenty-one different foods—at least twelve times during the second and third trimesters. You can do this by being sure to get just one each day, during any one of your three meals that day, and two on Sundays.

You may find foods on the list, such as bananas or mushrooms, that you just don't like. You may want to try them once during the second or third trimester, in case your tastes have changed, but there is no need to force anything. The goal now is to expose your baby to a broad variety of the flavors you *do* like (and to minimize exposures to junk foods you don't want your child drawn to). It's fine if you only choose eighteen or twenty (or fewer) of the families during pregnancy. After your child is born, there will be key windows where you can teach him to enjoy flavors you wish you liked but don't.

This twenty-one-family biodiversity safety net ensures getting at least some of the many as-yet-unnamed phytonutrients—the myriad of molecules created by plants that can nourish us and improve our health—from the major plant families that our species grew up with. It also helps in

Feeding Baby Green Tip

Experience Biodiversity in Your Own Kitchen

Generation upon generation of our ancestors ate foods from these twenty-one plant families—a rich collection of the delicious plant molecules that support our health. I've included some examples of the kinds of wonderful foods in each family. There's a checklist at the end of the book to help you keep track of getting at least twelve servings during pregnancy from the families you choose.

1. **Mushrooms** *(Agaricaceae):* shitake mushroom, crimini mushroom, oyster mushroom, portobello mushroom
2. **Amaranths** *(Amaranthaceae):* spinach, Swiss chard, beet (greens and root), quinoa
3. **Umbrellifers** *(Apiaceae,* also known as *Umbrelliferae):* carrot, celery, cilantro, dill
4. **Cruciferous vegetables** *(Brassicaceae,* also called *Cruciferae):* broccoli, cauliflower, mustard
5. **Bromeliads** *(Bromeliaceae):* pineapple (the *only* common edible bromeliad)
6. **Composites** *(Compositeae* also known as *Asteraceae):* artichoke, lettuces, sunflower seeds
7. **Bindweeds** *(Convolvulaceae):* sweet potato
8. **Gourds** *(Cucurbitaceae):* cucumber, pumpkin (and other winter squashes), watermelon, zucchini (and other summer squashes)
9. **Heath plants** *(Ericaceae):* blueberry, cranberry
10. **Legumes (Peas or Beans)** *(Fabaceae,* also called *Leguminosae):* black beans, chickpeas, lentils, peas
11. **Lilies** *(Lilaceae):* asparagus, chive, garlic, onion
12. **Woody trees** *(Musaceae):* banana
13. **Sesames** *(Pedaliaceae):* sesame seeds
14. **True grasses** *(Poaceae,* also called *Gramineae):* barley, oats, brown rice
15. **Rosy plants** *(Rosaceae):* apple, apricot, blackberry, cherry, peach, pear, plum, raspberry, strawberry
16. **Citrus plants** *(Rutaceae):* grapefruit, orange, lemon, lime
17. **Nightshades (Potatoes)** *(Solanaceae):* eggplant, peppers, white potatoes, tomato
18. **Grapes** *(Vitaceae):* grape

> 19. **Laurels** *(Lauraceae):* avocados (a great first food), cinnamon, bay leaves
> 20. **Myrtles** *(Myrtaceae):* guava (packed with nutrients), cloves, allspice
> 21. **Loosestrifes** *(Lythraceae):* pomegranate (packed with antioxidants)

learning new flavors. Variety begets variety. The more flavors a child likes, the easier it is to learn to like new flavors.

During this time, additional nutrients become important.

Protein Protein needs during the final two trimesters go up more than 50 percent—from 46 grams a day for most women before they are pregnant to 71 grams during pregnancy—and getting plenty of protein during pregnancy has been linked to healthier babies. In one study, the babies whose mothers got a normal amount of calories but got too little protein ended up having increased body fat, decreased lean body mass, higher cholesterols and triglycerides, increased insulin resistance, decreased leptin (a hormone that controls appetite), and increased appetite compared to the babies whose mothers got the protein they needed.[32]

Even with these increased protein needs, most American women get plenty of protein while pregnant. To give you an idea, two eggs contain about 12 grams of protein; one cup of cooked black beans has 15 grams, a quarter pound of lean ground beef, 22 grams; and six ounces of wild salmon contain about 46 grams of protein.

Fats Certain fat requirements also go up, notably one of the omega-3 fats involved in the growth of your baby's brain and the retina. (The brain is 60 percent fat!)

DHA is the omega-3 that has the most research regarding brain benefit. Women should average at least 300 milligrams per day during pregnancy and nursing (up from 220 milligrams per day during the rest of adulthood). The other omega-3 recommendations don't change during pregnancy or nursing, but include at least 220 milligrams per day of EPA and at least 650 milligrams per day total between EPA and DHA.

Most pregnant women don't get enough! Two six-ounce servings of wild salmon each week would easily do the trick. Pregnancy is also a great time to choose heart-healthy fats such as olive oil, avocado oil, and peanut or other nut oils—while minimizing unhealthy fats, especially trans fats.

Choline Choline is another brain nutrient that many women are likely to miss out on, because it is not contained in most prenatal vitamins. It's linked to memory and brain development in the fetus. The total needed is 450 milligrams per day.

Food choline is the best source, and it's not hard to come by. Eggs have high levels of choline, and just an egg or two a day is usually enough. Soy is another good source of choline (soy lecithin contains choline), and so are potatoes, cauliflower, tomatoes, bananas, oranges, lentils, sesame seeds, and flax seeds, among others.

Calcium Calcium is another nutrient that deserves close attention. Babies are born with a whopping 30,000 milligrams of calcium in their bodies—all of it from Mom's diet. If an average nonpregnant woman needs 1,000 milligrams a day to replace her losses and stay in calcium balance, how much extra would a pregnant woman need?

Surprisingly, perhaps none. Pregnant women absorb more of the calcium in their diets and lose less than nonpregnant women. That's why 1,000 milligrams of calcium a day remains the recommended amount.

Still, getting enough is important. And a bit more may be better—for a different reason than most people think. Heavy metals that you have been exposed to before pregnancy, such as lead, have probably accumulated in your bones. In one study, women getting 1,300 milligrams a day of extra calcium supplements significantly helped to prevent that lead from coming out of their bones and into their blood—and into the baby.[33]

Iron As we've seen, iron needs go up a lot during pregnancy. It also has an important effect on blood pressure (see "Hypertension" further on). But it can be tough to get enough from food alone—another reason that a good prenatal vitamin can be wise.

The World Health Organization (WHO) estimates that between two-thirds and four-fifths of all people on our planet suffer from iron deficiency.[34] Although 90 percent of those with low iron live in the developing

Feeding Baby Green Report

Eat Only Safe Fish and Shellfish

Here's a list of some healthy, eco-friendly seafood options that are high in omega-3 fats and low in contaminants like mercury:

- Farmed abalone
- Farmed catfish
- Farmed caviar
- Farmed clams
- Blue crab
- Dungeness crab
- Snow crab
- Stone crab
- Flounder
- Haddock
- Atlantic herring and anchovies
- Atlantic mackerel (NOT king mackerel)
- Mahi mahi
- Farmed mussels
- Farmed oysters
- Wild Alaskan or Pacific salmon
- Canned wild pink or sockeye salmon
- Sardines
- Bay scallops
- Farmed scallops
- Northern shrimp, Oregon shrimp, spot prawns
- Farmed striped bass
- Farmed sturgeon
- Farmed trout

Avoid: King mackerel, Atlantic salmon, Chilean sea bass, shark, unidentified or farmed shrimp, swordfish, tilefish, canned white tuna (at least), and fish caught in local lakes and rivers—unless you've checked the advisories. These same recommendations will apply for your baby later next year.

world, that still leaves 400 to 500 million iron-deficient people in developed areas.

Customize Needs for Every Body

Depending on specific dietary or health concerns, the foods you choose during pregnancy may vary. We'll discuss a few of these custom needs below, from families who want to reduce the risk of allergies, to those with family health issues, to those who are pursuing a vegan lifestyle.

Allergies There is scant evidence, as we've seen earlier, that when moms avoid specific foods during pregnancy they reduce allergies to those foods in their babies. The issue of whether or not avoiding peanuts during pregnancy reduces allergies in children has been quite controversial. In 2008, two major studies purported to settle the question—but they came to opposite conclusions.

Yet there is some evidence for reducing allergies by eating certain foods. Three food choices in particular seem to be beneficial:

1. *Probiotics:* I'm a big fan of probiotics (beneficial bacteria, such as those found in yogurt or kefir) for pregnant women because their consumption is linked to decreased eczema and other allergies in the babies.
2. *Omega-3 fats:* Foods rich in omega-3 fats, such as wild salmon, omega-3 eggs, walnuts, and flaxseed.
3. *Organic milk:* Studies of organic milk have found healthier fat profiles in the milk—more omega-3s and CLAs (conjugated linoleic acids), which may help reduce body fat and hinder tumors and inflammation. Studies of nursing mothers who switched from conventional to organic milk found more of these healthier fats in the mothers' breast milk. One study of pregnant and nursing women who switched from conventional to organic milk found a third less eczema in their babies.[35]

Eating according to what is called the Mediterranean diet has also been advised to prevent or lessen allergies. Although the jury is not yet in, a January 2008 study published in *Thorax*, an international journal of respiratory medicine, found that elementary school kids in Spain whose mothers had followed a Mediterranean diet during their pregnancy were less likely to develop asthma or allergies. Their peers, whose mothers had not eaten

Feeding Baby Green Report

The Mediterranean Diet

The authors of the Spanish study defined a Mediterranean diet as high in plant foods (fruits, vegetables, whole grain breads and cereals, legumes, and nuts), high in olive oil and fish, with moderate amounts of dairy products and eggs, and very little beef. Here are some typical specific daily and weekly amounts:

Fruit or fruit juice daily

Another serving of fruit daily

Fresh or cooked vegetables more than once a day

Legume more than once a week

Fish at least two or three times a week

Wholegrain as part of breakfast daily

Pasta or rice at least five times a week

Two dairy products (for example milk, cheese, yogurt) daily

Nuts two or three times a week

Olive oil used at home daily

Fast food less than once a week

Sweets and pastries less than once a day

this way, were about twice as likely to have positive allergic skin tests, more than four times more likely to wheeze, and more than three times more likely to have both positive allergy tests and wheezing. What separates this study from others on the same topic is that it was a forward-looking (prospective) study. The researchers put forth their hypothesis in advance, and then followed families from pregnancy until the children were six-and-a-half years old. (To avoid bias, the participants were not told this study was about the Mediterranean diet.)

The Mediterranean diet has also been recommended for prevention of cardiovascular problems. This is a delicious style of eating to consider, even if asthma or allergies do not run in your family. (For specifics, see "The Mediterranean Diet.")

Diabetes By working to keep your own blood sugars in the normal range throughout pregnancy, you could be reaching into the future to give a gift to your baby as an adult. Diabetes can be a vicious cycle—when the mother develops uncontrolled diabetes before giving birth, it makes it all the more likely that her offspring will develop diabetes later in life, and on and on and on.[36]

In a large Norwegian study of almost 140,000 new mothers, those whose own mothers had had diabetes during the months before they were

Feeding Baby Green Report
A Sweet Tooth

Some women are genetically and metabolically predisposed to develop diabetes. And if that weren't enough, during pregnancy your taste buds aren't necessarily your friends in avoiding it.

One study of pregnant women with and without gestational diabetes measured their responses to milk sweetened with sugar (10 percent sucrose) throughout pregnancy and after giving birth, and compared the responses to matched nonpregnant women. The nonpregnant women tended to have a sweet tooth. Those with gestational diabetes also had a sweet tooth throughout pregnancy and after giving birth.

The women who never developed diabetes, though, liked the sweetened drink less on average during the third trimester. By report, they tended to drink fewer sweetened beverages. Their sweet tooth had returned to normal by twelve weeks postpartum.[37]

If you are craving sweets in the third trimester, be sure you are getting plenty of exercise (see next section) to help keep your blood sugar under control.

born were almost eight times more likely to have gestational diabetes when they were grown and pregnant themselves.[38] Gestational diabetes is the result of our current obesity-diabetes epidemic, and it also helps to fuel it for the next generation.

It's no wonder that gestational diabetes (diabetes that comes and goes with pregnancy) is now so common—and getting more so. The rate varies in different ethnic groups, from as low as 2 percent to as high as 17 percent.[39] But it has been rising rapidly over the last ten years in most ethnic groups studied.

Keeping your blood sugars normal tends to reduce the risk of obesity and diabetes in your baby. In one long study that's been in progress since 1965, investigators looked at the offspring of pregnant women who had developed diabetes after they'd already had at least one child. Those babies born when their mothers had already developed diabetes were almost four times as likely to end up with diabetes as were their siblings born before their mother had abnormal blood sugars.[40] (There was no difference in siblings born before or after their dads developed diabetes.)

Another study looked at healthy elementary school kids whose mothers had developed diabetes either before or after they were pregnant. Even though none of these kids had diabetes, their glucose and insulin levels were significantly more likely to be healthy if Mom's sugars were normal during the months before they were born.[41]

Don't restrict calories too much or exercise too much in an attempt to prevent diabetes. Yes, too much weight gain in pregnancy is associated with later diabetes in the babies as adults—but studies show that too little weight gain could be an even bigger cause.[42]

The relaxing good news is that it is the comfortable middle zone of moderate weight gain and moderate physical activity that is healthiest for you and for your baby.

Hypertension Like diabetes and obesity, adult blood pressure correlates with how much weight the baby (and by extension, her mom) puts on before birth. But in this case, surprisingly, *low* birth weight is the strongest predictor of later hypertension.

In one Harvard study of over twenty-two thousand adult men, those who were underweight at birth were 26 percent more likely to have high blood pressure as adults—independent of their family history of high blood pressure or of their own weight as adults.[43] If cardiovascular disease runs in your family, you have an opportunity before your baby is born to help break that cycle by your healthy food and activity choices.

Getting plenty of iron during pregnancy has been linked to healthier blood pressures for the babies as adults. This has been demonstrated in animal studies where everything was identical except prenatal iron.[44] Getting plenty of calcium may also help to prevent high blood pressure.[45] And plenty of protein may also help.[46]

Obesity You've probably heard about the "obesity epidemic" in school-age kids and even toddlers. But you may not know that a tendency to pack on excess fat can be passed on from mother to baby during gestation. (In medical literature, this is called the epigenetic intergenerational maternal-fetal transmission of adipogenity!)

Likewise, the obesity epidemic in kids shows up not just in school-age kids or toddlers who are gaining too much weight too quickly, but also in today's fetuses. Weighing too much at birth increases the odds of being overweight as an adult.

Average birth weights are going up too quickly (4.7 percent in a recent twelve-year period).[47] But more important, newborns' relative weights (which estimate body fat) are going up even faster—birth weight is increasing nine times faster than birth length.[48]

Aiming for a healthy weight gain for your body type (see "How Much Weight Gain Is Right for You?" earlier in this chapter) during the second and third trimesters gives your baby the best odds for healthy weight as a child and as an adult.

Keeping blood sugars normal can also help make it easier for your baby to stay on course for healthy weight as he grows. For siblings growing up in the same family, those whose moms had diabetes during their pregnancy averaged half a pound heavier per square foot of skin as they grew.[49] For a typical four-year-old boy, that could be the difference between being ideal weight and being obese.[50]

Vegetarian or Vegan Choosing a vegetarian or vegan lifestyle can be very healthy both for the body and for the planet, even though it is not the way most humans have historically eaten. It's possible to have a healthy vegetarian or vegan pregnancy as well, but there are a few important considerations to keep in mind.

Vitamin B$_{12}$. Because this nutrient is essential for your developing baby, and because it is not found naturally within plant-based foods, it's important to find another reliable way to get it. For vegetarians, this might be dairy products or eggs. For vegans, choosing fortified foods is one possibility—such as fortified breakfast cereals or soy milk—but it is important to eat something containing B$_{12}$ consistently. Another option I like is Red Star Nutritional Yeast Vegetarian Support Formula. It tastes good as a seasoning sprinkled on soups and salads. You could also choose a prenatal vitamin that contains at least 2.6 micrograms per day of B$_{12}$.

Calcium and Vitamin D. Although there is some evidence that eating less animal protein may help the body absorb more calcium (from spinach, for instance) or reduce calcium losses,[51] there is no information to convince me that vegetarians or vegans need less calcium than others when pregnant. I still recommend getting at least 1,000 milligrams per day; 1,300 milligrams may be even better—and is strongly recommended if you are under age nineteen. This is tougher for vegans than for vegetarians.

Include rich sources of calcium in your diet, such as tofu (especially if it has been processed in calcium sulfate), tempeh, sesame seeds, dark leafy greens, and figs. As with B$_{12}$, you can find many calcium-fortified foods, such as soy milk, orange juice, or even whole grain waffles. Or choose a calcium supplement. If you are not getting enough vitamin D from the sun, you may also want 400 International Units (IU) of vitamin D with you calcium—in addition to 400 IU of vitamin D in your prenatal vitamin.

DHA. This omega-3 fat is found mainly in fatty fish. If you don't eat fish, you can find DHA supplements made from a vegetarian source (microalgae). Sometimes this is sold in gelatin capsules, not suitable for vegans, but it can also be found in vegan capsules or in a simple powdered form that can be sprinkled on food or in a beverage.

Protein. One of the most common concerns expressed to pregnant vegetarian moms by well-meaning friends and family members is about getting enough protein. Typical vegan women may get about 65 grams of protein daily before getting pregnant.[52] To increase to the 71 grams recommended during pregnancy isn't too tough.

I recommend not relying too much on one protein source—such as soy—during a vegetarian pregnancy. You can also get protein from other sources, such as seeds, grains, beans, and other legumes. This broadens the focus from phytoestrogen-containing plants, while also helping to ensure that you get a healthy variety of nutrients.

Exercise!

Exercise can prevent or even treat two of pregnancy's most common complications.[53] Brisk walking and other moderate physical activity is associated with a lower risk of preeclampsia, a pregnancy complication where the mother's blood pressure rises and blood flow to the baby decreases, often resulting in preterm delivery. In one study, those who walked at a rate of at least three miles per hour enjoyed the best results. Among the women who didn't intentionally exercise, those who climbed one to four flights of stairs each day still had a lower risk of preeclampsia than those who didn't.

Up to one in eight women will develop gestational diabetes during pregnancy. In one study of women who had already developed gestational diabetes, half of the women got the recommended insulin. The other half got personal trainers, who supervised them on exercise bikes.

Three twenty-minute sessions on the exercise bike weekly was *equally as effective* as insulin! And the blood sugar benefit was still detectable five to seven days after the last session.

Exercise during pregnancy has many other benefits, including stronger muscles, bones, and joints; less chance of urinary incontinence; easier labor and delivery; and enhanced ability to enjoy your new baby by helping to ward off the baby blues of postpartum depression.

For most pregnant women, I recommend thirty minutes of moderate physical activity every day or at least on most days, once the early pregnancy fatigue has worn off.

I suggest brisk walks (alone or with others), dancing, swimming, low-impact aerobics, or prenatal yoga.

Of course, no scuba diving, sky diving, contact sports, or anything where you might expect a collision or a fall (such as skiing). Nor do I suggest lying on your back to exercise when pregnant—this can constrict blood supply to your baby.

Be sure to discuss your plan with your pregnancy health care team.[54] Some exercise is marvelous. Too much or the wrong kind is not. Pay attention to your body's signals. Bleeding, chest pain, cramps, contractions, dizziness, or headaches are all good reasons to stop and check in with those caring for you.

And some pregnant women should not exercise, or should do so in an even gentler way than most. This is especially true for those with heart disease, lung disease, or who have been diagnosed with an incompetent cervix.

Reap the Benefits of Green

The fruits and vegetables you eat while pregnant should be as flavorful and nutritious as possible. There are a couple of strategies for achieving this that are good for you, good for your baby, and good for the environment.

Choosing produce soon after it has been picked often provides peak flavor and peak nutrients. And because this is easiest if the food has been grown locally, there are environmental and social benefits. Produce that was frozen shortly after being picked helps make that just-picked goodness available at other times and other places.

Non-GMO. Another advantage of organic food is that it is grown without the use of genetic modification. Just over a decade ago, genetically modified organisms (GMOs) were not part of our food supply. Today, about 30 percent of our cropland has been taken over by GMO crops. During the same time, food allergies have increased rapidly. I'm concerned that GMO foods may be one of the reasons.

The Italian government's National Institute of Research on Food and Nutrition published a study in 2008 comparing mice given feed containing corn with and without genetic modification. The two types of corn were grown at the same time in two neighboring fields in Landriano, Italy. Everything about the different sets of mice was the same, except that some sets' feed contained the genetically modified (GM) corn variety (common in the United States), some starting as pups, others starting later in life. Everything was the same but the results.

The GMO-fed mice had altered levels of immune T and B cells in their guts, their spleens, and their blood. They had elevated inflammation triggers, called cytokines, in their blood. Their allergy and inflammatory systems were revved up. This effect was significant in the mice that didn't start the GM foods until they were older, but it was most pronounced in those who started as pups.[55]

This report came on the heels of a study commissioned by the Austrian government showing that the same GM corn reduces fertility in the offspring of those who eat it.

Although most Americans believe they have never eaten GM foods, most eat them every day. Most of the soy, corn, canola, cottonseed oil, and papaya in the United States have been genetically modified. Much of the livestock has been fed large quantities of GM food. I hope the law changes so that the use of GM products in foods appears on the label.

In the meantime, especially while pregnant and nursing, you can reduce GM foods by cutting down on foods that contain corn syrup, high fructose corn syrup, corn meal, dextrose, maltodextrin, corn oil, cottonseed oil, canola oil, unspecified vegetable oil, soybean oil, soy protein, soy lecithin, or textured vegetable protein.

Or simply select organic foods. By law, these plants cannot be grown from genetically modified seeds, and the animals cannot be cloned or fed genetically modified feed. And as an added bonus, grass-fed organic beef cannot be given artificial hormones.

Artificial Dyes. The British Food Standards Agency (the FSA) decided to fund two careful, randomized, double-blind, placebo-controlled studies to see whether artificial dyes in typical amounts consumed by typical kids actually worsen children's behavior. These studies were on healthy British kids, not those diagnosed with ADHD or suspected of having sensitivity to the dyes.

The researchers found significant problems with the dyes, and prompted the FSA to call for the elimination of the dyes. "It is the Agency's duty to put consumers first. These additives give colour to foods but nothing else.

It would therefore be sensible, in the light of the findings of the Southampton Study, to remove them from food and drink products."[56]

These steps are already spreading beyond Britain. Recently, the Environment Committee of the entire European Union voted to ban artificial colors in foods for babies and small children throughout Europe.

Companies that do business both in the United States and in England have taken voluntary action ahead of legislation. Mars, for example, has removed some or all of the artificial dyes from M&M's, Skittles, and Starbursts—but not for American children. Kraft has removed artificial colors from Lunchables—but not for American children. Kellogg's has removed the dyes from their cereal and Pop-Tarts—but not for American children. McDonald's uses caramel and strawberries and beet juice to color shakes and syrups in England; here in the USA, they use Yellow No. 5, Yellow No. 6, and Red No. 40.[57] I've joined with a number of physicians and research scientists to send a letter to our FDA urging them to begin proceedings to end the use of artificial food dyes, which mounting evidence suggests are not safe for our children. The FDA's own regulations say that for a dye to be allowed there must be "convincing evidence that establishes with reasonable certainty that no harm will result from the intended use of the color additive."[58]

Excellent natural food colorings exist. Here in the United States, Whole Foods and Trader Joe's markets have taken a leadership role and do not sell foods that contain artificial dyes. And, as we already know, organic foods do not contain such dyes.

The impact of artificial dyes on the developing brains of school-age and preschool children has been the subject of major studies, but we don't know the dyes' impact during the rapid brain growth during the second and third trimesters. I suggest to err on the side of caution: these months are a good time to cut back on chemical food dyes.

∾

No matter how much you have enjoyed your pregnancy, the last weeks can sometimes seem endless. But soon enough, these months will rapidly become a fond memory, and you'll get to enjoy the wonder of seeing your baby face-to-face. You'll move from the unique ease, joy, and responsibility of feeding your baby *within you* to a new set of joys and responsibilities as you snuggle and gaze into each other's eyes as she nurses for the first time.

3

Babies

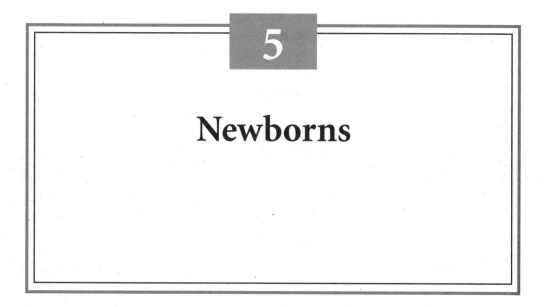

5

Newborns

Finally, the big moment has arrived! The umbilical cord is clamped and cut. You and your baby are able to look into each other's eyes for the first time, to touch skin-to-skin. In this truly magical moment, all of the worry and planning of pregnancy, and the struggle and pain of childbirth, seems to dissolve into the euphoric present. Your baby is home, with you.

Take time to savor her first moments on earth. She is meeting the world—and you—for the first time, face-to-face. The first weeks of your baby's life are like a private world inhabited just by you, your infant, and your immediate family. Bonding is stronger and stronger, nursing or feeding routines are begun, and often you just want to snuggle up together and soak up the shared beginnings of an amazing new life.

And that's just what you should do.

The Essential Steps for Teaching Nutritional Intelligence

During the first days and weeks of your newborn's life, your pastel (or muted earth-tone) visions of motherhood will likely be replaced by the reality of a real, live human being who looks to you for *everything*: shelter, protection, care, love—and food. It's natural, especially if this is your first child, to be overwhelmed by this new sense of responsibility.

Give yourself time to adjust to your new role as a mom—that's what these first days are all about. It's a learning process between you and your baby, a "getting to know each other" dance. As far as nutritional training, your job is especially easy now—all you have to do is what you've been doing: eat healthy foods that you love, and know that your baby is benefiting too.

Take Charge!

Many moms discover that all of their great attempts to take charge of their child's birth seem to dissolve when the child is actually ready to be born: perhaps they are at a hospital or birth center, and far from the wonderful room they had readied for a home birth; or perhaps complications mean the natural childbirth you planned so carefully is suddenly not an option. But all these issues disappear the first time you and your newborn gaze into each other's eyes.

Now, with your new baby naturally depending on your good care, is the perfect moment to recognize that you are indeed in charge. As you'll see in the next section, you can begin taking charge in the birth environment the first time you feed your baby.

Use Windows of Opportunity

Baby's first feeding after birth is often a very special opportunity. If for some reason this does not work for you (for example, if you or your baby need immediate medical attention), there will be plenty of other opportunities later to feed your baby. But if breastfeeding is something you want to do, and you *do* have the opportunity to let your baby nurse the way I will describe, it can be a wonderful time for all of you.

We know that if breastfeeding is attempted before a baby is taken out of the room and away from his mother (for postnatal testing, for example), the chances of successful nursing in the long run are higher. There's something powerful and almost mystical about those first moments together, just after the infant has emerged into the world after a lifetime of living inside her mother. Because of this, some nurses are eager to put the baby to breast to initiate this intimate journey.

I've become a big fan, though, of letting a baby decide when it's time for that first meal, and of letting him come to the table himself. Taking charge, in this case, means taking charge of the birth environment to create a space for nature to follow its course.

Sometime during that golden first hour, usually about forty minutes or so after birth, you are likely to notice a change in your baby's attention. His peaceful contentment—gazing at your face and listening to your voice—often shifts to an intense concentration on his own mouth movements. He may start smacking his lips. You might notice a glisten as his saliva starts to increase at the prospect of his first meal.

Rather than rushing to scoop him up and latch him onto the nipple right away, you might try leaving him on your tummy. You may feel a shiver of wonder as he starts to make his own way up your body, along the path of the dark line, the linea nigra, intent on reaching your darkened nipple for himself.

Babies are born with several key reflexes, including a rooting reflex to help them find the nipple when it touches their mouth; a sucking reflex to enable them to get milk when they latch on; and a stepping reflex, the ability to push with their legs as if they were walking. The stepping reflex has been assumed to exist to help prepare babies to walk as they become toddlers. But as it disappears after only a few weeks, I believe it may be present at birth, at least in part, to enable them to make their own way to their mother's nipple to root and suck.

As babies journey along their mother's bodies, their progress is typically halting and slow. You may notice your baby licking and sucking his own hands. He's getting directions! Babies use the taste and smell of the amniotic fluid on their own bodies as a compass toward the oily substances secreted by the breast, which are seasoned with the same ingredients. If a baby's hands have been washed before this road trip, he will likely get lost and give up. In studies, if one breast has been washed, the baby will predictably head toward the other one. If both breasts have been washed, he will set his course toward one that has then been splashed with amniotic fluid.

With a little patience, the baby might navigate to the nipple by himself and latch on perfectly, tasting those first precious drops of colostrum. Those who rely on instinct and reflex and who work to get there on their own are more likely to take the whole areola into the mouth, nursing more effectively and hurting the nipple less.

This often works beautifully—the baby takes the nipple and begins to suck hungrily. Some babies, however, aren't quite sure what to do. They lick the nipple, or latch on incorrectly. Be patient! You've never done this before. It's often awkward and frustrating. But take your time. Keep trying. Savor the moment. Most nursing moms value this closeness with their baby, no matter how hard won.

Even if it's clumsy or brief, or needs to be with a bottle, this first feeding can be a magical moment you will long remember. For most healthy babies, it's well worth delaying the washing, eye ointment, shots, and other procedures for the first hour to be able to enjoy this moment that you have all been awaiting so long.

Engage All the Senses

The newborn's sense of vision is still imprecise, but the other senses—taste, smell, hearing, touch—are vivid. Of course, your baby is far too young to interpret the language he hears, but he is already adept at using his nose and his tongue to get the information he needs—in some ways, even better than you can.

Engage with Flavor Colostrum is what we call the milk that flows from your breast in the first few days of your baby's life, before the mature breast milk comes in. It is filled with nutrients and antibodies that nourish and

---

Feeding Baby Green Tip

The First Few Days

For the first several days of their lives, it is normal for babies to lose weight. Their bodies are designed with adequate fuel to carry them forward several days until their mothers' breast milk comes in, when they begin gaining weight. Whenever possible, I urge breastfeeding at least until the baby has regained her birth weight—even for women who have decided to bottle-feed later, for whatever reason. (If you are unable to breastfeed, don't worry. Later in this chapter we'll talk about today's formulas—the best in history.)

---

protect the newborn. Colostrum and breast milk are evocative of the flavors and aromas your baby has come to love over the last several months.

If you are nursing, my core advice is simple: eat the healthy foods you love. Choose your favorite tastes that you want to pass along to your newborn. These first weeks may make an even bigger impression than others. Of course, you also need lots of rest. So this means making a few meals in advance, or enlisting a helper to cook meals for the family.

If you are not nursing, my advice is the same: eat what you love. You will certainly be exposing you newborn to a few of your favorite aromas. If you adopted a newborn, you may also want to have a meal or two of healthy items from the birth mother's cuisine to bridge the current bonding to the familiar aromas from your baby's past.

Engage with Aroma If you or I were asked to distinguish by smell alone between two samples of breast milk, we would have a hard time doing it— unless one of the mothers had recently eaten something aromatic, such as garlic. And if both smelled of garlic, we would be lost.

But your newborn knows right where he is.

Immediately after birth, babies' sense of smell is far more powerful than our own. They can perform a feat that we cannot: by smell alone, they can select the breast milk unique to their mothers. As we saw in the last chapter, babies will turn toward pleasant odors, familiar from before birth. Aroma forges powerful memories and influences learning and behavior.

Engage with Sight Newborns were once thought to be uninterested in seeing. Today, however, we understand that newborn vision, though still imprecise, plays a powerful role in bonding and helps them form vital links to the future. And we'll return to that shortly. But first, we can learn a lesson about how babies see from, of all things, chick booties.

Baby chicks have long been believed to have a hardwired instinct to move toward, reach for, pick up, and eat mealworms if they happen to see them. But investigator J. Wallman had an interesting thought. He noticed that baby chick toes look a lot like mealworms. They're about the same size, same shape, and have similar segmentation lines. Wallman wondered if seeing their own toes might prime chicks to notice and recognize mealworms.

He tested his idea by hatching a bunch of chicks in a dark incubator where they couldn't see their toes. He slipped little cloth booties on the feet of some of the chicks so their feet were not visible; others he left barefoot. For two days, all the baby chicks were otherwise treated the same. And then the mealworms were introduced. While the barefoot chicks pecked and swallowed, the chicks at the sock hop stood around looking confused, staring at the mealworms, baffled, one eye at a time.[1]

Their feeding instincts weren't innately hardwired; they were linked to their early visual experiences—in ways we might never have suspected.

Here's another example from the animal world: squirrel monkeys are terrified of snakes. They are afraid of live snakes, stuffed snakes, and of rubber toy snakes. Again, this was thought to be an inborn instinct. But some squirrel monkeys who are raised in captivity have no fear of snakes when they first see them. The difference is they've never seen any insects— yes, insects! Those who have never seen an insect have no fear of snakes. Those who see and are fed a few insects, as are squirrel monkeys in the wild, react to snakes with terror at first sight.

For whatever reason, the monkeys' experience of seeing or not seeing insects changes their other likes and dislikes in profound and seemingly unrelated ways.[2]

Squirrel monkeys' eyes are naturally drawn to live insects; baby chicks naturally look at their toes. Given the opportunity, human babies love to look at faces and at breasts. And in the direction of familiar sounds and smells.

I remember a vivid demonstration of this from medical school. My professor explained that the medical community used to think that newborns didn't see well at all because they ignored doctors' fingers. Mothers

Feeding Baby Green Recipe

Naked Salad

Naked? Yep, no dressing needed! The key is to use a very ripe avocado to replace traditional dressing—saving calories, time, and money. Use your imagination! If you'd rather use pumpkin seeds than walnuts, please do. If you're not in an onion mood, leave it out and add some fresh blueberries instead. My favorite salad ingredients include peppers, toasted nuts or seeds, jicama (crunchy); berries, citrus, grapefruit, Fuji apples, pears, Fuyu persimmons (sweet).

1 very ripe avocado, small diced

5 ounces salad greens, washed and spun dry

½ red bell pepper, diced

½ small sweet red onion, thinly sliced

1 small basket (1 dry pint) cherry or grape tomatoes

¾ cup toasted walnuts

1 tablespoon grated Parmesan cheese

Freshly ground pepper, to taste

1. Combine avocado, salad greens, red pepper, red onion, and tomatoes in an extra-large bowl.
2. Toss the salad liberally so that the avocado breaks down and lightly coats all the vegetables. You shouldn't be able to pick out any avocado pieces when you're done tossing.
3. Pour into serving bowls and top with toasted walnuts, Parmesan cheese, and fresh ground black pepper.

Serves 4

NUTRITION FACTS (AMOUNT PER SERVING)

Calories: 219
Total Fat: 16.82g
Cholesterol: 1mg

Sodium: 38mg
Total Carbs: 13.13g
Dietary Fiber: 5.51g

Sugars: 5.31g
Protein: 5.52g

who insisted, "My baby looks in my eyes" were dismissed as having wishful thinking. My teacher flicked his fingers in front of a baby's eyes and the baby did not blink. He didn't seem to notice. I wondered if the baby couldn't see.

Then my teacher took a Ping-Pong paddle with a few bold marks he'd scrawled on it with a Sharpie: a couple of random dots, two straight lines, and a curve, in no discernible structure or representation. He waved it in front of the baby's face, and he showed no more interest than if he'd been blind.

Finally my teacher flipped the paddle to the other side. It had the exact same marks, but now they were arranged to make a simple smiley face with an angular nose. The baby was riveted by the sight, following it with his eyes as far as he could and unhappy when it left his field of view. The difference in interest was dramatic.

Thankfully, no one will ever do an experiment to see what happens when babies with normal eyesight have the faces and breasts of their parents hidden from view by big, cloth booties. I suspect, though, it would change their relationship to food in ways we don't imagine.

The moral of all this? Newborns *can* see, and they want to look at *you*.

I'm a fan of gentle eye contact (gazing, not staring, looking away when your baby looks away), including some magic moments of eye contact during feeding. I encourage you to let your baby watch your face when you talk to her. Let her see the nipple she is drinking from, breast or bottle, before she latches on, and let her see the sources of some of your favorite food aromas.

I don't know exactly what ripple effects this will have, but I do know that human babies are designed to be interested in these food-related sights.

Engage with Sounds and Language Many of the classic studies of babies' early interest in language demonstrate how they respond to familiar voices, tones, music, and even specific language during this early newborn period.

To help form her future relationship with healthy eating, these are great weeks to repeat any of the food rhymes or songs or stories you used during pregnancy. Your child may be all the more interested now that she gets to see the food and smell the food as well as listen to the rhymes!

Engage with Touch Before they are born, babies are snuggled inside their moms and their skin experiences gentle pressure and movement. When babies exit the womb early through preterm delivery, this comforting touch disappears. Researchers have shown that when premature babies are gently stroked or massaged for fifteen minutes, four times a day, the babies tend to eat better—and to grow better even if they eat the same amount of food.[3]

In the animal world, mother rats usually lick their pups, stimulating growth hormones and other key chemicals. When the pups are separated from their mothers, they don't grow well. Saul Schanberg at Duke University wondered if touch was central to the young pups' early relationship to food.[4] He couldn't get the lab technicians to actually lick the pups, but stroking them with a wet paintbrush did the trick, restoring feeding, growth, and brain chemistry.

Whether your baby is bottle-fed or breastfed, allowing her to enjoy skin-to-skin contact can be quite powerful, especially during these first weeks. And you will like it too.

Choose the Right Amount

Earlier, we saw how a mother's weight gain and eating patterns during pregnancy can affect the child's lifelong weight. How a baby eats during the first week of life is another window where you have the chance to establish lifelong eating patterns that can lead toward a healthy weight in the future—or toward a life of struggling with obesity.

In a fascinating study from the Children's Hospital of Philadelphia, 653 formula-fed babies were each measured on seven different occasions while they were babies.[5] They were contacted again when they had grown to be adults in their twenties or thirties, and a chart of their weight over the course of their lives was plotted for each of them. About 32 percent of them had become overweight adults.

Feeding Baby Green Recipe

Calabecitas

This dish is a hearty blend of beans and vegetables, seasoned with chili. It is a delicious main dish for the whole family that can be easily mashed for baby when the time comes.

1 cup dried black beans (when cooked, equals 2 cups)

3 ears corn on the cob, fresh or frozen

2 tablespoons extra virgin olive oil

1 large onion, diced

3 medium zucchini, diced

¼ teaspoon chili powder

Kosher salt, to taste

½ cup shredded cheddar cheese

1. Wash beans carefully and remove any pebbles, sticks, and dirt that may still be in the beans. Place beans in a large saucepan, cover in cold water, and soak for 2 to 4 hours.
2. Drain the beans, cover with 2 to 3 cups of water, and bring to a boil. Reduce heat to a very slow simmer and cook on low heat for about 2 hours, or until soft.
3. Cut the corn kernels off the cobs.
4. In a large sauté pan, heat the olive oil over medium heat. Add the onions, corn, zucchini, and chili powder and sauté until zucchini and onion are softened, about 5 to 6 minutes.
5. Reduce heat to low, gently stir in black beans, and heat through. Season to taste with salt.
6. Sprinkle the cheddar cheese evenly over the top. Cover pan to melt cheese (about 1 minute). Serve immediately.

Serves 4 (Yield: 8 cups)

NUTRITION FACTS (AMOUNT PER SERVING)

Calories: 257	Sodium: 107mg	Sugars: 4.32g
Total Fat: 11.74g	Total Carbs: 29.68g	Protein: 11.04g
Cholesterol: 14mg	Dietary Fiber: 7.09g	

Submitted and reprinted by permission from *Fresh Baby*.

Strikingly, the speed at which the babies gained weight in the first eight days was very predictive of their risk of becoming overweight adults. For every 3.5 ounces of increased weight gain in those first eight days, there was a 28 percent increased chance of becoming overweight later. It seems that during that first week, babies are setting their internal sense of how much is "normal" for them to eat, how much it takes for them to feel full. Those who eat too much during the first week may be programmed to eat too much later on, without even noticing.

A baby's weight gain before birth that is either faster or slower than normal tends to lead to problems with being overweight later. Perhaps before birth the babies are deciding unconsciously whether the food supply is reliable (they can feel safe burning it for fuel) or threatens to be scarce (they should try to store all the fat they can).

Either way, the first eight days after birth seem to be another critical time for setting babies on the right nutritional path.

Thankfully, breastfeeding normally leads to correct amount and pacing of feedings during that first week. Your body naturally progresses from making colostrum early in the first week to milk in the second half. In a beautiful dance of supply and demand, you are designed to provide just what your baby needs. With formula-fed kids, care should be taken not to over- or underfeed, given the importance of these early days, weeks, and months.

How do you tell if a baby is getting the right amount? Your baby will tell you! First, she should seem satisfied after eating. And she should make a wet diaper at least once on the first day, twice on the second day, and three times every day thereafter. The first baby poops are the sticky dark green of meconium. By the end of the first week, babies may average eight to ten soft, seedy stools a day.

It is normal for babies to lose weight for the first several days. Sometime around day 3 to day 5, babies hit their lowest weight for the rest of their lives. Then, as the breast milk comes in (if you're nursing), they begin gaining. Whether they are taking breast or bottle they should usually gain about thirty grams (about an ounce) a day.

Choose the Right Variety

As of 2004, about 65 percent of the babies born in the United States start off breastfeeding; about 35 percent begin life on formula.[6] This is down a bit from the breastfeeding peak a few years ago, and the percentage seems to have slid a bit more since 2004. In 1971, breastfeeding hit its all-time low of 24.7 percent,[7] around the time that some of today's mothers were born.

Each year, more than one million babies in the United States will start life feeding in each of these ways. We'll consider breast milk first, and then formula.

Breast Milk It's no surprise—human milk is the ideal nutrition for human babies. Although formulas try to base their nutrients on breast milk, this is virtually impossible to achieve. Breast milk is dynamic and changing, tailored to a specific situation. Even if formula stores were like paint stores,

Feeding Baby Green Stories

"My World Was Turned Upside Down!"

My first two pregnancies, I didn't think much about what I ate other than a very generic "trying to eat a little healthier." I didn't realize at the time what a big impact food has.

When my son was born and had a lot of medical problems—partially stemming from what I was eating, since I was breastfeeding him—my thoughts on food completely turned around. I reluctantly tried to cook for him without milk, soy, eggs, wheat, nuts, or shellfish—and make it seem normal. This included avoiding anything with artificial flavoring (and sometimes even natural flavoring!) listed on the ingredient list. My world was shaken and turned upside down.

Things have improved for him, and we are able to eat a lot more standard food, but the way we look at food as a family has changed. It is now an important part of what we do to be healthy. We don't eat a perfect diet, but we make better choices. Fruit instead of candy when we're looking for something sweet, and whole grains instead of white refined grains have made a huge difference in my family's life.

Heather Cunningham
Cedar City, Utah

and you could go in and get a can shaken up to match your own breast milk, *your* breast milk transforms as the weeks go by, as the hours pass in a single day, and even over the course of a single feeding. The nutrient content changes, the flavors change, and the immune properties change to fit your baby's changing needs. For example, it has been found that, for the first few weeks after birth, mothers who had preterm deliveries make milk with a higher protein content than those who deliver at term.[8] Just what the tiny babies need!

Unfortunately, we can't just put "protein" into formula and call it a day. Why not? Because not all proteins are created equally.

Whey proteins (as in Little Miss Muffet's curds and *whey*) are the main proteins in human milk, accounting for about 70 percent of the proteins. Alpha lactalbumin is the main human whey protein. A number of nifty antibodies and immune molecules that resist digestion in the stomach are among the other key whey proteins.[9]

By contrast, cow's milk is about 82 percent casein (curds). Even if you were to artificially increase the proportion of whey that is present, cow whey is mainly beta lactoglobulin—the primary culprit in cow's milk allergy. And the immune molecules do us little, if any, good.[10]

The fats and carbohydrates in human milk are also ideally designed for human babies. Breast milk stools are softer and smell better. Breastfed babies tend to have healthier friendly gut bacteria and to absorb essential minerals more easily from their diets.

In addition to the nutritional benefits, we're learning more all the time about the immunization benefits of breast milk. In an exciting new study, scientists have worked out another piece of the puzzle about how mothers naturally help to protect their children. We can compare a mother's immune system to an e-mail system, where different molecules have been found that act as e-mail addresses, directing immune cells (the e-mail) to be delivered via her blood vessel network to the desired location.

A molecule called CCL28 is the address for the breast. If another molecule, CCR10, is attached when cells arrive in the breast, it's as if a Forward button has been clicked. The immune cells exit the bloodstream and begin pumping out antibodies into the milk in order to be forwarded directly to her baby on another network.[11]

Breast milk provides both general and situation-specific protection. There is now strong evidence that in the United States, breastfeeding cuts the risk of acute infections (such as ear infections) during infancy by two-thirds, and wheezing from any cause in the first six months by half. The benefits to babies in developing nations are even stronger. There is some evidence that early breastfeeding also reduces the odds of developing chronic illnesses such as diabetes, celiac disease, Crohn's disease, and some allergies.[12]

Beyond this, breastfeeding appears to confer intellectual advantages. A large meta-analysis of studies taking into account other possible explanations concluded that breastfeeding tends to enhance cognitive development.[13]

Breast milk can be expressed and stored to be fed to your baby later. It can be kept six months or longer in a deep freeze, three or four months in a regular freezer, eight days in a refrigerator, twenty-four hours in a cooler (at lower than 60 degrees F), or up to ten hours at room temperature (at lower than 72 degrees F). Thaw by running the container under warm water. Microwaving the milk or heating above 130 degrees F destroys valuable properties of the breast milk. Previously frozen milk that has been thawed will keep in a refrigerator for up to twenty-four hours, but should not be refrozen. Some antimicrobial properties of breast milk are lost with freezing, but frozen breast milk from you is still superior to any options other than breast milk.[14]

Breastfeeding can be very rewarding for mother and child, but it is also often difficult or uncomfortable for the first week or two. Get pointers, feedback, and encouragement from a lactation consultant to help with getting started and with troubleshooting along the way.

Donor Milk In 2005, the Human Milk Banking Association of North America provided 745,329 ounces of donated breast milk to babies in over eighty cities across the United States and Canada.[15] The banks serve babies who have been adopted or who are not able to use their own mother's milk for whatever reason. This can be especially valuable for special-needs babies such as those born prematurely or who turn out to have severe allergies to formulas.

The milk is pasteurized to eliminate infections and the milk is rigorously tested to ensure quality and safety. The donor mothers are also tested to be sure they are healthy, similar to the way a blood bank tests donors. The women must be nonsmokers, not on any regular medications, and must not have had any alcohol in the period before donating.

Feeding Baby Green Report

When Breastfeeding Is Not an Option

When my wife, Cheryl, had to stop breastfeeding because of her treatment for breast cancer, I saw firsthand how important it is that mothers never be made to feel guilty for not nursing—whatever their reasons. I'm sure we have all known wonderful mothers who just couldn't or didn't want to breastfeed, for personal reasons of their own, or because they were unable for medical reasons.

Just as immunities can be passed to the baby through breast milk, so can some illnesses. Most women in the United States with HIV should not breastfeed, because safe alternatives are readily available. For these women, breastfeeding a little seems to be even riskier than exclusive breastfeeding. Mothers with active herpes lesions on the breast shouldn't breastfeed. Nor should mothers with some types of active tuberculosis.

For women taking certain medications (including chemotherapy), the risks of the medications in the breast milk being passed to the baby can outweigh the many benefits. Discuss any medications you are taking with your health care provider.

Sometimes, breast milk isn't right for a particular infant. Babies with a rare metabolic disorder called galactosemia can't thrive on breast milk, or any lactose-containing milk. Babies with some other rare metabolic disorders may need to limit breast milk.

Whether you choose not to nurse for any reason, or not-nursing has chosen you, or whether you opt for a bottle or another method, such as a nursing supplementer attached to the breast or to a finger, you deserve to be supported in your efforts to feed your baby.

Donated milk isn't tailored to a specific situation like just-in-time breast milk, but it does offer outstanding nutrition, easy digestibility, and some immune protection. According to the World Health Organization (WHO) and the United Nations Children's Fund (UNICEF), "The best food for any baby whose own mother's milk is not available is the breast milk of another healthy mother."[16] This can sound strange to the modern ear, but keep in mind that most commercial formula is pasteurized "donated" milk from a mother cow.

If you are interested in learning about getting human milk for your baby, or in donating extra milk for a baby who needs it, contact the milk bank closest to you. A doctor's prescription may be required to get the milk.

Commercial Formulas If human milk is not going to be used, iron-fortified infant formulas are the best alternatives for feeding healthy term babies. In fact, today's formulas are better than any other breast milk substitute in history.

Although breast milk is the model for these formulas, it is the *effect* of breast milk, not only the *composition* of breast milk that is most important. For instance, because the forms of iron and calcium added to formulas can't be as well absorbed as the minerals when they naturally occur in breast milk, formulas must contain higher levels of iron and calcium in order to end up with the same amount absorbed by the baby. The Infant Formula Act, updated in 1986, sets minimum required amounts of twenty-nine nutrients (and maximum amounts of nine) in order for a formula to be approved in the United States. For nineteen of these minimums, the amount required is more than would be found in breast milk—in order to get the breast milk effect.

Of course, breast milk is far more complex than twenty-nine nutrients. It's fresh and alive and isn't shelf stable (as formula is, even with no preservatives) for over a year. Breast milk contains enzymes and antibodies, hormones and growth factors, and entire living cells that formula may never reproduce.

But the formulas are a good enough approximation for the millions of babies who thrive on them each year. And the formulas have been steadily improving since they were first introduced in 1919.

Of the current options available for healthy term babies, I prefer choosing an organic, milk-based formula with added DHA and ARA.

Examples include Bright Beginnings Organic (made by PBM), Earth's Best Organic Infant Formula with DHA & ARA (made by PBM), Parent's Choice Organic Infant Formula (made by PBM), and Similac Organic. I've seen some of these in some stores for as little as $15 for a big 25.7 ounce can—and the same size of an equivalent formula by the same manufacturer for $30 in a different store. Shop around. Or online.

Whether you choose human milk or formula, healthy newborns don't need anything else to eat or drink during these first weeks. They don't need water or juice or anything else.

Customize Needs for Every Body

Now that your baby is alive and kicking (outside your tummy, that is), you can begin to make some adjustments in your diet.

Caffeine Even though your pregnancy is over, you may enjoy staying at a lower level of caffeine consumption, so you can relax or nap when the baby naps. But if you want to return to a previous level of caffeine that's higher, and are breastfeeding, be aware that caffeine has a long half-life in newborns. If you drink a cup of coffee, half of the caffeine will have left your body in five hours; half of the caffeine that passed over to your newborn will still be there in ninety-six hours: four days later.

It may take a nursing mom drinking a total of the amount of caffeine in five five-ounce cups of coffee before her baby is visibly affected with decreased sleep or increased irritability. Of course, with as long as it stays in the baby, you might get there pretty quickly with ten ounces of coffee a day.

Alcohol A glass of wine or beer used to be a common recommendation to help new mothers relax and encourage her milk supply. Although it may help her relax, alcohol actually appears to *decrease* milk supply. Nevertheless, the American Academy of Pediatrics concludes that the short-term effects of light drinking are not a problem for most healthy babies.

Heavy drinking (defined by the AAP as averaging two or more drinks per day), however, can slow a baby's development.

If you choose to enjoy a wine or beer after nursing, all of the alcohol that will make its way into your breast milk should have done so within two or three hours. If you want, you can pump the breast at that point and discard the milk. This way, you won't be introducing as much alcohol to your baby.

Tobacco As we've said earlier, having a new baby is a wonderful opportunity to give your baby and yourself the gift of no smoking (call 1-800-NO-BUTTS for help). But if you are smoking, you can reduce the nicotine you expose your baby to by ten times by choosing the timing and location of your cigarettes. Nicotine has a half-life of only ninety-five minutes. Smoke only right after nursing and smoke outside to deliver the least to your baby. Smoking in the same car or room where the baby will be later leaves behind third-hand smoke particles that can be quite toxic.[17] Anything you do to minimize the damage, however, is not as good for you or your baby as stopping altogether.

Tobacco smoke and its residues are among the most important toxic environmental exposures to children, linked to health concerns from behavior problems such as ADHD to sudden infant death. The smoke contains over 250 poisonous gases, chemicals, and metals including hydrogen cyanide, arsenic, butane, toluene, lead, cadmium, and polonium-210. Eleven of the components are group 1 carcinogens—the most potent cancer-causing chemicals. There is no known safe level.[18]

Depending on your baby's health issues or on conditions that run in your family, you may also want to adjust what type of formula your baby takes.

Types of Formulas

Partially Hydrolyzed Formulas A few infant formulas are available made from proteins (whey proteins) that have been snipped into smaller pieces. Some studies suggest that these customized formulas may be of some benefit in helping to prevent eczema or other allergies. They are not useful, though, for babies who already have a cow's milk protein allergy or allergy symptoms. Examples include Enfamil Gentlease LIPIL, Nestle Good Start DHA & ARA, and Nestle Good Start DHA & ARA Natural Cultures.

Extensively Hydrolized Formulas In these formulas, heat and enzymes are used to snip the proteins (casein proteins) into very tiny pieces. These formulas are very difficult to be allergic to. Extensively hydrolyzed formulas are also lactose free. They cost more and taste worse than the above options—but the babies don't mind (at least not at this age). These formulas might be used to prevent allergies, feed babies with allergies, or for babies with galactosemia or who are otherwise lactose intolerant. Examples include Nutramigen LIPIL and Similac Alimentum Advance. In the very uncommon event of an allergy to one of these, a formula with even smaller pieces—an elemental formula such as Neocate—should work.

Soy Formulas These make up about 20 percent of all formulas sold. They are all lactose free. About 85 percent of babies who are allergic to cow's milk protein have no known problems on a soy formula.[19] They could be used to feed babies with allergies, or for babies with galactosemia or who are otherwise lactose intolerant.

Nevertheless, because soy contains such high levels of manganese, I do not typically recommend it during the first four to six months. The main use I see for it is for vegan families who are not exclusively breastfeeding.

Exercise!

You've been exercising during pregnancy; you'll be exercising soon with your baby. For this first week, though, it's time to rest and recuperate from the delivery—for both of you. This is especially true if you are nursing. You and your baby both burn calories just by transferring nutrients from your body to his. You'll burn about three hundred extra calories a day—as if you had been running more than a mile. And he'll work harder to pull milk from a breast than he would from a bottle.

Give yourself and your baby a break, at least for now—you've both been through a life-changing event, and your efforts deserve some well-earned appreciation and nurturing!

Reap the Benefits of Green

Breastfeeding is one of the greenest choices you can make as a parent—for your family and for the environment. It's the ultimate in eating local. You reduce your carbon footprint in terms of transportation, energy, and the costs involved in manufacturing, packaging, shipping, and storage.

Breastfeeding lowers the lifetime risk of cancer for you and your baby. It also reduces the odds that your baby will need antibiotics or surgery or need to spend the night in the hospital during the first year. It's a natural, sustainable, and renewable choice whose lasting worth we are still just beginning to understand.

Another bonus: continuing to eat green yourself makes this already spectacular choice even greener.

❧

Soon, however, you will all want to go out into the world and begin exploring. Your baby will look on your neighborhood as a brand-new world, and on the sights and tastes and aromas of fruits and vegetables and fish and grains and everything green as riches to be enjoyed. There is no better time to begin introducing her to everything you love and would like her to love also. So let's continue on our journey to better health and nutrition for your newborn.

6

The First Months

(ABOUT TWO WEEKS TO FOUR MONTHS)

The intimate world in which you and your baby live during these precious opening months is bound together by the rhythm of eating and sleeping. Much of your focus at this time is on feeding your baby, so you spend a lot of the day gazing at each other. During this time even tiny changes in your baby's behavior and growth are easy for you to notice, and your baby will notice changes you make in your feeding routine.

Mothers are busy adjusting to their new lives and changing bodies. If you are nursing, your breasts are heavy with milk. You may be struggling with your remaining pregnancy weight, and moving more slowly at home and at work because of sleep deprivation. Just sitting with your infant during feedings can be a welcome and restful moment, and a harbinger of shared meals to come.

However the baby is fed, it appears that these remaining months before starting solid foods are a unique window for introducing certain tastes—a window that may close before the first spoonful of food.

The Essential Steps for Teaching Nutritional Intelligence

Babies are hardwired to develop a few standard innate food preferences and food aversions. These may broaden and change throughout his life as he experiences new tastes—but they are especially easy to influence before the child is ever weaned.[1]

Take Charge!

We've already seen how mothers can make a big difference during pregnancy. Research suggests that these months between infancy and the introduction of solid foods provide another significant window of opportunity for introducing your child to the delight of healthy foods.[2]

Whether you are nursing exclusively, feeding your baby formula, or doing both, this is a unique moment in which you can take charge of your child's early flavor learning by being aware of the foods you are eating. Whether he experiences new flavors through your breast milk, or from the delicious cooking smells in your kitchen, or through simply watching the rest of his family enjoy their meals, your influence on how he feels about food is going to be huge.

Use Windows of Opportunity

Your baby will continue to grow very quickly during these months, gaining about one-half to one ounce a day. At this rate, it won't take many months to double his birth weight. But your baby isn't just getting bigger; in every area of development, he is making fundamental advances.

In gross motor development, he learns to raise his head and chest, working up to the ability to support his whole upper body with his arms when on his tummy. He learns to stretch out his legs and kick. In fine motor development, he learns to hold and shake simple toys (or foods), to bring his hands to his mouth, and to swat at objects in front of him. His cognitive development will center around what he sees and hears. When you hear your baby babbling consonants, it belies dramatic language and social development. He continues to study faces and learns to smile when you smile, and to turn his head and smile even at the sound of your voice.

Feeding Baby Green Recipe

Chickpeas and Tomatoes Provence

When you make this recipe, the aromas in your kitchen will bring to mind the south of France—even if you've never been there. As an added bonus, chickpeas are a fantastic source of protein. If you are limiting your meat intake, considering adding to your chickpea intake. A half a cup has about 19 grams of protein and 17 grams of dietary fiber to boot!

1 cup dried chickpeas (also known as garbanzo beans)

½ cup onion, chopped

3 medium-size Roma tomatoes, chopped

1 medium-size zucchini, chopped

1 tablespoon olive oil

½ teaspoon dried herbes de Provence

Kosher salt and freshly ground pepper, to taste

1. Rinse chickpeas and soak in 4 cups of cool water overnight.
2. Drain and cook in 4 cups of water until tender. Depending on the dryness of the chickpeas, cooking can take anywhere from 1 to 2 hours. Chickpeas should be soft but not mushy when done. Drain and set aside.
3. In a separate pan, sauté the onion until translucent. Add the zucchini and herbs, and cook until the zucchini is tender, but not mushy. Gently stir in the tomatoes.
4. Gently stir in the drained, cooked chickpeas. Season to taste with salt and pepper. Delicious hot or at room temperature.

Serves 4 (Yield: 4 cups)

NUTRITION FACTS (AMOUNT PER SERVING)

Calories: 227	Sodium: 16mg	Sugars: 7.09g
Total Fat: 5.70g	Total Carbs: 33.80g	Protein: 10.38g
Cholesterol: 0	Dietary Fiber: 9.59g	

Provided by and reprinted by permission from *BoboBaby*.

He wants to interact. And you can see him trying to imitate your facial expressions, your movements, and even some sounds.

This same imitation is happening in his nutritional development, even though you can't see it yet. He's using his senses to study and learn about the foods you enjoy so that he'll have a map for his early forays into the world of eating.

As this stage unfolds, your baby's attention between feedings begins to turn more and more to the outside world. The early explorer travels with his eyes, ears, and nose.

Meanwhile, in the months after giving birth, women's own changing bodies and taste preferences can help teach their growing babies about a variety of foods. We saw in Part One that a mother's food preferences often change when she becomes pregnant, and continue to change over the course of pregnancy. In one study, 93 percent of pregnant women experienced these changes.[3] More recent research describes how they often change again after birth.

After giving birth, salt often tastes less pleasant for at least a couple of months—less so than before or during pregnancy. Your body is working to return to a body just for you, and it no longer needs the water or extra blood volume retained by extra salt in your diet.

Meanwhile, too, the increased enjoyment of bitter compounds in foods that you may have experienced in middle and late pregnancy continues during these postnatal months, perhaps to allow you to enjoy a wider variety of vegetables and other foods than you did before becoming pregnant.[4]

Your increased pleasure in a variety of foods can result in getting the nutrients you need to best restore your body and to feed your baby. In addition, if you are nursing, this natural change can help teach your baby to enjoy a broader variety of flavors.

Just as you would be able to pick out your baby's unique scent blindfolded, to your baby, your breast milk tastes uniquely like you—and also varies from meal to meal to taste like the foods and spices that you have been eating.[5] No two meals will taste exactly alike. If your diet is sufficiently varied, this could mean that your baby will experience countless subtly different flavor combinations before the first bite of solid food.

Meanwhile, a completely formula-fed baby will become used to just one flavor, every meal, every day, every week, every month. But some variety can still come to him—through aromas.

Whether your baby enjoys the marvelous gift of exclusive breastfeeding for some or all of this period, grows strong on an infant formula, or, like most babies, partakes of some of both, what you eat for these next few months will help teach your baby about food.

Engage All the Senses

The senses of taste and smell remain especially acute during these months. Meanwhile, your baby's vision is rapidly improving. At one month, he can only see clearly for a foot or two. By four months, you may catch him enjoying looking across the room or out a window.

Engage with Flavor Konrad Lorenz became famous for his description of imprinting in geese. He taught that there is a critical and sensitive period early in life when key exposures have lasting influence in animals. He described how newly hatched goslings are programmed to follow the first moving objects they see. They quickly become imprinted on this object and will move their little feet fast to keep up with it.

Most of the time, this moving magnet is the gosling's mother. Lorenz showed, however, that if he were the first mover that a gosling saw, it would be imprinted on Lorenz and follow him about, refusing to follow a goose. Papa Goose Lorenz won the Nobel Prize for this work in 1973.[6]

Imprinting is a special kind of learning where an early life exposure at a particular time influences behavior later in life. Sometimes the early exposure is so ordinary that it happens without our noticing. But to the youngsters, some exposures are particularly stimulating, pleasurable, or comforting. They get a rush of endorphins, the brain's own opiates, which make them feel good and reinforce the desirability of that exposure. When they encounter that experience often enough, it becomes familiar and welcome.

Note: the taste and even the aroma of milk from a baby's own mother is a powerful trigger for releasing endorphins. So powerful, in fact, that study after study has shown the taste and even the aroma to be effective pain relief for minor medical procedures, such as injections or blood draws.[7] Imagine the imprinting power of food flavors and aromas in breast milk!

Lorenz taught that imprinting was rapid and permanent and must always occur in the critical window. We've learned since then that imprinting is often more gradual than he thought, more forgiving, and can take place later in life. It's just easiest when they are young.[8]

We've also learned that when geese imprint on a human or other animal, the lasting effect can be more profound than just whom they will follow. Imprinting can change the goose's sense of self; those who imprint on humans (or toy trains) seem to believe themselves to be humans (or toy trains). They can "fall in love" with other humans when they grow up.[9] Or toy trains.

We've known for at least thirty years from animal studies that very early flavor experiences change which foods will later be preferred. Within five years of Lorenz's Nobel Prize, food imprinting had already been demonstrated in snapping turtles, chickens, gulls, dogs, and cats. In one classic study, researchers tried to tease out which route of exposure made the difference.

Here, the nursing mama lab rats were fed either standard powdered Rat-Mouse Diet or the same diet seasoned with McCormick brand onion powder. Some of the pups got their mother's milk, but no other exposure to her diet. They hung out with their aunts. Others drank their mother's milk and got to hang out with her and smell her breath, her body odor, her poop, and any food particles clinging to her fur. Then, after the pups had been weaned, the investigators gave them a chance to eat some onion chow for themselves.

The researchers concluded, "Exposure to onion taste in mother's milk leads to enhanced preference for onion." Getting onion-flavored milk, *even with no other cues at all*, increased the pups' acceptance of onion later on. As you might expect, exposure to the other cues strengthened the effect. If several food bowls were available, the babies ate from the same bowl that they saw their parents eating from.[10]

Flavors in human breast milk have also been shown to influence babies' early flavor preferences. Remember that landmark study that showed the power of prenatal carrots to increase acceptance of carrots by babies after birth? The same study included women who drank ten ounces of carrot juice four times a week for three consecutive weeks sometime during the first two months of nursing. Their babies had both increased acceptance and enjoyment of carrots.[11]

Repeated exposure to a flavor in a positive context can help children learn to enjoy it. Breastfeeding is your last opportunity to offer these tastes through the uniquely nurturing and comforting context of your own body, before you start putting them on a spoon.

It's not just the intrinsic flavors of vegetable that come through breast milk, but seasonings and spices as well.[12] We observed that my oldest son clearly noticed the change in breast milk flavor after we had enjoyed a dramatically garlic-infused meal one evening. Garlic flavor in the breast milk appears to peak about two hours after the meal.[13] He didn't much like his first sample of garlic milk, but he since had many more samples, and he's a garlic lover today. Scientific analysis of flavors in breast milk confirmed this impromptu observation of garlic-flavored breast milk by the time my youngest son was born.[14]

Feeding Baby Green Report
When Does the Flavor Hit the Milk?

As you might expect, different flavors appear to take a different amount of time to enter breast milk. In one recent study, researchers gave breastfeeding mothers capsules of banana, caraway seed, licorice, or menthol flavors, and tested their breast milk to see when the flavors arrived and when they left.

Banana peaked and was gone within an hour. Caraway and licorice peaked in two hours and diminished after that. Menthol remained at fairly stable levels for about two to almost eight hours. The timing varied a fair amount from woman to woman, but all four flavors were gone from all of their breast milk by eight hours after the mother swallowed the flavor (without tasting it herself as she swallowed the capsules, by the way!).[15]

Interestingly, babies tend to suck more vigorously when a new flavor is introduced into their mothers' diet (even if the mothers don't notice the change in nursing, researchers can measure it). The babies' bodies seem eager to learn new flavors. When that flavor has been repeated a few times, nursing returns to normal, suggesting that babies have indeed learned the new flavor. Note: this same effect has been shown when a bit of vanilla is added to infant formula.[16]

Though the ability of breast milk to provide babies with exposures to a series of specific flavors is exciting, perhaps even more exciting is the ability of the variety of flavors in breast milk to help kids be more accepting of vegetables in general.

One interesting study looked at breastfed babies versus exclusively formula-fed babies and how quickly they learned to enjoy their first pureed vegetable. The babies were given either peas or green beans every day for ten days. Both groups of babies could learn to like the veggies with repeated exposures. But the breastfed babies learned to like them faster, even though their mothers hadn't focused on either of these flavors during nursing. And after the full ten days of the experiment, the breastfed babies still tended to eat more of the veggies than did their counterparts with limited flavor experience.[17]

There's no law that says a formula-fed baby needs to stay on the same formula month after month. Off-the-shelf infant formulas do taste different from each other.[18] Parents I speak with are often surprised to hear that research suggests that which formula a child drinks as a baby might influence what vegetable she likes in kindergarten. In one such study, four- and five-year-old children underwent a fun taste-testing game. Those who had been raised on a hydrolysate formula, such as Nutramigen or Alimentum (which taste sour to me!), were significantly more likely to enjoy sour flavors in the test than were the kids raised on milk-based formulas. They were also significantly more likely to enjoy broccoli, as attested to by their mothers. And they were less likely to make negative facial expressions on any of the taste tests. (They were also more likely to like the flavor or aroma of formula.) Those raised on soy formula as babies were more likely to enjoy bitter-flavored apple juice than were those raised on milk-based formula.[19]

These changes are not evident while the kids are still drinking the formula. In fact, those taking a hydrolysate formula may be even less likely to take broccoli or cauliflower at the same time.[20] Perhaps they are sated; enough is enough of the bitter-sour flavors. But years after their last sip of formula, those same bitter-sour flavors may be a welcome treat.[21]

For formula-fed babies, I recommend changing formulas at least once or twice, just to teach the child to enjoy more than one flavor. In particular, I suggest feeding a hydrolysate formula for at least three weeks sometime during this period. The bitter taste of a formula like Nutramigen or Alimentum is readily taken when first introduced by two months of age—and often permanently rejected if first introduced in the second half of the first year.

Feeding Baby Green Report

The Invisible Bouquet

Plants are surrounded by a small cloud of molecules—hundreds of thousands—that signal other plants and animals in amazingly complex ways. Some are designed to attract or repel others at specific stages of the plant's life. Some draw insects to pollinate for the future. Or, when a plant's leaves are being nibbled by bugs, the plant may produce signals to attract that bug's predators.[22]

A small subset of these volatile molecules falls in the spectrum that we humans can detect with our noses—the "flavor fingerprint" of that fruit or vegetable. The aromas in nature that tempt us to take a bite are often packed with nutrients. It's a win-win situation: the plants send us a come-hither smell, we eat and are nourished, then we protect or cultivate those plants. Consider the tomato. The typical tomato produces about four hundred volatile compounds, but few that we can smell—until the tomato ripens. Then the tomato emits a cloud of molecules, almost all of which are specific, powerful human nutrients.[23] Together, they blend to smell to us like a "tomato"—a childhood aroma I can still recall from picking tomatoes in the backyard with my father. It's a lovely dance: we plant the tomato seed and nurture the plant to maturity; it flowers and fruits and calls us to pluck it when packed with the most goodness for us.

Engage with Aroma Try this: while your baby is watching, simply pass a ripe vegetable or fruit under your nose and smile. Then pass it under your baby's nose and smile. Slice into the item and do it again (freshly breaking cell walls can greatly increase the available aroma molecules, especially in vegetables). You are teaching your baby to enjoy these lovely aromas, as you do.

Many of the unique aromas of spices and herbs are also signals of specific health benefits. You might want to try a little whiff of some of your favorites—rosemary, sage, clove, thyme, ginger, turmeric, mint, garlic—but remember that your baby's sense of smell may be much more vivid than your own. You want pleasing, fun, shared smell experiences, not an aroma assault.

Feeding Baby Green Stories

"My Mom Made GORP"

My mom did not allow us to have candy, soda, or regular snacks in the house. Instead, she offered us healthful food and made us fun, nutritious alternatives for sweets—like granola, GORP, whole grain French toast . . . you get the idea. She also didn't buy items that had things that sounded like chemicals on the ingredient list.

My sister and I felt a little outside the norm, but we grew up with really different and better, healthier habits that became normal to us—like a fruit bowl on the counter instead of a cookie jar; like ordering a glass of water in a restaurant instead of soda; like heading outdoors for fun; and the big one: not being sick often.

Well, eating our veggies and having fruit for dessert resulted in my lifelong interest in cooking and health. I'm now a naturopathic doctor with an organic food company, and my sister is a veterinarian who focuses on holistic health for cats and dogs. We both have children now and were avid about breastfeeding our babies and eating well during pregnancy. Just like us, our kids eat a lot of homemade meals with veggies, whole grains, and fruit.

Laryn Callaway, N.D.
Scottsdale, Arizona

And this is a great age to have some of your favorite flavor threads simmering (see "Enjoy Flavor Threads" in Chapter Four). This is especially true for formula-fed babies, who won't be getting tastes of your favorite foods yet. And breastfed kids have been shown to especially enjoy toys freshly scented with things their moms have been eating (a drop of vanilla?).[24] You certainly don't need toy fragrance, but do be aware: they're paying attention to aromas.

Engage with Sight During her first months, your baby's visual attention will gradually move from a focus on faces and shapes to paying attention to hands and then—food. Her vision is still mostly in black and white, so the colors of food are not terribly interesting yet. Towards the very end of this period, though, color vision may start to emerge, opening up a new world of experience. We'll discuss this much more in the next chapter.

Right now, the biggest visual impact comes when you combine glimpses of faces, hands, and food: pay close attention to what you are eating in front of your baby as these months progress—your baby certainly will.

Engage with Sounds and Language The sounds of cooking and eating will interest your baby. So will the sounds of your voice. But perhaps the biggest impact you can make through hearing and language at this age is to combine these sounds with hand signals.

Baby signs can be a wonderful way to make language more accessible to your baby. Especially when they start to focus their eyes on hands (theirs or yours), they can begin to learn your meaning when you show them the same hand or head movement along with the same sound.

The signs used by your family don't need to match anyone else's. Each sign is most effective if it is natural, simple to perform, and if everyone in the family uses both the word and the sign together most of the time. You might want to choose a simple sign for "eat," such as bringing the hand to the mouth. And choose signs for some of the first foods you decide on.

American Sign Language (ASL) is a great source for these signs—and they have the added advantage of being usable with others. Many of the food signs are simple, evocative, and fun. For example, for the ASL sign for a banana you point the left index finger up and peel it like a banana. The sign for an avocado involves bringing one fist into the curved palm of the other in a mashing motion. The sign for a carrot is reminiscent of peeling a carrot.

Choose the Right Amount

During these first months babies learn how to eat just the amount of food they need. The trajectory of weight gain in the first four months continues to predict pretty well which kids will later become obese.[25]

I often hear moms who are concerned about feeding the right amount say that bottles are easier because you can tell just how much they are getting. It turns out, though, that it is easier to be sure babies are getting the right amount if they nurse.

Nursing is a conversation. Your body and your baby's body send signals back and forth that help regulate how much milk is produced and how much they swallow. Cascades of hormones on both sides influence your feeding rhythms. The milk itself changes during the course of each feed, the milk at the end—after-milk—sending satisfaction signals to both of you. Babies are active partners in this process. They don't just suck your breast; they milk it with their tongues and palates. The interplay between the two of you is designed to provide just the right amount for their needs.

In contrast, sucking from a bottle can be much more passive than milking a breast. They can get milk with much less effort, there is no after-milk to signal the meal is done, and it is easier for them to be overfed. Some evidence suggests that they do tend to drink a bit more on average than breastfed kids—not something they need.

Formula-Fed Scheduling Most formula-fed babies start out taking two or three ounces every three or four hours. Over the first four weeks or so, they usually increase to about four ounces per feed every four hours. By two months, the feedings often stretch out to every five hours or so, and most no longer need a middle-of-the-night feeding. By six months, usually they are up to six or eight ounces per feed, with bottles no more than four or five times a day.

My rule of thumb is that most formula-fed kids need about two to three ounces per pound of body weight per day, up to a maximum of about thirty-two ounces a day. Their needs will vary from day to day. Some babies do well with more or less than this; but if you and your baby are outside of this range most days, I recommend considering the reasons why with your health care practitioner.

Feeding Baby Green Tip

Is Your Baby Getting All She Needs from Nursing?

It's fairly easy to get a sense whether your baby is getting enough nutrition from nursing:

1. Pay attention to your baby's mood. Babies who are satisfied and content at the end of nursing tend to be well fed.

2. Check her diapers. Once breastfed babies are a week old, they will usually have many soft stools, averaging around eight to twelve a day. By four weeks, the number of stools drops in half. By eight weeks, the average is only about one a day—but some healthy, breastfed babies will poop much less often, even as little as once every eight days (breast milk is such a perfect food). A formula-fed baby who goes less frequently than every other day is likely constipated.

3. Every now and then, check her weight. On average, babies will gain about one-half to one ounce per day for the first three months, half an ounce a day for the next three months, and less thereafter.

Breastfed Scheduling The feeding schedule for breastfed babies varies even more than for formula-fed babies. When their mothers' milk first comes in, they often nurse eight to twelve times a day. As they grow, some mothers and babies settle into a routine. Some prefer larger feedings less often; others prefer frequent smaller feedings. You don't need to worry about the amount—that usually takes care of itself.

One of the most common reasons that mothers stop nursing is that they are afraid their babies aren't getting enough. Often this happens during a growth spurt—especially if it occurs during the weeks when babies tend to cry the most anyway. The baby's hunger increases first, triggering the mother to make more milk—but not immediately. There's a built-in lag. It's not unusual for supply and demand to be out of balance for two or three days. And mothers instinctively sense that their babies want more than they are providing.

As the growth spurt progresses, babies get stronger and more efficient at nursing. They are able to drink more in a shorter time. But from a mother's perspective, she feels that her baby wants more, is spending less time at her breast, and is crying more often. No wonder a sense of inadequacy can develop *if you are not warned to expect this possibility.*

Supplements Even though breast milk is the perfect food, the American Academy of Pediatrics recommends that breastfed babies receive an extra 400 IU of vitamin D per day, starting in the first weeks of life. As many as 40 percent of breastfed babies are not getting enough from their diet or the sun.[26]

Feeding Baby Green Report
Getting Vitamin D from the Sun

How much sun exposure does it take to get the vitamin D needed to thrive? The answer depends on skin color, clothing, location, time of year, and time of day. Because of the angle of the sun's rays, kids only make significant vitamin D after about 10 AM and before about 3 PM in most of the United States.

During this middle part of the day, the amount of sunshine needed varies from person to person and place to place, but it is always much less than the amount of sun that would turn the skin slightly pink. This slight-color-changing sun exposure is called the minimal erythema dose (MED). You don't want babies (or yourself) to get the MED, only a small part of it.

In Florida at noon in the summer, the MED might be four to ten minutes for adults with pale skin and even less for a baby. But it might be sixty to eighty minutes for people with dark skin. The MED could be much longer in the winter, or in Maine. To get optimal vitamin D, if the arms, legs, and head are exposed to the sun, all it takes is a quarter of the MED every day. With the torso also exposed it may take only one-eighth of the MED.[27]

Vitamin D is normally produced by the skin when exposed to sunlight. I agree with the AAP's recommendation of vitamin D for breastfed babies throughout the first year—not because breast milk is in any way inadequate, but because babies are outside today much less than they used to be throughout human history. And when they are outside, they are often protected by sunscreen, which blocks vitamin D formation. Although experts argue the costs and benefits of sunscreen, the value of getting adequate vitamin D is clear. Perhaps extra vitamin D may even be important for formula-fed kids as well.

Diabetes Prevention Taking vitamin D drops in the first year of life may help prevent kids from developing type 1 diabetes, according to a study released March 13, 2008, in *Archives of Disease in Childhood*. The study is a review and analysis of the combined data from five different studies. The conclusions support many other studies in recommending the extra vitamin D for breastfed babies. But this analysis also included additional supplementation for formula-fed babies, with the same results.

The studies in the current analysis weren't strong enough to prove a link, but there is other suggestive evidence as well. Type 1 diabetes is more common in kids living at higher latitudes (in the Northern Hemisphere) and at lower latitudes (in the Southern Hemisphere.) It's also more commonly diagnosed in the fall and winter, and least common in the summer. And well-designed, carefully controlled studies in animals show that giving only vitamin D supplementation does decrease their risk of diabetes.

Other studies suggest that adequate vitamin D levels might slash the risk of asthma as well as some cancers, hypertension, osteoporosis, and autoimmune and neurological diseases.

Probiotics Probiotics, or beneficial bacteria, are something to consider for babies who are exclusively formula-fed, born by C-section, or who need to be on antibiotics. Breastfed babies born vaginally tend to have a healthy complement of gut bacteria on their own.

Neither healthy breastfed nor formula-fed babies of this age routinely need other nutritional supplements or water.

Vitamins for Mom I do recommend that you continue taking prenatal vitamins during this period, as a gift to your own bodies and, if you are nursing, as a gift to your baby as well. In addition, I suggest taking calcium with vitamin D and omega-3s if you are not getting plenty of both of these from your diet.

Choose the Right Variety

Breast milk, by itself, provides all of the necessary variety at this stage, even if you never give it a second thought. As an extra bonus, though, try to eat one from each of the twenty-one plant families listed in Chapter Four at least twelve times during nursing. You may want to use the checklist at the end of the book to keep track. If you don't like one, don't eat it—or take this opportunity to try something new. Remember, all you are trying to do now is to expose your baby repeatedly to a broad variety of the flavors you *do* like (and to minimize exposures to junk foods you don't want to pass along).

For formula-fed babies, if you are varying the formula a bit, as described in "Engage with Flavor" earlier in this chapter, you are automatically adding variety.

Customize Needs for Every Body

There are several important things for you to do during this period regarding special needs you and your baby may have.

Diabetes Perhaps the biggest influence at this age on later getting diabetes is something we call catch-up growth. Kids who are born small and gain weight too quickly are at the highest risk of type 2 diabetes as adults.[28]

To prevent this, follow growth curves at least every month for the first four months, especially if your baby is born small. Nurse, if possible; and if not, be sure to alert your health care provider if your baby is taking more from the bottle than expected.

Eczema In recent years, eczema in children has been on the rise, now affecting about a third of kids. Often it is mild, but in some of them it is quite severe. Exclusive breastfeeding for at least four months seems to drop the risk of eczema by about a third in those babies who are at high risk for developing eczema.[29]

One set of studies suggests that for mothers who drink milk, switching from conventional to organic may further reduce eczema, but more work needs to be done to confirm this.[30] Some evidence suggests that mothers who avoid milk, eggs, and fish while breastfeeding might reduce eczema in their babies—but other studies have found conflicting results. Mother's taking omega-3s and probiotics while nursing may also be helpful.

For formula-fed babies, choosing a hydrolyzed formula may help to prevent eczema.

Food Allergy Some food allergens, including cow's milk protein, peanut, and egg, can come through breast milk. At various times it has been recommended that nursing women avoid these to prevent allergies. To date, there is no convincing data that mother's avoiding anything while nursing prevents food allergies in the long run. If a food allergy in the baby already exists, though, mother's avoiding that food while nursing is helpful.

For formula-fed babies, a hydrolyzed formula may help prevent some food allergies.

Feeding Baby Green Tip

Is Your Baby Allergic?

How do you tell if your baby is allergic or intolerant to something?

Usually, you will not see a quick, visible response to a formula or food. Instead, you might see eczema or another skin rash, fussiness, loose stools, hard stools, or blood in the stool.

In the case of celiac disease, which is an intolerance to the grain protein gluten—not a true allergy—you might see diarrhea, smelly stools, irritability, and poor weight gain.

Allergy testing can be done in babies. At this age, a negative result doesn't tell you much either way, but a positive result likely indicates a real allergy (as opposed to tests done at age four, when a negative result is likely real, and a positive result may only indicate a possible culprit). There is also specific testing for celiac disease.

If you think your baby may have an allergy, consult your health care provider.

Obesity and the Metabolic Syndrome Metabolic syndrome is a combination of health problems that indicate the body is in an unhealthy state and very likely to develop significant disease, such as heart disease and diabetes, unless something changes. Features of metabolic syndrome include abnormal blood sugars, abnormal cholesterol and triglyceride levels, high blood pressure, and obesity—especially belly fat.

A growing number of studies strongly suggest that breastfeeding provides a small but consistent protection from obesity and metabolic syndrome.[31]

As we learned from the protein and calorie story during pregnancy, kids thrive best when their mothers avoid the extremes of too much or too little. This continues to be true for nursing moms.

Animal research suggests that nursing moms' getting plenty of protein could also help protect against key components of metabolic syndrome such as obesity, type 2 diabetes, high triglycerides, and abnormal cholesterol levels.[32]

Exercise!

Exercise? For babies?

Yes! I recommend at least a minimum amount of healthy, fun, physical activity for baby (and for you) during these first months. Tiny babies may seem too small to need to move, but if you remember your baby kicking in your tummy before birth, you'll begin to get the idea.

Let me tell you about movement in tiny preemies, averaging about two-and-a-half pounds in weight, and born three months before their due dates. If they were still inside their mothers, they would be floating in fluid and kicking and pushing against the walls of the uterus. In a typical hospital nursery, though, these babies spend the day lying still, losing bone strength week by week, until they are big enough to start moving about on their own in the air.

In a remarkable study, published in the July 2003 issue of *Pediatrics,* half of the babies were put on a completely no-stress exercise program: for just five minutes a day, five days a week, someone moved their limbs through a gentle, passive workout. These babies were compared to another group who received only skin-to-skin contact and stroking for the same amount of time. In just four weeks, the premature babies in the exercise program group had significantly stronger bones than their inactive peers, just from the passive movement—something you could easily do with your baby.

Feeding Baby Green Report
Chickpeas

Like other beans, chickpeas (also called garbanzo beans) are a great source of fiber that helps to normalize both blood sugar and cholesterol.[33] American kids get far too little fiber today. Chickpeas and other legumes may be the best way to get what they need. As an added bonus, chickpeas are a good plant source of protein, with about half as much protein per calorie as ground beef.

We love chickpeas as hummus, an easy spread for whole grain bread or dip for vegetables (see "Veggie Dips" recipes in Chapter Ten). Chickpeas can make a nice addition to salads or pastas. You'll also find them in the "Chickpeas and Tomatoes Provence" recipe in this chapter.

After the umbilical cord has fallen off, it's time for full-term babies to be moving their muscles, pushing against something firm, continuing a lifetime balance of calories-in versus calories-out that they began before they were even born, fed through the placenta and pushing against your belly.

The first newborn activity is simple and natural—spending time on the tummy, awake, for at least thirty minutes a day. Some babies instinctively love tummy time. For others, it takes getting used to. There are several ways you might help speed up this period of adjustment:

- Divide the thirty minutes into shorter bursts several times throughout the day.

- Give her a sense of power by putting your hand behind her feet so she has something to push against.

- Try rolling up a small towel and placing it under her chest to get her head up higher—especially if she seems frustrated by having her face down.

- Your baby might love it if you try getting on your tummy too, so you can look at each other and laugh.

- Use a mirror. It can be fun for her to watch herself move.

Music often helps as well. Her favorite, though, might be tummy time lying on top of you so she can push and kick against you, just like those special days before she was born.

And don't forget the importance of exercise for yourself at this time. You'll want at least half an hour of physical activity a day. It could be something as simple as a walk outside with your baby. This can help with

Feeding Baby Green Report

Spinach

Calorie for calorie, leafy greens pack more nutritional punch than any other food—and spinach is one of the all-stars. A cup of cooked spinach is loaded with vitamins, easily giving you a full day's supply of vitamins K and A, and at least about a third of your day's folate, iron, magnesium, and vitamin C. It contains almost as much protein as an egg, and almost as much calcium as a glass of milk (though only about a third as much is absorbed). Among its many health properties, it can help prevent cancer[34] and improve cognitive function in the brain.[35]

And it can be a delicious flavor to teach your child. Spinach salads are simple side dishes to complement many meals, or they can be a great meal themselves—especially during the spring and fall crops. I also like sautéing spinach with a bit of olive and garlic, sometimes with lemon juice for a fresh taste, sometimes with some mushrooms for an earthier dish. A bit of Parmesan cheese might be nice either way. Or pine nuts. And, to me, spinach can also be a nice addition to almost any pasta. You'll also find spinach in the Spinach Potato Puree recipe elsewhere in this chapter. Enjoy!

losing your pregnancy weight, giving you more energy, and helping to improve your mood. It can also help you sleep better—which in turn helps you eat better, feel better, and exercise more. This is a virtuous cycle to jump into at any point you can.

Reap the Benefits of Green

The hints of food that come through breast milk are tiny hints, so try to eat the most flavorful fruits and vegetables that you can find. As you've already learned, this often means choosing foods that were picked when ripe, that are in season, and that are eaten or frozen soon after being picked. All other things being equal, organic produce often is tastier than its conventional counterparts.

Pay attention to any plastics used in storing or preparing breast milk or formula for your baby, or in storing or cooking food for yourself. Certainly choose BPA-free bottles and phthalate-free plastics for anything that might go in your baby's mouth. By the time this book is published, I am hoping that some or all of the baby products will be routinely free of BPA or phthalates. Another plastic ingredient to pay attention to is dibutyltin (DBT), still widely used in PVC plastics. This plastic ingredient has been shown to disrupt hormones and immune cells even at nano doses.[36] Its cousin tributyltin (TBT) is also a bad actor. And even tiny amounts of exposure could be important, because babies' young livers aren't mature enough to detoxify it yet. Babies under age two can have levels of BPA in their blood *eleven times higher* than that of adults who are exposed to the same amount. This may be true of other toxins as well, and is another reason why *Feeding Baby Green* may be even more important than starting later in life.[37]

One of the biggest ways to reap the benefits of green is to make connections with where food comes from. Breastfeeding, of course, remains the best way to do that, and to reduce packaging, food miles, and all aspects of our carbon footprint as well.

But whether or not you are nursing, I like idea of planting something during this fleeting window of time that you'll be able to pick and eat with your baby when she starts enjoying solid foods. It might be something as small and simple as a kitchen window pot. Or if you have even a little outdoor space, you can get a self-contained kit (such as the Earth

Feeding Baby Green Recipe

Spinach Potato Puree

You and your family can enjoy this delicious puree as a side dish during your pregnancy, during those few short months that your baby is eating pureed foods (she'll recognize the wonderful flavor of thyme and onions in this delicious and healthy alternative to creamed spinach), and well beyond—our teenager loves this dish.

1 tablespoons extra virgin olive oil

¼ medium onion, peeled and sliced

2½ cups sweet potatoes, peeled and cubed

2 cups water

1 sprig fresh thyme, remove leaves from stem

2 sprigs fresh Italian parsley, remove leaves from stem

1¼ packed cups spinach leaves, cleaned

Kosher salt, to taste

1. Preheat a large saucepan over medium-high heat.
2. Add oil and onions, and cook for 2 to 3 minutes until onions are soft and starting to brown.
3. Add sweet potatoes and cook, stirring frequently for another 2 to 3 minutes.
4. Add water, thyme, and parsley and bring to a boil.
5. Lower heat to a simmer and cook uncovered for 15 to 20 minutes, or until the potatoes become tender.
6. Add the spinach and simmer for another 2 to 3 minutes.
7. Puree the mixture in a food processor, blender, or in the pot with a hand emulsifier, until it is a puree consistency. Season with salt to taste.

Serves 4 (Yield: 2 cups)

NUTRITION FACTS (AMOUNT PER SERVING)

Calories: 148	Sodium: 20mg	Sugars: 1.09g
Total Fat: 3.45g	Total Carbs: 28.07g	Protein: 1.91g
Cholesterol: —	Dietary Fiber: 4.48g	

Submitted and reprinted by permission from *Petite Palate*.

Box; see http://howtogardenguide.com/2007/05/23/earth-box/) with almost everything you need to grow a little crop of food, or you can do some window box or backyard planting, cultivating, and nurturing of an edible garden. It's a real thrill to grow your own healthy, nutritious, toxin-free food, even in an urban or suburban environment.

❧

As your baby grows, he will become more and more active—sitting up, looking around, and generally enjoying all of the wonderful sights, smells, and sounds that the world has to offer. And he's going to want to put many of these wonderful things in his mouth to see how they taste! In the next chapter, you'll learn the best foods to begin with.

7

Starting Solids

(ABOUT FOUR MONTHS
TO NINE MONTHS)

The table has finally been set. The first bite of food is on its way. Your baby has been learning about food, absorbing preferences, and establishing habits since long before birth. Now comes a very powerful period of direct experience.

A baby's first spoonful of food is the beginning of a new era. This can be an especially bittersweet landmark when a baby has been exclusively breastfed. Up until now, everything the mother sees when she looks at her baby—the toes, the smiles, and everything in between—have come from nutrients that were once a part of her own body. She has been fueling this amazing growth ever since that tiny fertilized egg embarked on its journey to plant itself in her womb.

With the first spoonful of food, your baby is beginning to partake of the world like you do, alongside of you—not through you.

This is a new era for formula-fed babies as well. They graduate from a single-flavor, off-white, liquid-only diet to a new, expanding world of taste, texture, and color.

Wow.

The Essential Steps for Teaching Nutritional Intelligence

However your baby was fed before this, the first spoonful signals a change in season from the quiet magic of cradling your newborn in your arms, to a new season of smiling, laughing, strong opinions, and increasingly rich, active interactions.

Of course, that first spoonful will likely end up on the face or on the floor.

Take Charge!

When is the best time to start solid foods? Advice on this issue has varied quite a bit over the decades. And even today, you'll find very different answers from different experts. One reason for this, I believe, is that babies have unique digestive systems that mature at different rates. There isn't a single best answer for everyone.

Don't let someone else's calendar or arbitrary schedule dictate this important moment. Instead, take charge by paying attention to the unique needs of your baby and your family.

Usually, the best time to start solids is when babies are asking for it with their body language. They become visibly eager to be initiated into the mysteries of taking the world into their bodies.

At some point, most babies will beg you to start solids—not with words, of course, but by the way they lean forward or strain or fuss or stare longingly at your food as you take a bite. I give great weight to this signal, especially in babies who are starting to try to sit up, even if they haven't mastered it yet.

Another indication that a baby is ready for solid foods is when you notice that she still seems hungry after getting plenty of milk (thirty-two ounces of formula, or nursing at least eight times). Often the baby weighs at least thirteen pounds and has doubled his birth weight.

These things frequently come together when a baby is between four and six months old. This is also a time when calorie needs are going up, and the iron reserves with which babies were born are becoming depleted.

I've met many parents who push to start feeding solids earlier than this because they think this will help their baby sleep better. Some even add rice cereal to their baby's bottle. There is no good evidence that this helps, and it could really hurt. Among other things, this practice can distort a baby's ability to tell how many calories are enough, predisposing him to overeating later in life.

For breastfed babies, I prefer waiting for solids until the babies are pretty adamant about starting; there is value in exclusive breastfeeding for six months. For formula-fed babies, I am more apt to start as soon as they appear interested after four months; I want to give them as many months of sampling veggies and fruits and whole grains as possible before this window of opportunity closes.

Sadly, most children in America begin their long-awaited solid food adventure with a taste of bland, processed white rice flour. What a wasted opportunity! It's not surprising that refined carbohydrates have become the centerpiece of nutrition in older children.

In many cultures, the first bite of solid food has been a mash made of a whole grain and mother's milk. I like this idea. Rice, oats, or barley, for instance, could make a nice first choice. Leverage your baby's eagerness to eat by making the first grains whole grains. You could cook some whole grain rice for the family, without salt (you can salt your own at the table), and puree some in a little food processor. If you mix oatmeal, barley, or rice cereal from a box, make it very liquidy at first.

I wouldn't object if you chose a vegetable or even a fruit as a first food (see "Choose the Right Variety," later in this chapter). In fact, there could be real advantages to offering an avocado: your baby could see an actual food, see it being cut open and mashed, and see you eating some as well. Or share a sweet potato. Bake until soft, mash with a fork, and mix with breast milk or formula.

There's no solid science pointing to which first food is best. What we have to go on is history and common sense. Whatever you choose, mixing it with mother's milk provides a wonderful bridge to the new flavor, and as

Feeding Baby Green Report

Brown Rice

In Thailand, the words for "to eat" (kin khao) literally mean "to eat rice." In Thai, the question, "How are you?" (*Kin khao yang?*) could literally be translated, "Have you eaten rice yet?"[1] You can find similar indications of the centrality of rice in Chinese and Japanese phrases.

Over half of the world's people get half of their calories every day from rice.[2] It's hard to overstate the importance of rice as a human food.

The difference between whole grain brown rice and white rice is more than just color. Brown rice can be milled and polished to turn it white. The bran, the germ, and the aluerone layer (rich in protein) are all removed. This removes most of the vitamins, half of the minerals, all of the fiber, and all of the essential fats from the rice. This greatly extends the shelf life, but leaves an empty, starchy food.

---

you would expect, increases babies' initial acceptance of the food.[3] Adding formula seems to do the same for formula-fed babies.

Spoon-Feeding Your Baby Bring the whole grain cereal (or whatever you choose) to your baby's mouth in a small spoon. This is a brand new skill for her. Designed for liquid feeding for the first months, babies have a strong tongue-thrust reflex. They instinctively push their tongues against anything that goes in their mouths. This instinct helps with nursing (when they suck at the same time) and helps protect them from getting unwanted objects in their mouths.

It may take a while to get the hang of eating from a spoon. For the first few days, more may end up on the bib than in the tummy. Be sure to have the camera out for some of these moments. They will be long-cherished treasures of the beginning of this new era.

If your baby objects to the spoon or seems uninterested, feel free to go back to liquid-only for a week or two.

We will talk about what to feed your baby below, but first let's consider some more keys to success.

Use Windows of Opportunity

Babies on the cusp of starting solid foods are going through big changes in their view of the world. Somewhere around four months old, they experience a gradual transformation that is as profound as that scene in *The Wizard of Oz* when Dorothy leaves the black-and-white world of her Kansas farmhouse and emerges in the Technicolor splendor of Oz. Babies are born seeing mostly in black-and-white, along with a few red tones. By the time they are starting to eat solids, their world is becoming drenched with color. Like Dorothy, they're not in Kansas anymore!

Meanwhile, your baby is gaining language and social skills. She responds to sounds she hears by making sounds of her own, and may begin performances of babbling lines of consonants. She recognizes her own name and may begin to understand other simple words ("Good!"). But it goes deeper. She is learning empathy. She studies mirrors. She is learning to interpret emotions underlying your tone of voice. She is learning to read your facial expressions and to make you smile.

Your baby is also making strides in gross motor development, gaining control of the big muscles in her body, learning to roll both ways, to sit, and then to move across the floor. She is developing the fine motor skills to manipulate the world from wherever the muscles take her: grabbing objects, moving them from hand to hand.

These advances are fueled by curiosity. Your baby is no longer content with just seeing, smelling, and hearing his surroundings, but wants to explore with hands and mouth, to look for objects hidden from view, and to struggle to obtain objects just out of reach. She wants to touch, to grasp, to connect physically with her world.

Her new, deeper curiosity about you, and her heightened fascination with objects in general and colorful objects in particular, creates unique opportunities to introduce her to colorful foods that you enjoy.

These events are fueled by another huge window of opportunity. Between the time that babies start trying to move across the floor and the time they have begun to walk with confidence, there is a marvelous, unrepeatable stage of nutritional development. The tongue-thrust reflex disappears, and babies begin to put almost anything in their mouths to sample and explore. It may not matter whether it looks palatable or not. It could be a rock or a snail or a piece of lint: they'll give it a try, make a face, and spit it out. If you let them sample something enough times, especially if it's something they see their parents eating, they can more easily acquire a taste for it than at any other period in life.

It reminds me of the scene in *The Chronicles of Narnia* when the world is young and the soil is so fertile that even a piece of a lamppost will grow. In this season, children are so young, and their minds and taste buds so open to possibilities, that an abundance of tastes and preferences can grow.

Neophobia—Fear of New Foods Inevitably, this window will shut. Usually sometime after they have been walking well for a while, the foods that toddlers will readily accept become limited to some of those they have already come to trust. This is called neophobia, and it can be quite intense. Again, this makes sense: you wouldn't want a more mobile youngster to toddle away from Dad and Mom for the first time and eat a strange berry—it might be poisonous. Or an unfamiliar leaf. Or a dead animal. Toddlers are designed to be suspicious of new fruits, vegetables, and meats. As they should be.

In recent times, many parents have squandered this precious window, introducing their babies to a narrow range of processed flavors. Most of these flavors don't taste like the real foods we want them to eat later. Jarred baby-food peaches, for instance, often taste more like canned peaches than like a real peach. Chances are that when a child who loved baby-food peaches as a baby tries a fresh peach as a toddler, he will reject it as foreign.

The window before neophobia sets in is a very special time when babies are primed to learn the food culture of their parents and of their society, using every avenue available to them.

Feeding Baby Green Tip

Poop!

When babies start solids, their poop often changes. Changing the balance of the diet is the most natural way to change the consistency of the stool to a comfortable happy medium.

Different changes work best for different kids, but to achieve softer stools you might try adding one or more of the following to their diet:

- Water
- Peas
- Peaches
- Pears
- Plums
- Prunes
- Apricots
- And if need be, juice

And perhaps try decreasing:

- White rice cereal
- Bananas
- Carrots
- Cheese

To make firmer stools, do the opposite of the above.

And if those food changes don't work—in either direction—consider the possibility that your baby has a cow's milk protein allergy. It more commonly causes loose stools, but it is also often a cause of constipation.

Engage All the Senses

With the sharpness and color of the visual world, vision comes to the fore. The sense of smell takes its place as a subtle but important background sense—except when it comes to foods. But the sense of taste is perhaps the most dynamic right now, as preferences are being set, much as you would set your preferences on a cell phone. You can pick your ringtone for each person in your contact list; your baby is setting what messages each taste will send to the brain.

Engage with Flavor We used to think that taste buds were passive and fixed, simply detecting certain molecules in a food and sending that information to the brain—the same way every time. Emerging science, though, has shown that the taste buds actually play an active role in how we taste our food. Under different conditions they can transmit a variety of information to the brain *in the presence of the same food.*[4]

They can change throughout life, but the taste buds and neural pathways are especially open to change for babies.[5]

Babies don't have to learn the basic tastes: the core sensations of sweet, salty, sour, bitter, and unami are hardwired. It's countless combinations of these primary tastes that will be learned.

Babies are naturally drawn to foods that are sweet from long before birth, and to foods that are salty by four months old.[6] They naturally shy away from sour or bitter foods—at first.[7] Genetically, some babies (and adults) have heightened taste perceptions, which can make bitter accents even more noticeable to them.

But babies can come to love even sour and bitter foods. It *normally* takes between six and sixteen experiences with a flavor before it becomes accepted. Somewhere between six and ten times is the most common. This is as it should be: a protective mechanism, to make them less likely to eat something toxic or spoiled.[8]

The magic word with new foods is *patience*. It's very important to understand that it's normal for babies to make a face or reject a new food the first time it's introduced. Sadly, in a large study of thousands of children, about a quarter of parents gave up on a food after only one or two tries, concluding that their baby didn't like it. The great majority gave up by five tries. Only 6 percent of parents would stick with a new food six to ten times. And only 1 or 2 percent would try more than ten times.[9]

Even when they initially reject a flavor, most babies can come to love it. In a recent study, researchers identified babies whose mothers had given up on some particularly protested vegetable after the babies had rejected it on two or three occasions. This disliked vegetable was then offered again every other day. At first, the babies' intake of the disliked vegetable was low. Yet by the time the babies had sampled it seven or eight times in the study (nine to eleven times in their lives), over 70 percent of the babies not only accepted the previously spurned vegetable, but really liked it—readily eating as much of it as they did of their previous favorites.

And here's the exciting piece: nine months after the study was over—and the babies were now toddlers—more than 75 percent of them were still readily eating that vegetable. For 15 percent we don't know what would have happened: the families never served that vegetable again.[10]

And that's just one vegetable, selected because it was particularly disliked by that baby. Compare that success with the fate of the typical American toddler. About a third of them eat no vegetables at all on any given day. Among those who do, French fries are easily the most common "vegetable." With just this one tool (repeated taste exposures during a critical window) and just one vegetable, your baby's taste range could surpass that of the typical American toddler. Imagine if you tried ten vegetables!

You've already given your baby a head start with flavors experienced during pregnancy and nursing. This is a great time to teach your baby to love flavors you *don't* like, but wish you did, whether they're beets or brussels sprouts.

And don't miss the opportunity to give your baby his first direct experience with something from each of the twenty-one plant families listed in Chapter Four—they're almost like a library of nature, containing a wealth of phytonutrient wisdom in every section. You may want to use the checklist at the end of the book to keep track.

Children live in a different sensory chemical world than we do. They can detect minor variations in taste that would elude us. And one child's sensory chemical world is not the same as another child's. Just as some of us experience colors differently from each other, we know that some of us experience taste differently from each other. Probably, all of us do.

Many studies have looked at pairs of identical versus fraternal twins to try to tease out what part of taste preference is hereditary and what part depends on how a child is raised.[11] These studies don't always take into account that identical twins not only share more genes, but may be treated more similarly.[12]

It seems clear that for most of us, differences in experience are just as important, if not more important, than differences in heredity—especially when it comes to our enjoyment of fruits and vegetables. How much more important is still open to disagreement, though I believe it is quite a bit. Either way, though, having a child who is genetically less likely to enjoy vegetables is not a reason to give up—if anything, these kids need a varied taste experience at this age all the more.

Engage with Aroma In the early days, the sense of smell was so intense and so precise that your baby could use it as a map of the room. Now, the primary smells he pays attention to are the aromas of food.

Sometimes you may want to bring food close to your baby's nose briefly as you are preparing it, to increase his desire for the food and help him connect the aroma with what he sees.

Other times, you may want to let the waft of an aroma alert your baby before he gets a chance to confirm his guess with sight and taste—sort of an olfactory game of peekaboo.

Engage with Sight I suggest feeding your baby something green at every single lunch and dinner (there's more than one reason this book is called *Feeding Baby Green*!). I also suggest trying for another bright color at every meal: breakfast, lunch, and dinner. The colors in plants, designed to attract us, often contain especially powerful nutrients.

And color is fun! If babies become accustomed to color, it could make it easier to keep their diet varied and balanced in future years. For these kids, brown-beige meals, such as grilled cheese and potato chips, or burgers and fries, look boring—they know intuitively that something's missing.

The color could either be in the food itself (think carrots) or in the peel, especially if the baby sees you peel it (think bananas). At a given meal, you might choose red (tomato, red bell pepper, watermelon, strawberry)

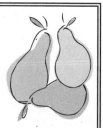

Feeding Baby Green Tip

Four Ways to Influence Your Baby's Food Preferences with Sight

1. Model the Behavior You Want

Let your baby see you relaxed, enjoying healthy food. This is the time to eat the way you really want to and that you want to pass along. Even if you've had difficulty changing the way you eat in the past, you may be able to do it now. Doing something for our kids as well as ourselves sometimes taps into deep motivational power.

2. Avoid Advertising

Take charge of avoiding exposing babies to commercials for empty food. This could mean turning off the TV (not a bad idea), watching PBS, choosing DVDs, or using a digital video recorder to fast-forward through commercials. Babies won't understand much of what they see and hear on television, but they will pay attention to the food. Babies at this age see TV as a kind of reality. If close enough, they may even reach for food on the screen.

3. Let Your Baby See the Colors of Nature Being Opened or Eaten

If you open an avocado or banana for yourself or for the baby, use the opportunity for visual learning from time to time. Even if you only feed your baby jarred bananas, hold up a real banana next to it from time to time to try to make the connection.

4. Play a Game

If your baby likes peekaboo, you might also want to try peekaboo with a piece of fruit or veggie, or an egg that you are about to prepare.

---

or orange (carrot, sweet potato, squash, cantaloupe) or yellow (yellow bell pepper, banana, yellow tomato) or purple (beets or plums or berries).

Another important part of engaging the sight is by modeling your own eating behavior for your baby to see. How do baby monkeys decide when given the choice between reaching for a marshmallow or an almond? If they have seen their parents faced with the same choice, the answer is easy. They will choose whichever food they have seen their parents choose, and will avoid the other.[13]

Animal studies suggest that even a single experience of watching an adult eat a specific food can increase the odds of a child wanting to eat that food when given the opportunity much later—the equivalent of a year later or more.[14]

Note: Just seeing a food repeatedly in a bowl or in the pantry does not seem to increase acceptance of a food if the baby hasn't seen it go into a mouth.[15] Seeing the food eaten readies them for other reinforcing visual experiences.

Most of us would shudder at the thought of giving our little baby a bowl of pureed fast-food French fries or of putting cola in her bottle. But if we enjoy a bag of French fries in front of her while slurping our soda through a straw, we are doing almost the same thing. Once she has made the switch to table foods, she will find a way to convince you to give her these same items.

Besides watching what their parents eat, babies pay a lot of attention to what other people in their lives are eating in front of them: siblings, grandparents, friends—and also people and characters they see on television or in commercials.

This is especially true of colorful foods and packages. The food industry has learned that adding coloring to food and packages increases desire for them. This is something many plants learned long ago. Their fruit has bright colors, especially when ripe, to attract us to eat the fruit and help protect and spread their seed.

Engage with Sounds and Language Taste preference acquisition occurs during the same developmental arc as language acquisition, and creatively combining the two can help both sets of skills. Early on, simply naming a food each time a child eats sets the groundwork.

Single words are the easiest to learn, and a great place to start. Soon, as their repertoire of food is expanding, so will their interests in words, rhythms, and rhymes to encourage their love of fruits and veggies. Now is the time to bring back those food rhymes you read or recited before your little one was born (see "Engage with Sounds and Language" in Chapter Four).

Kids love little playful word games at this stage. Making word games around healthy foods becomes especially important now, as learning language becomes a top priority for your child. A self-perpetuating circle of familiarity and delight can form with objects when they recognize its name.

If you are using baby signs, it might be time to introduce some new ones. Watch and observe what your child seems to want to communicate about. Most children would like simple ways to express basic requests next, such as "I'm hungry," "I'm thirsty," "Change me," "Pick me up," "Put me down," or "Take me outside."

You can easily model some simple signs to lay the groundwork for this communication. You might touch your hand to your mouth whenever you say "eat," and tilt your head back when you say "drink."

Transitions can be significant for children at this age, so a simple sign for "all done" can be very useful (perhaps your outstretched palms or tapping a wristwatch).

These very simple maneuvers create rewarding ways for parents to connect with their children. They make an already magical time even richer, further deepening family bonds.

Engage with Touch Just as there is a critical window for developing certain flavor preferences, there is also a window for learning to enjoy different texture preferences.[16] You don't want all of your baby's foods perfectly pureed. Have an eye toward providing soft chunks and irregularities that are easily managed and swallowed (remembering to be mindful of choking hazards). This variety will prepare them to accept more foods later.

When it comes to toddlers being willing to eat chopped carrots, for example, their willingness appears to depend as much, if not more, on their texture experience than on their flavor experience.[17] As your baby nears and reaches the toddling stage, texture will be a bigger issue than it is now. But even at the beginning of solids, an occasional fork-smashed banana or avocado is an exciting addition to a diet of pure purees.

Choose the Right Amount

During these early days of solid foods, a strong foundation of nutrition is still coming from breast milk or formula. So, as we've seen, there is no specific official amount of solid food your baby needs to get.

Most kids who take solids between four and six months do well having meals of solids once or twice a day. And two or three times a day after six months—usually at the same meal as breast milk or formula.

For breastfed babies, I usually prefer that they nurse first and then take solids until full. Nursing when hungry can help to keep up demand for Mom's milk supply, and fill up the baby with the splendid and unique properties of breast milk.

For formula-fed babies, I usually prefer offering solids first, and then topping off with formula, if desired, until full. Because they have less past and present taste experience, I want them to get the biggest taste variety now, and finish with formula when they are tired or bored.

Once your baby has gotten the skill of closing his lips around the spoon and swallowing easily, it's a great idea to support him in monitoring his own body's cues to determine the right amount to eat. *There is no preset*

Feeding Baby Green Tip

Just One More Bite?

Healthy babies who are growing well do not need to be coaxed to try more than a bite of anything. Although it can be fun to fly a spoonful of mashed bananas to your baby's mouth while making airplane noises with your lips, if they're not hungry it will be counterproductive. Similarly, you don't have to take a bite of her food yourself and exaggerate a happy reaction: "Yum, this is sooo good."

Desperation is out, enjoyable mealtimes are in.

Relax. When your child is hungry, she will let you know. When it comes to food, throughout childhood *pressure tends to backfire*. It usually decreases a child's enjoyment of the particular food, and even if it does appear to succeed in the short run, it can lead to overeating because it teaches her to ignore her body's cues.

amount. It will depend on his size, metabolism, activity, and so forth, and may naturally vary from day to day and from week to week.

To find out what is right for him at this age, move the spoon toward his mouth and observe his response. As long as he keeps opening his mouth and looks interested, slip the spoon in. Pause for a brief rest between bites, and bring the spoon back up. Watch for signs that he is losing interest. If he turns his head away from the spoon, scrunches his lips shut, or just looks bored, it's time to stop. He's not using words, but he's telling you his needs loud and clear: "All done!"

Babies who eat well at this stage may sleep better. Babies who sleep well at this stage may eat better. Emerging science suggests that poor sleep can decrease levels of leptin, an important hormone that moderates both the appetite and the metabolism. This is true in babies and adults. Too little leptin can lead to overeating and a slowed metabolism, resulting in too much weight gain.

Vitamin Supplements. Breastfed babies should continue to take 400 IU of vitamin D daily until they are clearly getting enough from other sources, such as sunshine, whole milk, fatty fish, or formula. You may also want to consider starting vitamin D drops for formula-fed kids who drop below thirty-two ounces a day of formula.

Choose the Right Variety

Babies learn new flavors best when they come in rapid succession. In one fascinating study, babies in France and Germany were assigned to one of three groups. Group 1 was given one vegetable for nine days in a row. Group 2 was given three vegetables, each for three days in a row (similar to what often happens in the United States). Group 3 was also given three vegetables, but they were changed daily (the rapid change group).

As you might expect, those who got three vegetables—those in Groups 2 and 3—significantly increased their acceptance of all new vegetables compared to those in Group 1. Strikingly, though, those who had a daily change were even *more* likely to enjoy all new vegetables. And the frequency of change was even more important than the total number of vegetables offered.[18] Variety begets variety.

If your baby doesn't like something today, there's no need to force it. Move on to something your baby does like, and try this one again tomorrow or the next day. Keep the new flavors coming.

Feeding Baby Green Report

Diapers

While we're discussing how solid foods are now going into your baby, we should also consider the waste coming out. Diapers are a frequent reminder that our actions have consequences.

The biggest environmental consequence from disposable diapers comes from their manufacture, especially the use of chlorine and the destruction of trees. And of course they cannot, for the most part, be recycled. The biggest impact from reusable diapers comes from the energy and detergents used in their laundering.

When you choose disposable diapers, choose those made in an eco-friendly way, without chlorine bleach or the chemical TBT, and with sustainably harvested trees. And when you choose cloth diapers, choose an eco-friendly detergent and washer, or a diaper service that does.

Another new alternative is called Elimination Communication, or the Diaper Free Movement. Here, parents learn to recognize clues that their baby is about to "go" and provide him with a receptacle just in time. Several readers of *Raising Baby Green* have reported that they started doing this when they introduced solid foods and greatly reduced the number of diapers used—and got their kids out of diapers entirely not long after they started walking. This takes a lot of work, but it can be good for the environment and for the pocketbook.

Many parents are still told to wait three to five days between starting new foods in an effort to prevent or identify allergies. I strongly disagree with this notion. There is no good evidence that this pattern reduces allergies, as you'll see in the "Allergies" section toward the end of this chapter.

After the first food, should you add fruits next or vegetables or other grains? The AAP suggests meats, then vegetables, then fruits—but admits this is just one of many possible good orders.[19] Conventional wisdom says that it's best to add a bunch of veggies (such as carrots, sweet potatoes, squash, peas, green beans, and potatoes) before starting fruits—because once they start tasting the sweetness of fruits it may be harder to get them to go back. With breastfed kids, I do like beginning with the green veggies first, at least one new one every day, because these are often the toughest flavors to learn to really enjoy. They make take to them with gusto at first bite, especially if you choose veggies you ate during pregnancy and nursing. Or learning may be a process. Go through every green vegetable in your family's repertoire (see the "Foods to Avoid" tip further on to learn about food allergies, nitrates, and oxalates). Decide as a family if there are new green veggies you want to incorporate into your life together. If you think you want to expand your own food tastes at some point, this is a great time to begin.

Babies need as many weeks as possible of really enjoying green vegetables before the neophobia sets in. These are often the most difficult foods to learn to enjoy later. I want babies to get accustomed to a green vegetable at every single lunch and every single dinner before they are toddlers, so it feels strange to eat a lunch or dinner without one. I wish that had happened for me!

For formula-fed kids, I'd also start with green veggies, such as peas or green beans. Many will be thrilled at their first veggies, but in the event they don't readily take to them, you might switch the first focus to orange veggies, such as carrots, squash, or sweet potatoes, a new one at least every day. These are often easier to take, and perhaps getting some variety under the belt will help them take the green beans! I wouldn't give up on the green veggies in the meantime, just plan to offer a bite and then move on if the baby rejects them.

This doesn't necessarily mean holding off on fruits or grains. The new foods don't need to be single foods or one at a time. Just be sure to get lots of them in. You can start cycling through them soon after you've begun cycling through the green veggies.

I tend to start meat after introducing a variety of some whole grains, veggies, and fruits—just because enjoying meat appears to be the least influenced by repeated early experiences.[20]

Allergies Thankfully, most food allergies developed in the first year of life are soon outgrown, though allergies to fish, seafood, nuts, and peanuts are less likely to be outgrown and may take longer if they are.

When people want to prevent allergies in young children, they usually do it by attempting to avoid or delay certain foods. However, this may not be as important as we once thought—and perhaps not important at all when kids are otherwise healthy.

The 2008 guidelines of the American Academy of Pediatrics (AAP) say that there is no convincing reason to avoid any food beyond four to six months for the purpose of reducing allergies. This includes even the foods most commonly associated with allergies: cow's milk, eggs, peanuts, nuts, wheat, soy, fish, and shellfish.

There is even some evidence that starting these foods *in infancy* may help prevent allergies. One study showed that peanut allergies are ten times more common among Jewish babies in the United Kingdom than among Jewish babies in Israel. In the United Kingdom, the babies averaged zero servings of peanuts per month; in Israel, they averaged eight servings of peanuts per month.[21]

Neither is there any evidence to support the old jarred-food pattern of waiting three to five days before each new single food. This does nothing to prevent allergies; it's just a way of finding out what they might be. Yes, it's true, if a child does display allergic symptoms, it's easier for the parents to guess which food was the culprit—but this minor ease of detective work comes at far too high a price.

The science of preventing allergies is still young, and many studies are contradictory. Here are my suggestions:

1. Breastfed babies seem to develop fewer allergies later in life. Breastfeed for at least six months, longer if possible.
2. Take probiotics (or eat yogurt) and omega-3 supplements (or eat fish) if you are nursing.
3. Avoid the most allergenic foods (cow's milk, eggs, peanuts, nuts, wheat, soy, fish, and shellfish) when your baby is sick or on antibiotics.
4. Avoid genetically modified foods, at least until your baby is older.
5. Consider a Mediterranean style diet for you and your family (see "The Mediterranean Diet" in Chapter Four for details).
6. Consider choosing organic foods, especially dairy products.

Are Carrots Safe? Parents are often told that it is not safe to feed your baby carrots, spinach, beets, turnips, or collard greens that you make at home: skip the root vegetables and leafy greens, give them what comes in a jar. *I disagree!*

Feeding Baby Green Tip

Foods to Avoid

1. Foods That Your Baby May Be Allergic To

If your baby seems to develop an allergy to any food, err on the side of safety. Signs might include spitting up, diarrhea, constipation, blood in the stool, irritability, or skin rashes. Avoid feeding your baby that food for now, and discuss it with your doctor before trying again.

2. Honey

It's wise not to give your baby honey at least until she's one year old, to help prevent infant botulism.

3. Raw and Undercooked Food

Undercooked or raw eggs or meat might harbor unhealthy bacteria.
I do not suggest feeding babies raw or undercooked produce at this stage, unless (like an avocado or banana) it is peeled before it is eaten. Cook the vegetables you serve your child, at least until she is six months old, to get rid of possible bacteria and to make the veggies softer and easier to swallow.

4. Choking Hazards

Perhaps the most important foods to avoid are those in a form that could lead to choking. Babies can't be trusted to chew effectively, even after a couple of teeth have come in. Avoid:

- Meats (unless well shredded)
- Nuts (unless ground)
- Peanut butter
- Popcorn
- Raisins
- Whole grapes
- Food chunks that require chewing

The foods should either begin to dissolve in the mouth or be soft, mashed, ground, or shredded enough to be easily swallowed without chewing and without getting stuck.

The worried warnings go something like this: "In some parts of the country, these vegetables contain large amounts of nitrates that can cause an unusual kind of anemia (low blood count) in young infants. Baby food companies are aware of this and screen the produce they buy for nitrates. . . . Since you cannot test for this chemical yourself, it's safer to use commercially prepared form of these foods."[22] This reminds me of the message behind the baby food and infant formula ads from when I was young: You can't feed your baby as well as we can.

Even the scientific literature sometimes supports this warning. "There seems to be little or no risk of nitrate poisoning from commercially prepared infant foods in the United States. However, reports of nitrate poisoning from home-prepared vegetable foods for infants continue to occur."[23]

But do they? It's time to put this myth to rest. The kind of nitrate poisoning of concern is a rare form of anemia called methemoglobinemia. The symptoms are obvious: the baby's skin has a bluish tinge. There has only been *one* reported case of a baby with nitrate poisoning from home-prepared vegetable foods in the United States. In 1973. It was a young baby boy who drank too much contaminated carrot juice.[24] And around the world, there have only been a small handful of other reports in the past forty years.[25] Moreover, *commercial baby foods* in the United States can also contain these high levels of nitrates—and it's not just the roots and greens.[26]

Methemoglobinemia in babies is almost always caused by drinking infant formula, not by eating homemade baby food. This can happen when the formula is made with water (usually well water) contaminated by nitrates from synthetic fertilizer runoff. Breastfeeding is safe from nitrates, even if mothers drink this water.

Beyond this, breastfeeding is protective. The predominant beneficial bacteria in the digestive systems of breastfed babies protects against methemoglobinemia even if the baby is exposed to nitrates.

The official AAP guidelines on nitrates say: "Home-prepared infant foods from vegetables (e.g., spinach, beets, *green beans*, squash, carrots) should be avoided *until infants are 3 months or older.*"[27] (Emphasis mine.) I wish these guidelines were more widely repeated. Nitrates are mostly a risk to the lingering fetal blood cells that are gone by around three months of age. By six months, the stomach acidifies, and the risk plummets further.

To avoid any nitrate problems in your baby, I suggest that you do the following:

1. Breastfeed.
2. Don't mix formula with well water, unless it is known to have low nitrates.
3. Avoid feeding your baby commercial *or* homemade vegetables before three months.
4. Choose organic vegetables (see "Reap the Benefits of Green," near the end of this chapter).
5. Use or freeze opened or homemade baby food within twenty-four hours. Refrigerator storage can increase nitrates.

Feeding Baby Green Stories

"One Bite"

Peas, carrots, and turnips were the main vegetables available when I was a child. Although I loved all vegetables raw, I can remember sitting at the table for hours trying to force down the cooked vegetables that were on the plate in front of me. To this day I cannot convince myself to eat cooked peas, although I do love them raw. I vowed that if I ever had children, I would not force them to eat vegetables, nor make them sit at the table for hours trying to force down food they did not like.

When my children were small I kept to my pledge. Although I would put a variety of vegetables on their plates, the rule was one bite and if you still don't like them then you do not have to finish them. I am pleased to say that all of my children like and eat all vegetables.

I am on a new food adventure now with my youngest grandchild. The first few bites of vegetables produced a crinkled-up nose and a turned-away head. We did not force the issue, but we would try again the next meal—normally, his reaction was not as negative. Sullivan, who is almost eleven months old now, will eat any vegetable we offer him, even preferring peas to peaches!

I often say I have a "texture" aversion to vegetables—I don't like the mush feeling that is produced by cooking. Perhaps babies and children are the same. I say if they won't eat vegetables cooked, offer it to them raw, grate them up fine if you need to—they just might surprise you.

Beverly Richardson
Vancouver Island, British Columbia, Canada

Variety in Sauces and Seasonings You also want your baby to learn to like a few sauce or seasoning combinations you enjoy—the flavor threads we discussed in Chapter Four—such as Italian red sauce, Chinese bean sauce, Mexican salsa, or Indian curry. You can start trying hints of your favorite seasoning combinations and sauces that you enjoyed together when you were pregnant and nursing. Remember, their brand-new taste buds may need *much* less of the seasoning than you do.

Breakfast Consider a whole grain and perhaps some fruit or eggs at breakfast. Or yogurt. A frittata or quiche (mashed up, of course) could be a nice weekend treat. Berries go nicely with yogurt or with a whole grain. Bananas, grapefruit, kiwi, oranges, papaya, or pineapple can make a nice start to the day.

Vary the fruits, vary the grains. (Bob's Red Mill is one online source for lots of varieties of whole grains—I've eaten at the original mill in Oregon with my family, and we continue to rely on them quite a bit at home.) You might try buckwheat, corn, quinoa, millet, rye, or spelt.

Breast milk or formula is also good at breakfast. Limit or avoid added sweets, or breakfast treats made from refined white flour—those are easy to acquire a taste for anytime, if you want.

Besides fruit for breakfast, I suggest fruit as a dessert at least one meal a day. You might try berries again (blueberries, raspberries, strawberries) or cherries, apricots, plums, or watermelon. Apples and pears can make a great snack, perhaps plain or with a little cinnamon. Whole grains can also make nice snacks, such as a finger-manageable piece of cereal (again, minimizing any added sugar).

Breast Milk and Formula The backbone of the baby's diet at this point is still breast milk or formula—about sixteen to thirty-two ounces a day. More than thirty-two ounces will discourage getting the needed variety. Less than sixteen ounces might result in too little of key nutrients. Most of the rest should be fruits and vegetables, followed by whole grains, followed by beans, eggs, yogurt, meat, poultry, fish, and so forth.

Variety in Beverages Even though your baby gets liquid in the form of breast milk or formula, she can also enjoy other beverages. Water in a sippy cup is ideal (see "Hydration Solutions" in Chapter Three for ideas about making flavorful water available for your family at any time).

> ## Feeding Baby Green Tip
>
> ### Your Baby Can Join the Family Table
>
> There's really no reason your baby can't join in family meals at this stage. Simply bring your baby food mill (see next section for details) to the table, add a small amount of your food, perhaps with some breast milk or formula, grind, and serve!

I'm not a fan of fruit juice for babies—and certainly not in a bottle. In a pinch, juice can be a gentle medicine for constipation, but kids don't need the nutrition. The high sugar content and calorie count can teach kids to consume too many calories. Juice in a bottle can also be damaging to the teeth.

I'm even less of a fan of sweetened or artificially sweetened drinks for babies. These dial up their sweet tooth, while adding nothing of value. Sadly, in a major study of American babies, almost half of our seven- and eight-month-olds consume a daily sweetened beverage or a sweetened dessert.[28]

Customize Needs for Every Body

You may have thought that the foods described earlier in "Choose the Right Variety" sounded more like family meals than like baby food. This was intentional. The goal of baby food is to be a bridge for your baby from breast milk or formula to eating the way you eat as a family.

The best baby foods available are the ones you make yourself using the healthy, nutritious, and environmentally friendly foods that I hope you are already eating as a family. You may need to adjust the seasonings in order to share these food with your baby. The carrots and other crunchy foods may need to be cooked softer than the way you would normally eat them. But feeding some version of your real meals seven days a week is a logical continuation of the theme you began before your baby was born and when you started nursing.

Feeding Baby Green Recipe

Caul Me a Pear

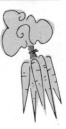

The cauliflower and pears have lots of vitamin C, vitamin K, folate, and fiber. This versatile recipe can be soup (puree until smooth and add enough reserved cooking liquid to make it "spoon consistency"); baby food (puree until smooth), or for an older baby (leave a few small lumps).

1 head cauliflower, cut into small florets and left to sit 10 minutes to preserve the effects of the enzyme myrosinase

3 pears, peeled, cored, and quartered

¼ teaspoon cinnamon

¼ teaspoon ground turmeric

1 cup cooking water

1. Soak the cauliflower and pears for minimum of 5 minutes in water, to remove dirt and bacteria. Drain.
2. Steam the cauliflower for 15 minutes. Add pears and steam for another 10 minutes until both are fork tender.
3. Drain, and reserve cooking water for blending.
4. Add the steamed cauliflower, pears, cinnamon, and turmeric to the food processor with ½ cup reserved cooking water. Puree to desired texture. You may want to add more water, a ¼ cup at a time, to achieve desired texture.

Serves 4 (Yield: 4 cups)

NUTRITION FACTS (AMOUNT PER SERVING)

Calories: 113	Sodium: 47mg	Sugars: 16.54g
Total Fat: 0.19g	Total Carbs: 28.48g	Protein: 3.37g
Cholesterol: 0	Dietary Fiber: 7.85g	

Provided by and reprinted by permission from Jack's Harvest.

Making Your Own Baby Food Here's the simple secret: most of the time your baby can eat the same food you are eating at home or away. This can be much easier and more fun than most parents imagine. And it's a great way to take charge. Start with a great tool like the KidCo BabySteps Food Mill or their Electric Food Mill, both BPA and phthalate free (www.kidco.com). The regular food mill is great for bringing to the table at home and on the go. In seconds, your baby can be eating a softer version of the same foods you're eating, with almost no extra effort.

For those times when you are not sharing the same meal as a family with just a few twists of the food mill handle, you can still easily make your own baby food. The electric version is nice for making food for the week.

You can learn how to make all you'll need in just thirty minutes per week. My friends Joan Ahlers and Cheryl Tallman have a great resource for helping you do this at www.Freshbaby.com.

Compared to even the best commercial baby foods, making your own can result in less waste (no disposable jars or containers), less energy (no factory, just a blender and a little energy to steam the foods), and minimal food miles (no trucking containers from an average of fifteen hundred miles away—just pick up some produce at your local farmers market or CSA). And it can save money.

For your family, choose produce at the peak of ripeness if possible. No matter what has gone on before, the longer the time between harvest and eating (or freezing), the greater the loss of good flavors. And the greater the odds of acquiring off-flavors or extra bitterness.

We all know that the appearance of a fruit or vegetable will eventually deteriorate after it has been harvested. Generally, both flavor and nutritional bounty suffer considerably before any noticeable change in appearance.

Feeding Baby Green Report

Organic Baby Food

In the last few years a number of excellent fresh and frozen organic baby food brands have been showing up on store shelves, providing great food that doesn't taste like it came in a jar.

Bobo Baby (www.bobobaby.com) has some very nice vegetable-and-grain combinations. **Jack's Harvest** (www.jacksharvest.com) makes use of cinnamon, ginger, lime, and thyme to enhance their flavors. I'm impressed with **Petite Palate's** (www.petitepalate.com) use of spices. Some flavors include onion, garlic, oregano, thyme, vanilla, cinnamon, and lime (not all in the same recipe, of course). **Plum Organics** (www.plumorganics.com) has the largest offering of flavors of all of these companies (and I sometimes enjoy eating their Super Greens Multigrain as a convenient way for me to eat organic vegetables on the road). They also have toddler foods, as does **Happy Baby** (happybabyfood.com). I especially like their fish bites for toddlers.

Homemade Baby (www.homemadebaby.com), found in the refrigerator case, not the freezer aisle, is sold in stores in New York and Los Angeles, and is moving into communities across the country. You can check their Web site to find a store near you or to "complete a request certificate" to request a store near you to carry their products. I particularly like their Yummy Yammies and Baby Tex Mex flavors.

If you want to go all out, consider **Bohemian-Baby** (bohemian-baby.com). It's made in small batches and delivered to your home. You can order it from their Web site, but be prepared to pay top dollar.

You may also want to try some of the larger national brands, such as **Gerber Organic, Earth's Best,** and Safeway's **O Brand.**

The key is to pop one open and see if it tastes reminiscent of something your family now eats or wants to (perhaps with seasonings adjusted). If it's a match with your family, it makes sense.

Commercial Baby Food Thankfully, today there are a number of excellent pre-made organic baby foods on the market for when you are on the go, or if you just want to open something and serve. You could even do the reverse of making your own baby food, and take one of these baby foods and put it over some brown rice or chicken or fish or pasta as a meal for you.

Exercise!

Baby's big activity during this period is learning to move across the floor. This doesn't necessarily mean learning to crawl. Rolling over, sitting without support, cruising (walking while holding on to furniture), and walking independently are important developmental milestones. Crawling isn't.

Crawling isn't even mentioned in my favorite pediatric development textbook.

This probably seems strange—of all these behaviors, crawling is most associated with babies. The truth is, however, many babies never crawl. They do need to find some way to move across the floor. Each will do so at unpredictable times and in distinctive ways. Your child may be a scooter—one who likes to stay upright and scoot across the floor on his bottom. Many babies prefer creeping, or wriggling forward on the stomach. Many children will crab-crawl, moving backwards. And, of course, many children will get up on all fours and crawl forward in the traditional way. Each child's method is unique.

Some adults are concerned that children who don't crawl in the traditional way will be less coordinated. This is a myth. As long as the baby begins to move across the floor using each arm and each leg, there is no cause for concern.

You can encourage moving in whatever way your child prefers by spending time on the floor with her. Consider placing favorite toys just out of reach. If it's too close, it will be boring; too far, and it will be frustrating.

Our task as parents is to find that zone of moderate challenge—where learning is fun. Provide situations where he can teach himself through playful exploration. Forced teaching hinders development. These principles apply equally to "gifted," "average," and "special-needs" children.

As with healthy eating, healthy movement is best modeled by parents. I'm a fan of programs such as Stroller Strides, a workout group for moms

Feeding Baby Green Recipe

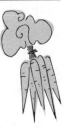

Black Bean Tomato Ragout

This delicious dish is a hearty and flavorful blend of vegetables, grains, and spices. It's a great source of dietary fiber for digestion, contains vitamin C for a healthy immune system, and is a complete vegetarian protein source.

1 cup dried black beans

¼ cup dried lentils

1 tablespoon extra virgin olive oil

2 large carrots, peeled and chopped

1 (14.5 oz.) can stewed tomatoes

¼ cup quinoa

1 teaspoon ground coriander

1 teaspoon ground paprika

Sea salt, to taste

Cooking dried black beans:

1. Wash and carefully remove any pebbles, sticks, and dirt that may still be in the black beans.
2. Place the beans in a saucepan or Dutch oven, cover beans in cold water, and soak for 2 to 4 hours.
3. Drain the beans and cover in fresh water. Bring to a boil, then reduce heat to a very slow simmer. (If you add salt to the beans before they are totally cooked, the beans will take about twice as long to cook—the salt prohibits them from getting tender quickly.) Cook on low heat for about 2 hours or until soft.

Cooking dried lentils:

1. Wash and carefully remove any pebbles, sticks, and dirt that may still be in the lentils.
2. Place the lentils in a separate pot with water to cover. Bring to a boil. Cover and simmer until tender. Drain and rinse. Set aside.

Ragout:

1. In a large saucepot, over medium heat, heat the olive oil and sauté the carrots until tender. This will take about 4 to 5 minutes.
2. Add the tomatoes with their juice and bring to a low simmer.
3. Wash the quinoa thoroughly and add it to the carrot-tomato mixture. (Quinoa tends to be bitter if you don't wash it before cooking.)
4. Add the coriander and paprika and turn heat to a simmer. Cook covered for about 10 to 15 minutes or until the quinoa is tender.
5. Stir in the black beans and lentils. Season with salt, to taste.

Serves 4 (Yield: 4 cups)

NUTRITION FACTS (AMOUNT PER SERVING)

Calories: 200	Sodium: 309mg	Sugars: 4.06g
Total Fat: 4.43g	Total Carbs: 31.77g	Protein: 9.42g
Cholesterol: 0	Dietary Fiber: 10.06g	

Submitted and reprinted by permission from Plum Organics.

with their babies. Stroller Strides was founded by fitness expert and mom Lisa Druxman after her son was born and she wanted a way to get back into shape that would include her baby.

Reap the Benefits of Green

As should be abundantly clear by now, choosing locally grown produce has many advantages for the environment, and for you and your baby. You should also be aware by now that I am a proponent of organic produce. One reason is because it is grown without synthetic fertilizers. And this can have significant advantages for you and your baby that go beyond flavor. Let me tell you a story.

Off the coast of the Gulf of Mexico is a dead zone about the size of New Jersey where aquatic life cannot survive during part of the year. This dead zone doubled in size between 1985 and 1999 and has continued to grow rapidly since then.

According to the Congressional Research Service, the main cause of this dead zone is synthetic fertilizer runoff that ends up first in the Mississippi River, and then dumps into the Gulf. Our conventional corn crop is the single biggest culprit.[29] Conventional corn appears to be cheaper than organic corn, in part because of government subsidies and in part because the true costs don't show up immediately in the supermarket. The dead zone is one powerful picture of the cost of industrial corn production.

Commercial agriculture uses about as much fossil fuels as we do in all of the cars on the road. And on a typical farm up to 40 percent of this fossil-fuel use is in the production of synthetic fertilizers and pesticides.

Nitrogen-based fertilizer not only depletes nonrenewable resources from its production and pollutes our water, but also tends to increase nitrates and decrease vitamin C in our produce.

In most conventional farming systems where nitrogen fertilizers are freely applied, the plants are basically overeating. But even though they have been overeating, they tend to be undernourished: the nutritional quality of conventional produce has fallen over the last fifty years.[30]

The plants tend to channel their excess nutrients toward making simple carbohydrates, starch, and carotenoids, and away from some important products for their (and our) health, such as vitamin C, quercetin, and total antioxidants.

Meanwhile, these plants can also experience a buildup of nitrates (a negative for food safety and nutritional quality).

Organic produce does not use these synthetic fertilizers derived from fossil fuels. As you might expect, in organic systems levels of vitamin C, quercetin, and total antioxidants are typically elevated, and there is little buildup of nitrates. This allows these plants to better deal with stresses from pests and the climate, giving them an enhanced ability to scavenge free radicals via vitamin C and other antioxidant systems.

According to the biggest matched comparisons of organic versus conventional produce available to date, compiled by my friend and colleague Dr. Charles Benbrook, organic produce averages just 55 percent the nitrate levels of its conventional counterparts, while it averages 10 percent more vitamin C, 140 percent more quercetin, and 24 percent more total antioxidant power per serving.[31]

This is another example of how eating green, especially for babies, is better for you, your family, and the planet.

These days of spoon-feeding your baby the best of what life has to offer will quickly draw to a close. Soon, as we'll see in the next chapter, she'll be pushing the spoon away and making choices for herself—another wonderful opportunity for both of you.

From Babies
to Toddlers
(and Beyond)

Becoming a Toddler
(ABOUT NINE MONTHS THROUGH EIGHTEEN MONTHS)

As your child moves from infancy to toddlerhood, the days of spoon-feeding your child begin to end. The timing of this event varies widely from child to child, but your baby begins to lose interest in receiving the spoon from you at meals, and ultimately refuses it altogether. This is not a cause for alarm, but actually the signal of an exciting new stage in your baby's journey.

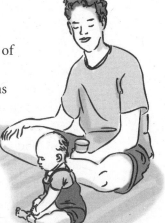

At this stage, changes in behavior come quickly. Your child is learning to pull himself up to stand and look around, to cruise along the furniture while holding on, to stand for one thrilling, wobbly moment without support, and finally, to toddle out and explore the world bravely, on his own.

This same desire for exploration and autonomy colors his approach to food. No wonder he's beginning to push away that spoonful of perfectly wonderful food you offer! When he has eight teeth—four on the top and four on the bottom (usually by eleven months)—and especially when those first molars come in (usually by sixteen months)—he's looking for more adventure in his food choices. (See "Teething Pain.") He wants more texture in mashed foods, and finger foods he can crunch and chew and even peel. He's at the beginning of a brand-new food adventure, and you're his trusty guide.

The Essential Steps for Teaching Nutritional Intelligence

With your child's growing independence, he needs your guidance now more than ever. Many parents, though, are at a loss on how to feed their new toddler. Here are some keys to guide you through this intense time.

Take Charge!

It's especially important to be in charge of your baby's eating during this crucial developmental period. Because no matter how careful you've been up to now, as she nears the end of her first year, your child can get out of the habit of eating good food so fast you won't know how it happened!

Here's a common scenario: A baby who has happily received every spoonful of hand-fed food from Mom and Dad suddenly begins to push away the spoon, lips pursed. Her parents try again, with the same result. Okay, they think, we'll try something else. They hand her a piece of real fruit, but she drops it on the floor and begins to cry. At this point, the frazzled parents—desperate for their baby to eat *something*—surrender their position as leaders: maybe, they say, we should buy her some toddler food. They run to the grocery store and buy a few boxes of manufactured, processed foods—high-fructose juice boxes, French fries, white-flour crackers, chocolate chip "toddler" cookies—advertised as something "toddlers eat." And *voilà!* Baby is eating and asking for more!

Unfortunately, it soon becomes clear that's *all* baby wants to eat. Baby is eating for a good reason: the salt and fat and sugar in commercially processed food tastes *great*. Preferences for those flavors are hardwired in our brains in order to lead us to natural foods like nuts and berries that provide the energy and nutrients we need.

Unfortunately, food companies have learned that by concentrating the calories, fat, sugar, or salt beyond what is found in natural foods, it can lead kids to prefer these manufactured goodies to real food. They're high in the taste sensations known to tickle the primary preferences but low in the nutritional value found in natural fruits, vegetables, or eggs. Without the loud distraction of these hyper-flavored and colored products, real foods— served in a way that respects babies' emerging independence—could still

Feeding Baby Green Report

Teething Pain

Although some babies never seem to notice any teething pain, for many babies teething is quite unsettling. The intrusion of a hard, sharp tooth through tender, swollen gums can be quite an adjustment. Some get used to it quickly, but at first it can be more attention-grabbing than a pebble in a shoe.

Babies bring their hands to their mouth when they are teething because pressure on the gums brings relief. Most massage tends to be more soothing when it comes from someone else, and teething is no exception. A great way to comfort a teething baby is to rub the gums firmly and gently with a clean finger. The first few passes are sometimes a bit uncomfortable, but babies get more and more relaxed as the massage continues.

Providing cool things to chew on is another gentle, effective way to treat teething. Clean, wet washcloths or terrycloth toys fresh from the fridge or freezer have been the most popular with babies and toddlers in my practice. Some are delighted with smooth, hard objects, like the wooden handle of a hairbrush. Few babies, in my experience, prefer soft plastic teething rings. If you do choose something plastic, be certain it does not contain BPA, phthalates, or DBT (dibutyltin) (see "Reap the Benefits of Green" in Chapter Six). Whatever you select, be careful that the object is not something your child might choke on.

be quite satisfying. But for many toddlers, these more subtle tastes are drowned out by processed foods.

The result of this common occurrence is troubling: In the United States, French fries have become the third most common vegetable eaten by children between nine and eleven months old; and by fifteen to eighteen months, French fries are the number one most commonly eaten vegetable.[1] For parents like you, who are concerned about raising their children to enjoy healthy food, the story gets worse. Also by nine to eleven months, more than 40 percent of U.S. babies are given cakes, pies, cookies, donuts, or pastries at least once *every day.* By the time they are two, more than 75 percent of these kids will be given these sweetened desserts or candy at least once a day. This huge sugar and sweet ingestion doesn't include the millions of toddlers in the United States who drink sweetened beverages (sodas and sweetened fruit flavored drinks) every day.[2] Almost half of American toddlers will be drinking them by the time they are two.

Many parents go for the short-term gain of making sure their baby eats. They figure it will be easier to get their children to eat veggies when they get older, as their taste buds "mature." Not so. It will likely get harder for the next seven years.

This is the opportune time. You're training your child's taste buds to enjoy good food *right now.* Just as it's almost magically easy to get young children to eat sugary, fatty, and salty foods, it's equally difficult to break these bad food habits. If you're not careful, their taste preferences for unhealthy food choices will become quickly ingrained for the long haul. By virtually mainlining these artificially heightened flavors to kids' taste buds, we take away their opportunity to learn how to enjoy the gentler and more complex rainbow of flavors in fruits, vegetables, and healthy grain products. Not taking charge during this transition means almost inevitably that your child's food style will soon become a blend of the way you eat and the predominant American kids' food culture—slanted strongly toward the latter.

It doesn't have to be this way. The prevailing current is strong; but by making conscious choices now, you can make a lasting difference for your child's health and ongoing enjoyment of a variety of foods throughout her life.

All of the healthy and flavorful choices you've already been making for your baby—during pregnancy, breastfeeding, and spoon-feeding—will pay off big time now, as he begins to make his own food choices. But even if you're starting right now, taking charge of how and what your baby eats can change the trajectory of your child's food future. It's not too late to start.

When you consciously take charge of your child's eating habits during this vulnerable transition from your spoon to theirs, you can usher your child into a bright future of healthy foods. As babies begin to push back, some parents find it hard to keep their guidance firm but gentle. In fact, some of the most common parenting choices have the opposite effect from the wide-ranging and healthy nutritional training we are striving for in this book.[3] These few caveats bear repeating:

- Pushing or coaxing healthy foods will decrease your child's desire for them.

- Restricting unhealthy foods that you are eating or that are in plain sight will increase your child's desire for them.

It's critical for you to decide to make a difference. The rest of the keys will show you how to carry out your decision.

Use Windows of Opportunity

As your baby transforms into a toddler, many new things are happening. He's intensely interested in exploring his world, he's quickly progressing from crawling to toddling around on his own two feet, and he's also getting a brand-new set of teeth. The opportunities afforded by this developmental stage are perfect for encouraging a fun and healthy relationship with nourishment.

Everything about your baby seems to be changing now. As your child begins to walk, he is also gaining fine motor precision with his hands, to grasp and manipulate small objects between thumb and index finger. He'll be eager to use this new skill when he eats—that's why finger food usually is so popular around this time, and why it's fun for him to put objects into containers and take objects out of containers—think half a banana slice into applesauce dip! (See "Treasure Trays" later in this chapter.)

He'll also be able to point with his finger and to let go of objects of his own free will, giving him greater freedom of choice. He'll use some of that freedom to imitate you—whether it's scribbling with crayons or learning to eat with his own spoon—another urge you can use to help teach him new eating skills (see "From Your Spoon to Her Spoon" for some tips).

Your child will practically be inhaling new information at this time, and his knowledge of the world is increasing rapidly. He explores the objects in his world by shaking, banging, dropping, and throwing. He'll be interested in finding hidden objects and will recognize what many objects (such as a cup, a plate, and a spoon) are used for.

Your child is also more interested in language than ever before, paying attention when you talk and even starting to respond to simple requests. He'll babble with style and inflection, use simple gestures (such as shaking the head) to communicate, and may even get out a "Mama," "Dada," or "Uh-oh!" And you'll hear him trying to imitate things you say. He'll also start to enjoy looking at objects—including foods—as you name them. Take advantage of this by continuing and evolving the name games you've been playing with food since before he was born.

Engage All the Senses

The last months of relatively easy learning to love healthy new foods often overlap with the growing interest in finger foods. Use this eagerness as long as it lasts to build a repertoire of fruits, vegetables, whole grains, and rich sources of protein that they can pick up on their own. Even when the desire to sample new items diminishes and the intense suspicion of new foods sets in, by enlisting all the senses in sync with this developmental window, you'll be able to increase enjoyment of healthy foods.

Engage with Flavor A focus at this stage is to teach new finger-food versions of familiar flavors and keep as many healthy tastes and flavors as possible from dropping out of the repertoire, rather than settling for tempting empty snack foods, junk foods, and desserts.

One key concept to help make this easier is that of using what I call "flavor threads" and "flavor bridges" to other enjoyed foods. The sauces and spices you've already taught are the flavor threads (see "Flavor Threads" in Chapter Four) that become especially valuable at this stage. A new vegetable (such as Swiss chard, if you never thought to serve it before) or a new form of a vegetable (such as spinach leaves instead of pureed spinach) is more familiar and more welcome if it comes in something they already love, such as a favorite pasta sauce or curry sauce. The "flavor threads" themselves are constant, leading children from one developmental stage to the next, from pregnancy onward.

Feeding Baby Green Tip

From Your Spoon to Her Spoon

You can help your baby extend her interest in spoon foods while she is learning finger foods. We've found three simple techniques that are fun and work well.

1. *Give Her a Spoon of Her Own*

    Keep feeding your baby from your spoon, but give her a tiny spoon of her own Once she has figured out how to hold it, you can dip the spoon in her food and let her try to get it in her mouth. Of course, at first, most of the food will end up anywhere but her mouth!

    Yes, dinners will become more of a lingering, European-style affair, but her experience is well worth the slower pace. Don't expect much, and don't worry if she doesn't seem to get enough: grabbing the spoon from her is usually a mistake. You want her to feel your patience and your confidence that she can feed herself.

2. *Alternate Bites*

    Early on, you can try alternating bites she feeds herself with bites you feed from a separate spoon you are holding. Many babies love this. It bolsters their confidence to try, knowing that they have this set of "training wheels" to keep them from falling. But pay attention to your baby's cues, and stop feeding with your spoon at any given meal when she doesn't want it. One day soon, you'll stop forever.

3. *Put the Food on Her Spoon for Her*

    Some babies still like it if you put a dollop of food on their spoon for them—it's quicker for them getting to the good part, and they still get to feed themselves. This saves time and messy clean up, and is fine if you both enjoy it. And she still has the opportunity to pick up the food herself if she wants to.

Flavor bridges, on the other hand, work within a single developmental stage. With "flavor bridges," you take a food they already enjoy and introduce something similar, but different. If they already like spinach omelettes, for example, you can broaden their repertoire gently by trying Swiss chard omelettes. Or if they like roasted carrots with ginger, you could try roasted carrots with sea vegetables, using the familiarity of carrots to encourage them to try something new. Children more easily acquire a love for new foods if they are combined with experiences they already enjoy. It's also a great way to keep the foods you want in the repertoire. Babies and toddlers need variety as well as consistency.

Still, learning to like new, finger-manageable forms of previously learned flavors often brings on a new round of repeated, low-pressure trials—the "let's-see" bite. Even if a baby loved pureed green beans with a little garlic, she may protest at her first sliced-up finger-food green beans—especially if she hasn't seen in the past where her purees came from. She needs to make connections.

Feeding Baby Green Report

Green Beans

Green beans (also called string beans) are native to the Americas, brought back to Europe by early explorers. These explorers found a treasure. Green beans are naturally loaded with nutrients: vitamin K, vitamin C, manganese, vitamin A, fiber, potassium, folate, tryptophan, iron, magnesium, riboflavin, copper, thiamin, calcium, phosphorus, protein, omega-3 fats, and niacin.

Given the chance, toddlers often love them. Steamed or lightly grilled with olive oil and garlic, or a favorite flavor thread, they make fantastic finger foods for meals or snacks (they're my toddler niece's favorite right now). And along with some sautéed mushrooms or slivered almonds or roasted red peppers to the sauté, they are great to serve individually in the Treasure Tray (see "Tip" further on).

And, of course, she is still watching you: "Momma likes these green beans. Someday I bet you'll like green beans. Maybe today! Let's see." And if she rejects them, offer again some other time.

Remember: it's *normal* for kids to refuse new foods or new forms of foods multiple times before learning to like them. We saw in the last chapter how younger babies often need to taste a new food six to ten times to really like it, and sometimes up to sixteen times. At age one, the *average* is eleven times, and it can take up to eighty-nine repetitions.[4] But these figures are for American kids raised according to what was popular in the last half of the twentieth century: your child will have been exposed to far more variety before ever reaching this stage.

As your baby's openness to new flavors wanes, starting in the months after they learn to walk, genetic differences in the sense of taste can become more important. The most studied of these so far are the variations in the ability to taste the bitterness of a food molecule called 6-*n*-propylthiouracil—or PROP, for short.

You may be a PROP taster if

- Grapefruit juice tastes bitter

- Coffee would be undrinkable without sugar or cream

- Sweet foods taste sweeter to you—and some sweets are sickeningly sweet

- Broccoli, Brussels sprouts, spinach, and cabbage taste more bitter to you than they do to your peers

- Hot peppers taste hotter than they do to your peers

If you inherited this trait from both of your parents, you may be a supertaster. PROP supertasters are often more able to distinguish subtle differences in bitterness and sourness in foods that would taste similar to non-PROP tasters.[5]

Feeding Baby Green Tip

If Your Baby Is a PROP Taster

If you think your baby may be a PROP taster, rejoice! She has a complex palette and may be able to appreciate a wide range of foods. But be forewarned: some foods—especially healthy green vegetables—may take much longer to learn to enjoy. Here are some tips for parents of PROP babies:

- Be extra patient—keep offering healthy green vegetables without giving up.
- Let her enjoy the many wonderful vegetables that don't trigger these bitter taste buds, including green beans, carrots, sweet potatoes, and many lettuces.
- Add a splash of lemon juice, salad dressing (especially one that contains vinegar), or anything sour to broccoli or spinach to help counteract the sensation of extra bitterness.

There are advantages to being a PROP taster. These people have more of *all* the types of taste buds—it's not just the bitter. The bitter just happens to be the most noticeable. PROP tasters tend to be less likely to drink too much alcohol as adults or to eat too many sweets, and they are more likely to be gourmets. On average, PROP-tasters tend to eat a bit less and weigh a bit less than their non-PROP-taster peers.[6] (See "If Your Baby Is a PROP Taster" for food tips.)

Engage with Aroma Hunger is your ally in getting your toddler to enjoy great foods. One way to make her aware of her hunger is to entice her with delicious aromas just before a meal is served. Something simmering or sautéing on the stove may trigger her appetite more than something warmed in a microwave. Whatever food aromas your family already enjoys, this is a great age to use them as tempting tools.

Also, when the foods she is eating look different than before (pureed lasagna versus whole lasagna) a familiar aroma can be a clue that the new version is an old friend, even before she takes a bite. And teaching the aromas of spices with their names is a great game to foster imagination and delight.

Engage with Sight If food looks inviting, chances are your baby will pick it up and want to eat it. Try serving him colorful foods like carrots and yams and green beans and blueberries—rich colors are clues to high nutritional value. And food cut into cubes or interesting shapes—with a paring knife, or with a cookie cutter—just begs to be handled. No need to go overboard here, but a little thought to the food's appearance can be a big help. "Treasure Trays" are one great example.

And don't underestimate the effect of family meals, even for babies. I've seen kids accept a new food many times just because it was literally on Dad's or Mom's plate first and then casually (or even reluctantly) transferred to hers. (It's important not to appear to be *trying* to convince her to try it. If you seem eager to get her to eat it, the unconscious message is that this doesn't taste good, it's just good for you. Kids are often very sensitive to any pressure in this regard, even if very subtle.)

Seeing parents, siblings, or peers happily eating the same thing can be a particularly strong way to entice children to try new foods or continue to enjoy old ones. When studied in monkeys, this social learning was shown to be the strongest influence.[7] Social influences can be huge—both in determining what is eaten and how much.[8]

Here's another example from the animal world. A group of mother cats was trained to do something unnatural: to eat bananas and to ignore meat pellets. When weaned kittens were then allowed in the room with their moms, fifteen out of eighteen of them joined their mothers in eating bananas and ignoring the meat! When observed later when their mothers weren't around, they continued to eat the bananas and ignore the meat. A control group of kittens the same age that had missed out on seeing the banana-munching all ate the meat pellets and acted as if there were no bananas in the room.[9]

Don't waste this opportunity by letting your baby's foray into the world of adult foods be potato chips, French fries, or sugary treats.

And remember, meals don't start with the first bite. Discover the importance of involving children, at least as observers, in meal preparation, as has been the habit in countless cultures for millennia. Whether peeling a banana, or cubing a sweet potato, be sure your child gets some opportunities to see and participate in, to whatever extent possible, how real food make its way to the plate.

Feeding Baby Green Recipe

Grilled Garlic Green Beans

These garlic green beans are finger food in our house (note—if you intend to puree them, save some out to cook until tender and use those). The long bean—cooked to *al dente*—is reminiscent of the French fry in eating style and crunch, but much lower in fat and higher in nutrition. And kids love 'em.

1½ pounds green beans, washed and trimmed

1½ teaspoons olive oil

½ teaspoon garlic powder

Kosher salt and freshly ground pepper, to taste

1. In a large bowl, drizzle the olive oil over the green beans. Toss with the garlic powder to distribute evenly.
2. Heat a grill, grill pan, or cast-iron griddle over high heat. Arrange the beans in one layer (you may have to do two batches) and cook without turning until hot all the way through but still crisp, about 3 to 4 minutes. Gently turn the beans over and cook for another 3 to 4 minutes, stirring occasionally. Season with salt and pepper and serve immediately.

Serves 4

NUTRITION FACTS (AMOUNT PER SERVING)

| Calories: 68 | Cholesterol: — | Total Carbs: 12.38g | Sugars: 2.47g |
| Total Fat: 1.8g | Sodium: 10mg | Dietary Fiber: 5.82g | Protein: 3.15g |

Engage with Sounds and Language At this age, everything is a game—and games are fun! Ask questions: "Where's the carrot? Where's the apple?" As kids learn to point, it's more important for them to learn the names of fruits and vegetables than it is to learn body parts! When they have a sense of mastery, they want to eat the food.

It's also time for descriptions. As babies start to comprehend phrases, the adjectives used to describe foods change their perceptions of taste, just like the enticing adjectives used on restaurant menus influence choices made by adults. Blue, blue, blueberries taste better than blueberries. Yummy yams taste better than yams.

Food adjectives can act almost as a flavorful spice, but be careful. Too much can spoil the taste. Discriminating toddlers don't like sales pitches. Be descriptive. Be naturally, verbally appreciative of good food. But don't try to "sell" your baby on anything.

Choose the Right Amount

Many of the most common questions at my Web site DrGreene.com have to do with how much a child is eating: Is she eating too much? Too little? Does she get enough meat? Enough vegetables? These questions become especially common as kids start to refuse being spoon-fed right around the time they are starting to learn to walk. Here are some of my thoughts about this.

Be careful not to react to picky eaters by overfeeding. A study of thousands of children found that many of their parents described that their babies (19 percent) or toddlers (50 percent) were picky eaters. When their diets were analyzed, on any given day the picky eaters in the study met or exceeded the age-appropriate calories *and protein* for the day. There is no need to give them something unhealthy just so they'll eat something! Getting enough calories (about nine hundred calories a day for a one-year-old) isn't a problem.[10]

For the next two years, your baby will need about 13 grams of protein a day[11] in order to optimize the building and remodeling needed to turn him into a preschooler. He will also need 500 milligrams of calcium each day.[12] This is not as much as you might think!

Just two cups of whole milk a day provides about:

- 16 grams of protein

- 550 milligrams of calcium

- almost 300 calories[13]

- about 16 grams of fat—about half the fat that's needed for the day

Feeding Baby Green Tip

Treasure Trays

I love Treasure Trays—a small muffin tin (or a few tiny bowls), with each individual muffin cup filled with a few tasty, bite-sized treasures. You can also repurpose the Fresh Baby baby-food tray with the snap-on lid, if you used it earlier, or use a Japanese bento box—these are also great for older kids' school lunches.

Finger foods are on your baby's menu at this stage, so use one or two of the cups for a dipping sauce. Applesauce, yogurt, and especially pureed fresh fruits or vegetables that were once favorite baby foods are all good choices.

Choices for other cups might include steamed sweet potato cubes, diced pears, small half-slices of bananas, half-medallions of soft-cooked carrots, diced soft-cooked green beans, shredded apple, diced kiwi, shredded carrot, small pieces of cheese, diced avocado, quartered grapes, diced peaches, bite-sized pieces of wheat toast, or oat cereal O's. Imagine all of the possible combinations!

Keep the number of bins at any meal small (perhaps a green vegetable, another vegetable, a grain, and some beans or meat, and some fruit "for dessert," though it doesn't matter in what order she eats). Choosing what, how much, and in what order are her decisions; choosing what goes in the bins is yours. Try to always include a green vegetable, and at least three colors of food total. Keep a balance of familiarity and variety.

One meal might include some pureed Black Bean Tomato Ragout (see Chapter Seven) in one bin, some green beans and carrots (both grilled or sautéed with a little olive oil) in two more. Some small pieces of whole grain toast and slices of banana complete the meal. You and your treasure hunter could explore this tasty and balanced meal in a number of different ways. Occasionally having Treasure Trays for the whole family (giving each person, child and adult, a Japanese bento box meal is ideal), or visibly loading the trays with food from your plate, can be a great way to eat together. You can tailor your Treasure Tray for breakfast, lunch, or dinner.

Your job is to provide and to model eating a varied selection of healthy foods: it's your baby's job to decide how much and what to eat. The biggest pitfall to letting him control the amount comes when he has easy access to calorie-dense, nutrient-poor snack foods, junk foods, or sweets. In this situation, most toddlers will eat too much. Their bodies are designed to desire the right amounts of real foods, not of these relatively recent creations.

This is especially true of liquid calories. It's best to avoid sweetened and artificially sweetened drinks altogether at this age. Even 100 percent fruit juice can lead to consuming too many calories. I agree with the American Academy of Pediatrics in recommending no more than four to six ounces a day through age six—and never juice in a bottle, to protect both teeth and the waistline.[14]

Taking charge doesn't mean doing your baby's job, it means creating an environment where he can succeed. The guidelines couldn't be simpler:

- Have three meals a day and a planned snack or two for the breaks in between.

- If you're watching for it, you'll learn to tell when he is done. It may not be subtle—when he shoves the Treasure Tray on the floor, he's done!

Choose the Right Variety

If getting the right amount isn't too tough, even for picky eaters, getting the right variety is the biggest challenge and holds the biggest reward.

Try to repeat as many of the twenty-one different plant families (listed in Chapter Four) that you offered your baby during pregnancy, nursing, and again during spoon feeding. Don't give up now! By continuing these flavors through this critical transition time you are creating deeply ingrained habits that will serve your child (and grandchildren!) well. Try to offer, as a finger food, something from as many as possible of the twenty-one families at least *sixteen times*. You may want to use the checklist at the end of the book to keep track.

Continue to make a green vegetable part of every lunch and dinner, cut into bite-sized pieces. They should be soft enough to match your child's chewing skill. Salads can be great finger foods, with the dressing on the side. So can green beans, peas, and broccoli. Reinforce this habit so that it feels strange to have lunch or dinner without a green veggie.

Add a different veggie at lunch or dinner. Carrots, tomatoes, tomato sauce, sweet potatoes, corn, or squash are good options. Try to avoid brightly colored convenience foods: use color to signal interesting real foods.

Three of the most commonly eaten fruits at this age in the United States are canned fruits (peaches, fruit cocktail, and canned applesauce). Unless you want the canned version to be part of your family's repertoire in the long run, opt instead for fresh fruit, cut or heated to make it easy to swallow. Bananas, grapes, apples, and strawberries are the most popular—but keep the variety coming.

Be sure to offer some whole grains every day. Breakfast can be a great time for cereal grains, and snack time can include some whole grain finger foods.

Here's a rough guideline. Every day, a typical one-year-old should get about nine hundred calories a day, in the form of about

- 1.5 ounces of lean meat or beans

- ¾ cup of vegetables

- 1 cup of fruit

- 2 ounces of whole grains

- 2 cups of organic milk (or a non-dairy equivalent)

Milk   Getting too much milk can be an obstacle to variety. I frequently come across children after the first birthday drinking twenty-four ounces of milk

Feeding Baby Green Recipe

Sweetie Pie

This luscious combination of sweet potatoes, apples, and cinnamon reminds me of Thanksgiving.

1 cup sweet potato, peeled and cut into 2-inch cubes

1¼ cups sweet apple (any variety other than Red Delicious), peeled and cut into 1-inch cubes

¼ teaspoon ground cinnamon

1. Steam the sweet potatoes and apples until soft, about 20 minutes. Reserve cooking water to add to puree.
2. In a food processor, blend the sweet potatoes, apples, and cinnamon, adding cooking water ¼ cup at a time until the desired consistency is reached.
3. Serve warm, or fill individual cups and freeze.

Serves 4 (Yield: 1½ cups)

NUTRITION FACTS (AMOUNT PER SERVING)

Calories: 45	Sodium: 18mg	Sugars: 4.87g
Total Fat: 0.03g	Total Carbs: 11.21g	Protein: 0.62g
Cholesterol: 0	Dietary Fiber: 1.53g	

Submitted and reprinted by permission from Tasty Baby.

a day, or even thirty-two ounces and sometimes more. The more milk they drink, the less likely they are to be hungry for different kinds of foods.

Water and Other Beverages If kids are only drinking sixteen to twenty-four ounces of milk a day, they will want more to drink. This is a great age for kids to learn to enjoy the refreshment of water as their other main beverage. (If you're not already using a family water jug, as we suggested in "Hydration Solutions" in Chapter Three, now is a good time to start!)

We sometimes buy bottles of a tasty pure peppermint tea, with no sugar or caffeine. Sometimes we brew our own. Other teas can be good choices as well, but avoid caffeinated or sweetened teas.

Customize Needs for Every Body

Just like the rest of us, your baby is unique—and getting to be more of an individual every day! You will continue to adjust healthy nutritional guidelines to what works best for your child and your family.

Milk Breast milk or formula forms the core of a baby's diet throughout the first year. I'm a fan of continuing to nurse beyond the first year, for as long as the mother and the child both want this. For most of human history, the majority of babies drank breast milk for at least two or three years. Milk is a great source of needed protein, fat, calories, and calcium, among other things.

For many kids, cow's milk enters the picture and replaces formula around the first birthday. It's fine to have some before this, but not yet as the primary beverage. When you do introduce cow's milk, I suggest starting it in a sippy cup in order to make the transition away from the bottle easier.

What about children who are allergic to cow's milk? Or who just don't like it? I'm asked something like this by parents almost every single week.

Those who can't (for whatever reason) drink breast or cow's milk after the first birthday might thrive on goat's, soy, rice, or almond milk (but avoid options with not enough calcium and vitamin D, and check the sugars on the label—the amount can vary quite a bit between brands). They may even be able to take cow's milk eventually: more than half of the babies who have had an allergy to cow's milk protein will have outgrown it by the first birthday. Most of the rest will have outgrown it by age three.

Toddlers, however, don't necessarily need milk at all. They do need sources of protein, fat, calcium, and vitamin D (in the amounts indicated earlier in this section), but these can be found in a variety of different foods.

- Calcium: yogurt, sesame seeds, cheese, spinach, blackstrap molasses, fortified foods

- Protein: chicken, salmon, beans, yogurt

- Fat: yogurt, olive oil, nuts, nut oils, chicken, salmon, sesame seeds

- Vitamin D: sunshine, vitamin D dots

Feeding Baby Green Report
The Lowdown on Toddler Vitamins

Both breast milk and formula contain plenty of vitamins (with the exception of vitamin D—which nature designed for us to get from the sun). When breast milk or formula is no longer a central part of your baby's diet, I recommend starting liquid multivitamin drops for your baby or toddler, which you can either give directly or add to food. This helps fill in any nutrition gaps, and may help you be more relaxed about feeding. I suggest choosing vitamins that provide the omega-3 fat DHA (many toddlers do not get the 150 milligrams a day they should) and that contain 400 IU of Vitamin D.

Exercise!

As kids begin to toddle, they thrill to the joy of walking. They often spend hours on the go, keeping their growing bodies fit with no help from us (other than to turn off the hypnotic TV). Once they have been walking for a while, they often sleep better than they ever did before—partly as a result of all this exercise. It's important for you to get exercise too, both for yourself and as a model for your toddler.

This is a great age to incorporate a daily walk with your baby in a stroller, if you haven't already. If you have a friend or two you walk with regularly, that's great! If you don't, think about joining a group like Stroller Strides (see "Exercise!" in Chapter Seven): having others to move with makes it easier (and more fun) to follow through on your intentions.

I'm a big fan of using strollers that allow your baby to face you. These rear-facing strollers give your child options: to look at you, or to look at the world—and perhaps to point at something for you to look at together. The first large study of the two different directions of travel supports this idea.[15]

The study shows that on average, kids who face their parents during a daily walk had twice as many conversations with their parents (one of the most powerful brain boosts there is) and laughed ten times as much—even though they spent almost twice as much time sleeping in the stroller! It's no surprise, then, that their parents' laughter tripled as well.

When the kids were turned to face away from their parents, their heart rates went up, their vocalizing dropped by a third, their mother's speech dropped by half, and the kids had a tougher time falling asleep or staying asleep. Only 5 percent of them laughed in the stroller during forward-facing walks.

What about exploring the outside world, though? Doesn't facing the parent limit the view? When the stroller faced the parents, the parents were more than twice as likely to show their child something ("Look, there's a dog!") and more than twice as likely to respond to something the child noticed ("Yes, that's an apple tree!").

The parents were also more than twice as likely to comment on the child's mood ("You look cozy in there"), to use the child's name ("Emma, are you getting hungry?"), and to talk about the future ("When we finish here, we'll enjoy some carrots").

Parents were much more inclined to enjoy the daily walk when facing their little one—and more likely to want to go for a walk again. Your baby becomes your workout partner. Children this age usually enjoy stroller walks or runs with their parents. In fact, none of the children in this study were reported as trying to get out of the stroller. (I'm sure some do, but probably fewer try, however, if they are facing their parents—but that's never been studied.)

Reap the Benefits of Green

As we have seen throughout this book, making connections—with where food comes from, how it is prepared, and with others who share the food—is a powerful way to instill love for real food. Eat seasonally. Eat locally. Grow something together.

You can help reinforce your child's connection with certain foods by taking her into the garden: help her reach out to pick an apple or a lemon from a tree, pull a carrot or lettuce from the ground, pick a tomato from the vine. Even if you have no room for a garden, you can grow herbs in your kitchen and allow her to pluck the leaves to put into a meal.

Yield Versus Nutrition The agriculture business—whether it's small farmers or huge conglomerates—is always faced with choices: the breeder's dilemma. In recent years many choices have favored whatever made the most money—the highest crop yields and the lowest costs—at the expense of nutrients and taste.

In just one example, we've bred cheap oil crops and animal feed grains low in omega-3s and other polyunsaturated fats.[16] Most Americans don't get enough omega-3s from the plants or animals they eat, a deficiency which has been linked to decreased heart, brain, and immune health in a variety of ways.

When we support sustainable agriculture and nutritious strains, we are not only caring for our soil, our water, our air, our climate, and our limited resources, but we also directly reap the benefit in our own bodies.

And each serving of fruit and each serving of vegetables or grains delivers more punch for fewer calories—and often tastes better as well.

Antibiotics Ear infections, most common between six and twenty-four months of age, are the number one reason that antibiotics are prescribed to children—millions of prescriptions each year. Not surprisingly, emerging strains of antibiotic-resistant bacterial strains are a growing problem. In 2008, for the first time ever, researchers testing multiple soil samples found bacteria that were not just resistant to antibiotics, but that could live entirely on the strongest antibiotics as their only food source![17]

The most conservative estimates agree that more antibiotics are given in the United States to fatten food animals (not to treat their diseases) than all of the antibiotics used to treat every man, woman, and child in the United States. Perhaps several times more.

Can antibiotic resistance spread from the farm to the rest of us?

Clearly.

In a 2008 study, researchers associated with the Center for a Livable Future at the Johns Hopkins Bloomberg School of Public Health reported

Feeding Baby Green Stories

"I Recommend Bento Boxes for All Toddlers!"

Two years marks an age when children explore their independence. They learn the word "no" and they use it liberally! During this time, parents typically experience the stress of their children becoming more finicky eaters. I know I worried about my first daughter, Hannah, when she was two!

With our twin daughters, Faith and Hope, people are often amazed at how well they eat a variety of foods despite being feisty two-year-olds. I truly believe the use of plates with multiple compartments has contributed to their love for eating. As soon as they could feed themselves, we gave them their food in colorful, partitioned plates.

The key is having four to five different compartments in which to separate their food. For us as parents, having to fill each section with a different food item challenged us to present our children with a variety of nutritious foods at each meal. For picky two-year-olds, it separated the food so that they wouldn't reject a certain food item simply because it touched another that they refused to eat. Finally, two-year-olds love their independence, and having choice made them feel in control of their eating (while in reality, we still controlled what was on their plates). Their perception of choice has really helped promote their love for eating nutritious foods. I recommend partitioned plates or bento boxes for all toddlers!

Khanh-Van Le-Bucklin, M.D.,
M.O.M. (Mother of Multiples)
Irvine, California

a new path of human exposure to antibiotic-resistant bacteria from animals—just driving in a car on the same road behind the trucks transporting broiler chickens! Increased levels of drug-resistant bacteria were found in the air and on the surfaces in these cars.[18]

These antibiotics don't improve the quality of the food or of the environment, and don't contribute to the humane treatment of the animals. They are used to provide cheaper food by enabling animals to be unnaturally jammed together in confined animal feeding operations (CAFOs) and by speeding weight gain.

By forgoing eating animals and animal products produced in this manner, we can support sustainable agriculture and animal welfare, and build the groundwork for our own health. As we've noted throughout this book, the best way to avoid food produced with antibiotics is for you and your baby to eat only organic foods. The routine use of antibiotics is not allowed in organic meat, poultry, eggs, and dairy production—by definition.

⁓

By introducing your young toddler to healthy, natural foods during this crucial stage of her development, you are helping lay the foundation for her to make her own good choices as she ventures ever further into the world outside your sheltering arm—the world of kids and American kid food. As we will see in the next chapter, your soon-to-be sturdy toddler is about to start making some loud distinction between what she wants and what prompts her to say NO! Standing your ground for your child's healthy food choices is more important than ever as he begins to venture out on his own.

9

Toddlers

(ABOUT EIGHTEEN MONTHS THROUGH TWO YEARS)

"Where did my sweet baby go?"

During this period, your baby's body is growing much more slowly than it has been, both relatively and absolutely. An average boy, for example, may gain seven pounds as a baby in the first four months (up 90 percent from his birth weight); but as a toddler he may only gain five pounds in an entire year (increasing his first birthday weight by only 20 percent).[1]

This growth isn't steady, but comes in spurts. Kids grow more in the spring, for instance, than at any other time of the year. We are seasonal creatures, even in our climate-controlled modern homes.[2]

Appropriate weight gain varies considerably from child to child. For all healthy children, however, average growth should slow down and continue at about this slower pace until the big growth spurt during puberty.

As growth slows down, his appearance is changing quickly. At his first birthday, even if he was already walking, he probably still looked rather like a baby. His head and the belly were the biggest parts of the body, and his arms, legs, and baby bottom were still small and softly contoured. His rounded face might belong to either a boy or a girl, confounding strangers.

By his second birthday, your child's body will have undergone a drastic makeover. His arms, legs, and bottom will all be more muscular, and his head (already 90 percent of its adult size!) will appear much smaller on this larger, sturdier new frame. His belly should no longer be prominent, and his overall shape will be straighter, more angular. Even his facial features will have changed. Strangers will likely be able to tell at a glance that he is a boy, not a girl.

Somewhere during the middle of the second year, it becomes clear that you have an independent-minded toddler who is experiencing conflicting drives: independence and imitation. He feels the urgent delight and terror of needing to make his own choices and decisions. At the same time, his desire to imitate you is very strong—as long as he feels he's in control!

Not surprisingly, conflicts will become more common. Inevitably, many of these conflicts will focus on eating. When he responds to your offer of what you thought was his favorite meal by screaming, "NO!" you may well wonder where your sweet baby went. Don't despair, he's still there. And don't give up! The groundwork you've laid until now has prepared your toddler to delight in a variety of healthy foods—he's just exercising his new choice muscles. Stay cool, and give him limited but real, healthy options he can choose from. Your relaxed, steady attitude now will give your toddler the security he needs to feel confident about his choices throughout his life.

The Essential Steps for Teaching Nutritional Intelligence

Many people call this important phase of development the "Terrible Twos." I prefer to call it "The First Adolescence." This period begins long before age two and actually continues long afterwards—and revives again during puberty. But for the majority of children, it is most intensely focused around the period from one-and-a-half to three years of age.

During this important transitional stage, your child is blossoming into an individual with her own needs and plans and ideas about the world. She will not always agree with you, nor should she. Instead of hoping to prevent the "Terrible Twos," or trying to bend your child to your will, your task at this stage is the same as it has been from the beginning: to wisely guide your child as she navigates her world, and to help her learn to make good decisions about the many choices she will face—including the food she eats every day.

Take Charge!

Without guidance, typical American kids at this age continue their slide into junk food habits and "kids' meals" like artificially bright-orange mac and cheese, reaching the long floor of the valley at around the second birthday. By this time, their eating habits—for better or worse—are likely to remain very similar up until at least age eight.[3]

The good news is that kids who eat a variety of fruits and vegetables at age two are likely to continue to do so. Those who will at least try new foods at this age will continue to do this as they get older, picking up new foods to enjoy along the way.

The bad news, of course, is that when parents don't take charge their children may get stuck in a rut of salty, fried, sweet junk that skews their tastes toward limited, unhealthy choices for years to come.

If I were a food marketer, I would do everything I could to market versions of my products to kids under two—and that's just what they do! If I were a parent of a child under two, like you, I would do everything I could to resist this kind of nutritional brainwashing and take charge of what my child is exposed to at this critical stage.

As you may notice at the first temper tantrum, taking charge at this age is very different from taking charge with a baby. Your child's ability to say "NO!" (and his clear delight in doing so) may be jarring to you; but taking this important sense of personal power away from him is not the goal of parenting toddlers. There are battles that you can't (and shouldn't) win.

Toddlers say "NO!" so often for a simple reason that has nothing to do with you: they are gaining skill at making choices. That's why your toddler needs you to take charge of what he eats as much as or more than ever: Although it's tempting to shout back "Yes you will!" to every "NO!" your role is not to be a dictator of what he *must* eat, but to be a gentle but firm guide helping him wisely navigate all of the wonderful choices in the world.

Use Windows of Opportunity

Toddlers alternate between being fiercely independent and desperately clingy, between feeling calmly confident and emotionally out of control, between sweetly calling "Mama" and screaming "NO!" You can help your child reconcile them by providing real choices between limited options, and by continuing to be a good role model.

The Urge to Imitate   The tug-of-war between your toddler's urge to imitate you and her need to assert independence plays a big role in the food realm.

Feeding Baby Green Stories

"Food Is a Passion in Our Home"

We have three children, seven years old, five years old, and nearly one. We have always fed them whatever we were eating. If we are having sushi at a local restaurant, so are they. They adore crab, avocado, sticky rice, salmon roe, and so much more. While everyone else was focused on carrots, beans, and peaches as first foods for kids, my husband and I were thinking about what foods we love.

Growing up, my mother made whatever was growing in the garden. So now we believe that if there's something good growing in your area, your body needs it during that season. Hundreds of years ago I wouldn't have been able get a banana flown in from Ecuador in December. So my body probably can probably get along without it now, at this time of year.

Food is a passion in our home, and I believe our children see the rituals we have with good food, and honor it similarly.

Kelly Guertin, C.L.C.
Warwick, Rhode Island

Although your child was born with a unique personality, her early experiences were profoundly influenced by her physical states and by her environment (primarily, you). Thus, early on, your baby's desires tended to be either responses to physical needs (she was hungry and wanted to eat, he was sleepy and wanted to sleep, or she had a soiled diaper and wanted you to change it) or reflections of your desires. She wanted things that made you happy, that engaged your attention. When you smiled, she smiled. When you became tense, she became emotionally agitated. Throughout that first year, a wonderful dance between parent and child developed as your child mirrored your moods. Because her moods were usually in sync with yours, she seemed like a "good baby."

Gradually, though, sometime after she had mastered walking, an irresistible urge to make her own choices began to well up inside her. This is an exciting development, but the difficulty for her in making an independent choice is that she must disagree with you in order for the choice to be her own. Now, when you ask him to do something, he may refuse. It is unpleasant to have anyone passionately disagree with you. When this opposition comes from your own little delight, the situation is decidedly disagreeable.

Another complicating issue is the fear of new food that arises at this time. It's important to understand that your toddler's fear of any new food is often greater now than in the past (and will continue to increase from here, for a while). Nevertheless, kids do continue to learn some new foods at least up until about thirty months old, when it becomes much more difficult until the stirrings of puberty.[4]

The bottom line, with this as with most issues during this stage, is that your child's desire to imitate you is very strong—as long as he feels that he is in control. The best approach—and it can be difficult—is to keep modeling the behavior you want to see and avoid taking "NO!" personally. Remember that you are in charge, remember your overall goals for her, and don't be deterred when she doesn't follow your every move the way she used to. Because even though it's not always obvious, she's still watching you to see what you'll do. Model the behavior you'd like to see in your toddler, and sooner or later you're likely to get it.

Offer Limited Choices Children in this phase of development have a great deal of difficulty making the choices they so desperately want to make. You may ask your child what he would like for dinner, and she says,

"Macaroni." You lovingly prepare it for her, and then as soon as it's made she refuses to eat it. For a child of this age, it is perfectly normal to reverse a decision as soon as he has made it, because at this stage, he even manages to disagree with himself!

Your toddler's task during this phase is to gain skill at making appropriate choices. To help him accomplish this, offer your limited choices at every opportunity. He will be demonstratively frustrated when he is given direct commands with no options. He will be overwhelmed if he has too many alternatives. Keeping him to two or three options generally works best.

Make sure the choices you offer fall within an appropriate agenda. Your child still needs the security of knowing that he's not calling all the shots.

For example, when it's time for a snack, don't expect him to choose from everything in the house! Instead, say something like, "Would you rather have a slice of apple or a banana?" He feels both the reassuring limits that you set and the freedom to exercise his power within those limits. If there are two things he needs to do, let him decide which to do first, when appropriate ("Would you rather drink your milk first or eat some cereal?").

If this phase is difficult for parents, remember that it is also hard for children. When children take a stand that opposes their parents, they experience intense emotions. Although driven to become their own unique persons, they also long to please you. Even now, when I do something that my parents disagree with, I feel very conflicted. I am an adult, living in a different city, with well-thought-out choices, and it is still quite difficult.

For a child who is tentatively learning to make choices, who is dependent on his parents for food, shelter, and emotional support, it's even more intense. Dissolving into tears is an appropriate expression of the inner turmoil that is so real for children who are in the midst of this process.

I like to think of the process as similar in some ways to childbirth. Labor is a very intense experience. Pain, after pain, after pain eventually produces something beautiful—a child is born. The episodes of oppositional behavior in "First Adolescence" are psychological labor pains—one difficult situation, then another, and another, and as a result your child's own persona is being born psychologically. This is a beautiful (but difficult) time with a truly worthwhile result.

As you see how rapidly they are developing in each sphere, you'll better understand the push-pull process of asserting themselves: their desires to do things on their own followed by their desires to return to you for help and support. You'll appreciate how to support them through the swings and rhythms, and even use these moments as windows of opportunity. A key theme will be to set a few limits, and go along with her choices within those limits.

Spoon and Fork This is the age for your child to learn to use the spoon well, and for early attempts with a fork. Inevitably, there will be drops and spills. Welcome—don't discourage—messes as they master these tools.

Kids need freedom to experiment with their utensils as they

- Work on fine-motor skills

- Improve hand-eye coordination

- Learn that independent actions lead to enjoyment

- Learn to choose for themselves between different textures, tastes, and colors

Choose foods and utensils that help your child be a success. She should have her own small spoon and small fork with dull prongs. Her unbreakable dishes should have sides that she can push the food against. Cut foods into bite-sized pieces that she can pick up with a fork. Serve some food that is soft or wet that she can pick up with a spoon. Be sure that the food isn't very hot.

No Coaxing, Bribing, or Rewarding Coaxing kids to eat their vegetables, or anything else for that matter, can also short-circuit their developmental need to choose what to eat from among the options you set out. It's your role to select and prepare the food; it's hers to choose which and how much of it to eat, and in what order.

Bribing or rewarding kids with food is also counterproductive. The plea, "If you eat your spinach, you'll get dessert" has been shown to teach kids to value dessert more and to enjoy spinach less.

Feeding Baby Green Recipe

Baby Tex Mex

Baby Tex Mex is a full-flavor, south-of-the-border taste experience. By combining black beans with brown rice, we have created a high-quality protein dish rich in B-complex vitamins, calcium, iron, magnesium, zinc, and soluble fiber—essential nutrients for sustaining on-the-go toddlers, and a healthy body-building protein option for vegetarian children. The brightly colored chunks of perfectly cooked vegetables provide a good source of the protective antioxidant beta-carotene as well as vitamins C and E.

This dish is terrific as a full meal or can be used as a side dish or delicious dip. Wrap it in a tortilla, melt some cheese over the top, and enjoy a super-nutritious on-the-go meal for the entire family.

1 tablespoon extra virgin olive oil	*½ cup peas*
½ onion, chopped	*½ cup corn kernels*
1 clove garlic, minced	*1/2 cup black beans, cooked*
1 carrot, halved lengthwise and sliced	*1/2 teaspoon ground cumin*
1 cup brown rice	*1 tablespoon cilantro, chopped*
3 cups vegetable stock	*Kosher salt and freshly ground pepper, to taste*
1 red bell pepper, roasted, seeded, and chopped	

1. In a skillet, heat the olive oil over medium heat and sauté the onion and garlic until softened.
2. Add the carrots and continue to sauté for 2 minutes.
3. Stir in the rice and cook for an additional 2 minutes.
4. Add the vegetable stock and cumin and bring to a boil. Reduce the heat, cover, and simmer for 20 minutes.
5. Gently stir in the roasted red bell pepper, corn, and beans, and stir until well incorporated. Continue to cook, stirring occasionally, for 15 minutes or until the rice is tender. Stir in peas and cilantro. Season to taste with salt and pepper.

Serves 4 (Yield: 4 cups)

NUTRITION FACTS (AMOUNT PER SERVING)

Calories: 404	Sodium: 812mg	Sugars: 4.66g
Total Fat: 7.83g	Total Carbs: 64.19g	Protein: 11.65g
Cholesterol: 3mg	Dietary Fiber: 7.26g	

Submitted and reprinted by permission from Homemade Baby.

Engage All the Senses

Engaging all of the senses can make this process even more pleasant for all involved. Although the senses themselves don't change much during the second year, kids' relationships to some of their senses change profoundly.

Engage with Flavor This is an age of food jags. Some children will seem to have a love affair with a few specific foods, wanting them morning, noon, and night. Some will display a passionate dislike for certain tastes. At the same time, fear of anything new continues to escalate.

Despite this aversion to new food, repeated, relaxed taste and aroma exposures can still be a powerful way to gently nudge children's taste options to be broader. This is an ideal time to employ the flavor threads and flavor bridges you learned about in Chapter Four and Chapter Eight.

You'd love for her to continue to try new foods and to continue tasting earlier favorites. But you can't force her to do what she doesn't want, especially with eating, particularly now that she's holding the spoon. Forcing doesn't work, and would be counterproductive if it did.

Present her with versions of what the family is eating that she can maneuver, even if you know it contains some things she isn't eating right now. You can tell her those things are "let's-see bites." Someday she'll probably like them, and today may be the day. She may accept this readily if she's used to this expectation. All you're trying to do is get her to taste it, not to eat it.

Some kids, though, will protest. If so, it's not worth a battle right now.

Don't remove the foods if she refuses them; don't be reluctant to put them on her plate again soon. Leaving them there keeps them as an option she can choose. It may be two dozen meals before she does it, but since you're relaxed and don't feel like you should be making her eat her veggies now anyway, it won't seem so long.

If *she* removes them, that's the time for a firm "No" from you. As we'll see below under "Choose the Right Amount," the right amount at this age also includes the right amount of table manners.

A combination of familiarity and variety when it comes to tastes tends to promote the broadest enjoyment of foods. As a family, try to eat your favorites from as many as possible of the twenty-one food families while your child is learning to manage her own spoon and fork. And continue to use sauces of favorite flavor profiles to introduce foods they might not enjoy otherwise.

Engage with Aroma Smelling the aroma of something cooking or being sliced can be one way to help your toddler make a decision. She might start wanting that for dinner—and feel that she's made the decision herself. Another advantage of aroma is that it's a way to allow her to sample something indirectly, without having to open her mouth and surrender her autonomy.

Engage with Sight The strong desire to imitate at this stage makes food modeling critical. This is an especially important age for family meals—even if it is only one other member of the family. Seeing what you eat and how you eat becomes almost as important as what she does. Try to find a high chair or booster seat that can get her at the right height to join you at your table (and that keeps her confined enough that she can focus on eating, not on all the options available if she were to climb down).

This is a great age for a child to become a kitchen helper—if she's not one already. When your toddler sees you going about your daily life, she may want to help—whether you are reading a book or talking on the phone. If you can find ways for your little helper to be involved in preparing food, all the better. Food that she's seen at the farmers market, and that she's helped you carry home and mash, is likely to be an even bigger hit.

Feeding Baby Green Tip

Appealing Fork and Finger Foods

Even though your toddler has been eating finger foods for a while, at this stage food presentation changes drastically. Finger foods should still be available, but now you want tidbits that look inviting for them to pick up with their own spoon or fork *without your help.* That's one of the reasons macaroni and mashed potatoes are so popular at this stage. You can add color by including peas or tomatoes in the macaroni and trying mashed sweet potatoes on occasion. This can be powerful—especially if you are eating the same thing.

Here are some more ideas for fun foods that have worked at our house:

- Salad as finger food, with dressing in a tiny bowl on the side for dipping
- Small burritos
- Elbow macaroni with ground beef or tofu and peas in a spaghetti sauce (much easier than spaghetti!)
- Small pieces of sautéed broccoli
- Peas, carrots, or green beans (keep frozen veggies on hand) make for fast forkable or spoonable veggies
- Half an ear of corn on the cob

Most of the recipes in this book are great as purees for younger children, and also as bite-sized or spoonable ingredients for your toddler.

And don't put away those Treasure Trays (Chapter Eight) just yet. For some kids, discovering hidden items on the plate at this stage can make them want to sample the treasures. Finding some softly cooked, bright-orange carrots under an upside-down small serving bowl can seem like a precious find.

Engage with Sounds and Language As language development races along, use the types of exchanges she enjoys to help her connect to real food.

For a while, kids love to be able to point to things that you name. "Where's the carrot?" and "Show me the broccoli" become occasions for you both to feel delight and mastery. The familiar becomes much more accepted.

In the clinic, when I'm seeing a child this age with an earache, simply asking, "Where is your nose? Where is your ear?" can make all the difference in how the exam goes. Once the toddler points to his ear, and we've both seen that he understands, he is much more likely to let me peek in without protest.

Pointing games can help kids want to eat what they've identified. At some point, this will become old—at least for a while. But old, familiar games often have later waves of popularity,

Some kids delight in following simple commands to demonstrate their mastery: "Please bring me the apple. Go get a lemon for our water." Not commands to make them go against their will, but polite commands that let them feel capable and part of what's going on. Again, they're more likely to want to snack on the apple they brought you to slice, or drink the water flavored by the lemon they brought you.

Feeding Baby Green Report

How Much Food Is Enough for Toddlers?

As a rule of thumb, calorie needs go up a bit from about 900 calories a day at the first birthday to about 1,000 calories a day at the second, but they still don't need very much.[5] Just two cups of milk continues to provide all of the necessary protein and calcium, and half of the needed fat.[6] After the milk's 300 calories, that leaves just 700 calories or so needed total between the day's meals and snacks. That'll be less than 200 calories per meal.

It's easy to see how kids who drink soda or sweetened drinks, or who eat lots of high-calorie snacks and sweets, could exceed that number of calories and become overweight. On the other hand, fruits, vegetables, whole grains, and lean protein sources can satisfy appetites and keep the calories in line.

Keep track of your child's weight curves and appetite cues, and make sure the food choices you give them are healthy ones.

Choose the Right Amount

For most of human history, food scarcity was a major threat. In many parts of the world, famine is still a fact of life. And even in the United States, children still go to bed hungry. It's no surprise, therefore, that our food customs handed down from generation to generation and even our ingrained parenting instincts are concerned with getting kids to eat enough.

But the deeper instinct is to protect and nurture our children. And when we "get it" that today's threats come more from overeating and from eating poor-quality foods, our parental instincts can quickly shift to help us raise our children in today's environment.

Many of us were raised to clean our plates. "Remember, children in (wherever it was when we were kids) are starving, so we don't waste food in this family." We learned to eat as much as possible when food is available, and often to eat just two more bites to get dessert. My grandparents gave candy to babies to get them to eat.

But the truth is, if you provide them with the same tasty, healthy choices that the rest of the family is eating, kids do a great job of getting plenty to eat. If the selections offered include too many calorie-dense junk foods or sweetened beverages, though, they will likely eat too much.

It's your job to select and offer the tasty healthy food options that work for your family (see "Choose the Right Variety," later in this chapter), but it's your toddler's job to choose how much of each item to eat, and how much to eat overall.

Keep providing these foods as long as your toddler is still eating. You'll be able to tell when mealtime is over when your toddler loses interest, refuses to eat, or says, "All done." He'll also be watching you for cues.

Snacks One of many toddlers' time-honored tricks is to forgo food at lunch or dinner and to come begging for a snack soon afterwards. They are so cute when they do this. And it's so tempting to give in. But don't.

I understand why you'd want to give a snack right away. We have deep instinctual desires to feed our kids; it can allay our (usually unfounded) fears and guilt that they are not eating enough, it will stop their pestering, and it will make them happy with us right now. But our role as parents is to keep the long view in mind, and to help them learn and grow. Giving in short-circuits all of that, and can get them stuck in an unhealthy cycle. It's even important (perhaps especially important) not to give in to kids who are growing too slowly.

That said, well-planned healthy snacks can be a parent's best friend. Toddlers usually do best with three meals a day, plus small planned snacks in between, timed so that they are not within about two hours after or before meals. This way, your toddler will not get overly hungry but will still be hungry for meals.

When she begs for a snack, you can then say, "Lunch is over. Now you'll have to wait until snack time." Of course, this reasonable reply might prompt a fit—toddlers are designed to test the boundaries. But if you can stay relaxed and firm, she'll soon learn the limits: She'll get to eat something good at least every two or three hours; you'll offer lots of tasty food; she'll get to choose whatever she likes from what everyone else is eating; she won't get to eat in between. Soon enough, her body will get used to this rhythm, and she'll be more likely to enjoy a broader variety of foods.

Choose the Right Variety

Make one meal for everybody in the family. All too often, parents fall into the role of short-order cook, feeling like they need to jump up and make something different for their toddler if she refuses what the rest of the family is eating. Falling into this trap means more work for you, and often leads to a childhood of making special kids' meals or just offering fast food or processed food. More important, it can undo all the taste-bud training you've done so far, and can allow her to skirt a central developmental task of this age: learning to feed herself like the rest of the family.

Choose the same meals you have been enjoying from pregnancy throughout the first year. For the portions your toddler eats, the spices and texture may be increased from the infant versions. Include variety throughout the day, but let your toddler choose which foods from those meals to eat.

Optimally, by age two a typical child should get every day about two ounces of lean meat or beans, about one cup of fruit, about one cup of vegetables, about three ounces of whole grains, and about two cups of organic milk (or a non-dairy equivalent). In other words, the target amount of fruit and milk stays the same between ages one and two. Vegetables and meat or beans each go up 33 percent, and whole grains go up 50 percent.[7]

But this is the age where your child is choosing what to eat. Earlier habits and rhythms and preferences will help inform his choices, but the fact remains, they will now be his choices.

Use the guidelines above to help guide you in what variety to put on your (and his) plate. Keep this up, keep modeling what you eat, and relax even if he skips vegetables entirely for a season. Don't take refusals personally, and don't call attention to it. Just leave the food on the plate. She may even take it later at the same meal. Continuing 400 IU vitamin D, DHA, and a liquid multivitamin at this age can support your toddler, and help you stay relaxed.

Eating should be a joy and a delight. Repetition is critical to acquiring tastes for new flavors, but so is novelty. You don't want to make the same meal so often you all get bored of it, or so rarely he has to learn to like it all over again. Serving the same choice about every three to fourteen days works pretty well.[8] If something was very popular for a while, and now he turns up his nose, try removing it from the rotation for two weeks before trying again. Then he may greet it as a familiar old friend.

One important exception to this: seasonal foods. When it's asparagus season, we may have asparagus every day for a while, and then look forward to next year when they return. Cherry season and tangerine season are also big in our household, and we don't have them much in between.

You'll learn to select foods that provide balance and abundant nutrition, while creating a framework for nurturing an adventurous eater. Make a point of including foods you know he likes, as well as some that stretch him a bit. Do include his passionately favorite foods, even if it seems like that's all he wants to eat, but don't provide enough of them to fill him all the way up. Keep a couple of other options in the mix as well.

Commercial baby food may be popular once again, because it is an easy consistency to spoon. This can be great in the spoon, or as a spread, sauce, or dip, but don't let it be the main food. Commercial baby food tastes about the same every time. They need variety, even the bit of variety you get when you pull out your old baby food mill and grind it yourself.

Over time, serve all of the fruits and vegetables you eat as a family. Serve them raw, or cooked the way you like them. I prefer my vegetables, for instance, roasted or lightly grilled with olive oil; I know other families who prefer to eat them steamed. Start raw vegetables with thin strips or slices (not rounds), until your toddler is quite proficient at chewing and swallowing.

Serve all of the grains you eat as a family—pastas, corn, tortillas, breads, cereals (without added sugar), and crackers (without added fat). Choose whole grains whenever practical.

By around eighteen months, kids are better able to digest beans than they were earlier. This is a good time to include them in the diet if you haven't already.

Serve all the kinds of meats, poultry, fish, and shellfish your family eats—but avoid products raised with artificial hormones or antibiotics, cured with nitrates, or supplemented with fillers and by-products. Choose fish lower in mercury and PCBs, such as those listed in "Eat Only Safe Fish and Shellfish" in Chapter Four. For some reason, tastes for protein foods are more genetically determined and less learned than the tastes for fruits or vegetables, even among PROP tasters (see Chapter Eight).

Don't be concerned if your child doesn't take to them. For kids, a vegetarian lifestyle can be as healthy as or healthier than the way most kids eat. (However, being a vegan raises issues in the first three years or so, unless the child is being nursed often throughout that time. Remember, most humans in history had milk from their mothers throughout the first years of rapid brain growth.)

Even though your child is learning to eat by herself, never let her eat alone. Choking remains a real risk at this age. They should eat sitting down—most choking happens when kids are up and moving (or having a tantrum, another reason to have pleasant mealtimes).

Gagging is normal and healthy as they learn more how to chew and swallow at their own pace, but avoid foods that might be swallowed whole and block the windpipe—large pieces of raw carrots, raw cherries with pits, whole grapes, peanuts, spoonfuls of peanut butter, popcorn, or hard candies. You can modify many of these foods to make them safe (quarter grapes and cherries, slice or cook carrots, quarter hot dogs lengthwise).

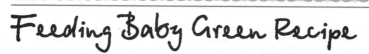

Feeding Baby Green Recipe

Chewy Oat Nuggets

Here's a recipe I used in college for tasty, lightly sweet "cookies" where all of the sweetness comes from fruit. I got it from a friend's mother, and we've been making it ever since. The sweetness is supplied by the banana only, so be sure to pick a ripe one!

2½ cups steel-cut oats

¼ teaspoons salt (optional)

1 teaspoon cinnamon

¾ cup walnuts, pecans, or macadamia nuts

2¼ cups sliced bananas (4 large bananas)

¼ cup walnut oil

1. Preheat the oven to 400 degrees.
2. Put steel-cut oats, salt, cinnamon, and walnuts in the workbowl of a food processor. Process until mixture looks like flour. Add the bananas and walnut oil. Process until well mixed.
3. Drop by the spoonful onto a greased baking sheet and bake for 8 to 10 minutes or until lightly golden.

Peanut Butter Oat Nuggets:

Omit the nuts, add 2 tablespoons of crunchy or creamy peanut butter, and substitute peanut oil for the walnut oil.

Serves 12 (Yield: 4 dozen)

NUTRITION FACTS (AMOUNT PER SERVING)

Calories: 252	Sodium: 49mg	Sugars: 5.25g
Total Fat: 10.51g	Total Carbs: 32.12g	Protein: 7.84g
Cholesterol: 0	Dietary Fiber: 5.19g	

Feeding Baby Green Tip

Make-at-Home Veggie Juice!

Store-bought juices are often loaded with too much sodium, but home juicing can be easy and fun. If we have extra produce around that's not quite as crisp as it was, we whir it up in the Jack LaLanne Power Juicer and (most of the time, anyway!) out comes a fresh, tasty drink. Plus, seeing and hearing the juice made—and getting to point to which items to toss in—can make this an easy way for kids to enjoy vegetables.

Use one vegetable, mix 'em up, or toss in a little fruit. Here are some combinations we like to make at our house. The amounts of each veggie are up to you—experiment!

- Carrot and celery
- Lemon, apple, beet, celery, cucumber
- Cherries and sweet potato
- Lime, red pepper, apple
- Asparagus, lemon, and cucumber
- Beet, lime, and ginger root
- Kiwi, broccoli florets, and green grapes

Hot dogs?!? I know, most hot dogs are made from unhealthy meat processed in an unhealthy way. But there are exceptions. Applegate Farms Great Organic Hot Dog, for instance, is made from quality muscle-cuts of grass-fed organic beef, raised without artificial hormones, cloning, antibiotics, or toxic synthetic pesticides. The hot dogs contain no artificial colors, no dextrose, no corn syrup, no gluten, no casein, no fillers, no nitrates, nitrites, or other preservatives. They have about half the fat of conventional counterparts. And they taste great.

What about dessert? Whatever you're having for dessert makes sense for your toddler as well. Don't use dessert as a reward for eating enough. In fact, if it's a healthy, nutritious choice—something naturally sweet such as berries, or pineapple sorbet (just puree some ripe pineapple and freeze, no sugar), frozen pitted cherries (one of my favorites), and chewy oat nuggets sweetened only with bananas (see the "Chewy Oat Nuggets" recipe)—it's fine to put dessert on the plate along with everything else (as long as the serving isn't enough to fill him up) and let your toddler decide whether to have dessert at the beginning, middle, or end.

As I noted at the beginning of this book, in the first two years I suggest minimizing any added sugar, sweetener, or artificial sweetener. Kids are designed to enjoy sweetness, but let them do this through real foods that are both sweet and nutritious—especially while their deep unconscious sense of good food is developing.

Water and Other Beverages. In addition to water, breast milk, cow's milk, or perhaps some other kind of milk, and some types of teas, vegetable juices can be another choice at this age. See the "Make-at-Home Veggie Juice!" tip to learn about making vegetable and fruit juices at home.

Customize Needs for Every Body

Even though you are making only one meal for everybody, the toddler portion will need to be prepared in a way that is easy to eat with fingers or a spoon, and easy to chew and swallow.

Cut foods into bite-size pieces. Meats need to be cut even more finely, because saliva doesn't start to work on them the same way it does on carbohydrates. Use unbreakable bowls or plates with sides that she can push her food against to get it on the spoon.

Please do not put your child on a low-fat or low-protein diet—in fact, they shouldn't be on any weight loss diet at all. If you are on a diet before your child is two, consider eating appropriate amounts of a variety of healthy foods rather than choosing low-carb, low-fat, and so on. Your children are watching and learning. Teach them how real foods can lead to a healthy weight.

Exercise!

Often when I go to the park, I see parents relaxing on a bench while their toddler dashes about the park. To be sure, parenting a toddler is a high-energy job, and you need your rest. The steady stream of interruptions and opinions can make even simple tasks an ordeal. Nevertheless . . . you need physical activity now as much as you ever did. It may seem counterintuitive, but getting regular exercise will actually give you more energy.

For many families, a daily park outing is a nice way to make sure both toddlers and parents get to have fun. As the child shoots to and fro, the parents can play with their children or keep walking laps around the play area for half an hour. Perhaps with hand weights.

Many communities now have "baby gyms" or activity centers where parents and young children can be active together. This can be great, especially if it is too dark or too cold to play at the park. You and your toddler will both make new friends that can last a lifetime. You can also put on music and dance at home.

Of course, you may want your own personal workout as well, but there is something anchoring about having at least thirty minutes a day where you are active within eyesight of each other. And, as always, you are modeling regular exercise as something that is fun and a normal part of daily life.

If you're a runner, you might consider getting a stroller built for just this purpose—you get to take your run while pushing your toddler, perhaps after he is tired from his own playtime.

Reap the Benefits of Green

When you purchase prepared foods of any kind, always read the ingredient label to know what you are getting. Many options on grocery store shelves are loaded with sweeteners, trans fats, and a long list of chemical additives. You can find tasty versions of most items with a short, clean ingredient list of real food, not chemicals.

For example, consider artificial colors. Added to make packaged foods more attractive than fruits or vegetables, these dyes can also affect growing brains and change behavior as much as drugs prescribed for attention deficit hyperactivity disorder (ADHD).

Researchers at the University of Southampton studied over 1,800 three-year-old children, some with and some without ADHD, some with and some without allergies. After initial behavioral testing, all of the children got one week of a diet without any artificial food colorings or chemical preservatives. The children's behavior measurably improved during this week. But was this from the extra attention, from eating more fruits and vegetables, or from the absence of the preservatives and artificial colors?

To answer this question, the researchers continued the diet, but gave the children disguised drinks containing either a mixture of artificial colorings and the preservative benzoate, or nothing—each for a week. The results were published in the June 2004 *Archives of Diseases in Childhood*.[9]

The weeks that children received the hidden colors and preservatives, their behavior was substantially worse. This held true whether or not they had been diagnosed with hyperactivity, and whether or not they had tested positive for allergies—good news for parents of young children everywhere!

Removing artificial colors and preservatives from the diet was dramatically effective at reducing hyperactivity—somewhere between the effectiveness of clonidine and Ritalin, two common ADHD drugs. It seems to me that this practice may be better for all children, whether or not they have behavior problems.

And of course, as you continue to eat in a way that minimizes your family's footprint on the earth, choosing foods that are grown locally, organically, thoughtfully, and that are without unnecessary chemical ingredients, you are helping to create an environment that will help nurture your child's generation and all those to follow. And having a delicious time doing it!

∽

The meals you enjoyed when pregnant, imagining what it would be like to have this child of your own, are especially meaningful now that you can enjoy them almost as equals as your child starts the fork and masters the spoon. In the final chapter, we'll take a look ahead to mastering the fork and beyond.

A Glimpse Ahead

(ABOUT TWO YEARS THROUGH EIGHT YEARS)

Congratulations!

You've made it through the first two years of your baby's life and worked to create a firm foundation for good health and food pleasure for the years ahead. There will still be some tasks and challenges to come, but important habits and tastes have been established. You're already enjoying many meals together, and looking forward to enjoying many more in the future.

Young children keep parents so busy every moment that it can be difficult to take time to look into the future. But that's exactly what we'll do in this final chapter.

The Essential Steps for Teaching Nutritional Intelligence

As your child grows from a toddler, through preschool, and into the primary grades, her development will, to some degree and for a large part of the day, be out of your hands. To hands-on parents who are used to having complete say over what their child does and doesn't do, this can be a bit of a jolt, to say the least. Like it or not, the school experience, her friends, and the media will now have increasing influence.

Take heart: you've done all you can to ensure that your child's earliest and strongest sensory memories have been well set, and you are continuing to help your child eat—and live—a healthy and green life.

Take Charge!

Taking charge during these years means different things in different families. Researchers often categorize parenting styles according to parents' level of expectations for their children and their responsiveness to their children's cues.

What would high expectations look like? Parents of first graders, for example, might expect their children to sit or play quietly while adults are talking, cooperate smoothly with unexpected changes in plans, stay in bed once put to bed, and so on.[1]

Those who have high expectations and demands but who are not very sensitive, warm, or responsive to their children are often called *authoritarian*. When it comes to feeding, they tend to be strict. They pressure their children to eat certain foods, while placing other foods off limits—at least until the veggies are eaten. This kind of taking charge is ineffective. High demands don't ordinarily produce the goals they want. In spite of such efforts, the children of authoritarian parents tend to eat fewer fruits and vegetables[2] and, when studied, have the highest odds of being overweight by first grade of any of the four groups.[3]

Parents who are very sensitive and responsive, but who don't maintain high expectations, may be too *permissive* or *indulgent*. It's a form of not taking charge. Their children may be a bit better off nutritionally than the children of authoritarian parents, but they may still be likely to emerge overweight and with an unhealthy diet.

Finally, parents with low expectations and low responsiveness are called *neglectful*. It's another way not to take charge. This group of kids, like the children of permissive parents, may still be about twice as likely to end up obese as the kids of authoritative parents.

None of these styles is ideal.

I recommend parents adopt the parenting style call *authoritative*. Authoritative parents are warm, sensitive, and emotionally responsive,

Feeding Baby Green Tip

Grocery Shopping with a Preschooler

Bringing your child grocery shopping can be an enjoyable experience for both of you, and a further education in food and nutrition for your child. Here are some simple "store rules" you may want to follow:

- If possible, bring your child shopping when she is neither tired nor hungry. Give her a healthy snack just before starting. That way, she'll be more interested in the process and less interested in wanting you to buy everything she sees.

- Stores are designed to entice your child to beg you for food; don't be surprised if she does. Conflicts are less likely if she sees you shopping from a list, rather than appearing to make arbitrary choices. You may want to avoid the cereal aisle, at least, while you are shopping with her.

- When she asks for something, you can add it to the list, telling her that at the end she could pick out one thing from among the things she's added. Or she could pick one fruit, one vegetable, and one treat for the family.

- If there are things you won't buy, try to tie it to a reason or policy so it doesn't seem arbitrary.

- Never give in to tantrums in stores. It's better to stop shopping and carry her out. If you do give in, tantrums are more likely on future shopping trips.

while maintaining high expectations for their children and setting firm boundaries. These parents are tuned in to their children's unique needs and temperaments. They are supportive of their children's successes, no matter how small. They understand and acknowledge their child's perspective. They interact warmly, and don't put their child down in any way. They don't get irritated easily.

This is the way you want to take charge. This is the feeding style you have been learning in *Feeding Baby Green*. None of us is perfect, but even little steps in this direction can make a big difference. Kids whose parents fall in this group are the most likely to eat vegetables, and least likely to become obese of any of the groups.

Don't Let the Food Industry Take Charge It's important to keep in mind that you are not the only one trying to take charge of your child's eating habits. I'll bet you remember food ads from when you were a child—I know I do. You may not be aware, though, that food advertising budgets for children have grown staggeringly since then, much like the growth of the obesity epidemic.

In 1983, all of the food and beverage companies in America spent about $100 million a year combined targeting kids. Today, Burger King alone spends almost that much.[4] In 2006, food and beverage companies spent more than $10 billion a year on marketing to children in the United States—up more than a hundred times (10,000 percent) for your child's generation.[5] Some already put the figure as high as $15 billion today.[6]

These companies know exactly what they want your child to eat and drink, and are very skilled at persuading her to do so. Food companies have a lot to gain if they can influence or control your child's eating decisions. And one study found that 83 percent of the food commercials during the most popular shows for elementary school kids were for fast foods, snack foods, or sweets.[7]

My colleague at Stanford, Tom Robinson, M.D., led a team that measured the effect of real-world marketing and brand exposures on young children three to five years old. They presented kids with five pairs of identical foods, one item of each pair in simple McDonald's packaging and the identical item in similar packaging without the McDonald's logo. The kids took a bite or a sip of each sample in each pair and were asked if the two foods tasted the same, or if not, to point to the one that tasted better.

Even though there was absolutely no difference between the foods, children said they preferred the taste of foods they thought came from McDonald's. This was true for fast food (burgers), for milk, and even for baby carrots (which were not sold by McDonald's at the time).[8]

This is sobering. It has also been shown that even a single exposure to a thirty-second television ad can change a preschool child's food preferences.[9]

(I'd love to see well-made ads for simple, healthy foods—fresh cherries in season, for instance—using all of the music, colors, fun, and messages so cleverly used to promote things kids don't really need. Not lame ads. Perhaps you could make some with your child and post them on YouTube?) However, another study points to a kind of taking charge that can make a real difference. Dr. Robinson and colleagues demonstrated recently that just reducing elementary school kids' exposure to television and video ads over several months can reduce their requests for advertised items.[10] This is good news indeed.

But our kids are faced with more than just thirty-second ad spots. It's more than you can control. In their superb article, "Calories for Sale: Food Marketing to Children in the Twenty-First Century,"[11] Susan Linn and Courtney Novostat detail some of the other common avenues of influence:

- Products are often branded with favorite characters. SpongeBob SquarePants became Kraft's top-selling macaroni and cheese. Shrek helped to sell Kellogg's Marshmallow Froot Loops cereal, Keebler E. L. Fudge Double Stuffed cookies, "ogre-sized" Peanut Butter M&M's, Cheetos, and Kellogg's Frosted S'Mores Pop Tarts, as well as McDonald's "ogre-tastic" Minty Mudd Bath Triple Thick Shake.

- Product placement can be very effective, even if you fast-forward through commercials. *American Idol* is one of the most popular shows on television for children. Ask a child if she knows what drink the stars of the show drink. Product placement is also common in films, at live events, on the Internet, and in video games. Product placement in games alone is expected to soon reach $1 billion annually.

- Contests and sweepstakes (win fabulous prizes!).

- Promotions (collect them all!).

- In-school marketing, including Channel One, vending machines, incentive programs (get free pizza, ice cream, and donuts from Papa John's if you get at least a C in all of your classes, or from Pizza Hut pizza if you read a certain number of books), textbook covers, sponsored educational material (such as Susan Linn's report of a school poster on nutrition put out by Frito-Lay that "exhorted kids to 'Snack for Power, Snack for Fun!' 'Did you know,' the poster asked, 'Cheetos, Doritos, and other Frito-Snacks give you the bread/brain

Feeding Baby Green Stories

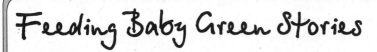

"Julia's Special Tomato"

Growing their own produce can make even the most stubborn young eaters become like bunnies and munch their way to healthier eating. As a dietitian and nutrition communicator, it's a concept I have long promoted. But even I was surprised at how young a child can be to be influenced by the excitement of a garden. My sweet little red-headed granddaughter, Julia Ruby, showed me just how.

Since Julia started eating foods, vegetables, legumes like garbanzos, and fruits were always her first choice. Nothing could please her more than getting some hearts of palm, avocados, or even cumin-spiced garbanzos. But tomatoes, as for many other children, were on her banned list. She would sometimes try them, unbeknownst to her, along with a favorite food. But somehow they were detected and she managed to spit out every piece. That is, until one day, when she picked her very own cherry tomato.

Each time Julia was at my house through the summer she was turning one, she and I had a ritual: I would carry her through my garden to see and touch my plants. One day, she picked a cherry tomato and guarded it in her tiny hand as though it was a very important treasure.

Since she only had four teeth, I was concerned that if she put it in her mouth she might choke. But I couldn't wrestle it from her hand. So I persuaded her that we needed to go into the kitchen and wash and cut up "Julia's special tomato." Her reaction as she ate it? "Mmmm" was all she could say. Now, at sixteen months, when she sees a tomato she squeals with glee in anticipation of a yummy treat.

Rosie Schwartz
Toronto, Ontario, Canada

power that the food guide pyramid says you need?'"), and fund-raising programs.

- New technologies. Fast-food companies are making their own video games and creating kids' marketing campaigns for cell phones and iPods. Social networking sites are also being exploited to advertise poor food choices to kids.

Do everything you can to decrease these attempts to manipulate your children, especially when they are young. As your kids get older, point out to them when others are trying to manipulate them. Some of this exposure will be beyond your control, but every bit of resistance helps. And if you want to get active to help change the rules and practices, consider the Campaign for a Commercial Free Childhood (www.commercialexploitation.org).

Use Windows of Opportunity

Engaging your child in food activities—from gardening and shopping to unpacking and cooking—provides opportunities to use all of the senses in positive ways to appreciate food. I've seen time and again that children who don't enjoy fresh tomatoes are much more apt to when given a knife (with supervision!) to help slice them. They're even more likely to enjoy the tomato if they get to pick it from the vine. But with both of these levels of involvement, the children are still consumers. The biggest change comes when they help plant tomatoes, nurture them, and watch them grow. They become co-creators—and tomatoes go from indifferent or negative foods to prized treasures. Growing cherry tomatoes can be easy, even on a small balcony, and is a real hit with kids.

But every level of involvement can be a plus. Use the produce section at the store to teach your child the names of all the foods. See if he can find the green beans or the red bell peppers. If you get a delivery from a local CSA (community supported agriculture) like I do, use unpacking to talk about the farms where the food comes from or what you will make with the treasures.

And this is a great age for your child to begin helping in the kitchen. He can tear lettuce for a salad and make a salad dressing. He can make dips for veggies—and of course the young chef will also get a chance to sample tastes as he prepares the food.

Over the next several years your child will go through many exciting types of growth and development. She will learn many of the rules and patterns of how the world and society work. Her imagination will emerge, and for a time the world will seem magical. She will develop a clearer sense of self, a gender identity, a moral identity. She will enter school. She'll adjust to obligations and expectations from outside the family. She'll learn to use symbols to explore and understand the world. She'll gain new competence and skills with each passing year.

Through all of these changes, each meal you share together is a chance to connect, a window of opportunity. And in today's busy culture, such chances become increasingly rare.

About half of preschool-age children don't have breakfast with a parent on most mornings. Instead, parents set something on the table and hurry about, getting ready.[12]

About 30 percent of preschool children in the United States spend part of the day with a grandparent or other relative who feeds them at least one meal. Another 40 percent get a meal at an organized daycare.[13]

And in the evening? As a culture we eat out more and more.[14] About 40 percent of family food dollars are now spent on meals outside the home.[15] Too many of these meals are drive-thru mistakes. Sitting down together at a restaurant can be a positive experience for the family—especially if you use it to model healthy eating in the broader world.

It's hard to overestimate the enormous potential benefit of families' sharing meals together. Even without giving extra effort or conscious thought, family meals are associated with better nutrition, better health, better behavior, and happier children, parents, and grandparents.

The table is one of the most important "classrooms" where kids learn from their parents. My simple prescription for all families: find a way to enjoy as many meals together as you can, especially at home together—at least seven meals a week.

Dozens of scientific studies have demonstrated an impressive list of benefits associated with eating together as a family. But some people have correctly pointed out that in the earlier studies it wasn't clear which was causing which. It made sense to suspect that eating together promoted the benefits, but it was also possible that the association found in the studies was because happier, healthier families were just more likely to eat together. The more recent studies have taken into account other measures of family connectedness and concluded that the benefits do indeed arise at the table together.[16]

The nutritional benefits alone are dramatic. Each meal at home is, on average, healthier than a meal on the go; it is also a lesson in enjoying healthy foods when not together. As kids eat more meals at home with their parents, they naturally begin to eat more fruits, vegetables, whole grains, and healthy dairy products than their peers do. They are significantly more likely to achieve their nutritional needs. And they eat less in the way of deep-fried foods and drink fewer sugared and carbonated beverages.

Increasing the frequency of family dinners is associated with substantially higher intake of several specific nutrients, including fiber, calcium, folate, iron, vitamins B_6, B_{12}, C, and E; with lower average glycemic index; and with lower intake of saturated and trans fats. The benefits are even greater if kids are involved in mealtime preparation and cleaning.

Youth who eat more family meals perform better in school. They spend more time on homework, get better grades, and spend more of their free time reading for pleasure. And they are happier. They are less likely to use alcohol, tobacco, or illegal drugs. They are less likely to engage in early sexual activity or to have eating disorders. Their self-esteem is higher, on average, and they are less likely to become depressed. Teens who eat many meals with their families are half as likely to think about suicide.[17]

Eating at home together with family around the table is different from eating take-out food in front of the television set. The more often that children eat in front of the television, the more likely they are to get more of their calories from fatty meats, pizza, salty snacks, and soda; and the less likely they are to get them from fruits and vegetables. Children in high television-meal families also average twice as much caffeine consumption as do their peers.[18]

And fast-food, on-the-run meals out can be even worse. As you know, the typical kids' meal in many restaurants is a nutritional wasteland. Fast-food meals more than twice a week are associated with increased obesity and type 2 diabetes.[19]

Each family meal can be a place of calm in the sea of busyness that roils around us. Family meals offer routine and consistency in the midst of change. Family meals are opportunities to learn together about communication skills, manners, nutrition, and good eating habits. They build family identity and memories to last a lifetime. Family meals may also provide an important time to "check in," when parents can tune in to the emotional well-being of their children and each other.

Clearly, for most families where someone works or attends school away from home, many, many meals will be apart. But even enjoying a third of your meals together represents enormous, gentle, lasting, quiet power. It's not clear which meals together—breakfast, lunch, or dinner—are most valuable. I suspect it would be different for different families.

Engage All the Senses

By the time kids have passed their second birthdays, they often carry within them an unwritten rule: foods I've already enjoyed are good; new foods are suspect and likely to taste bad. Learning to like new foods is uncommon but possible for typical American kids of the last generation between the ages of two-and-a-half and eight.

Ideally, of course, your children's version of this unwritten rule would be, "The foods I have enjoyed are varied, tasty, and satisfying; this new item might be more of the same"—something you have been teaching your child since pregnancy. Whatever an individual child's willingness to explore new foods at this age, the best strategies to help them be accepted are to convince kids either that, unlike other new foods, this one tastes good or to convince them that this new food isn't new at all.[20] Use the senses to communicate genuinely one or both of these messages.

Engage with Flavor The flavor threads you have already taught are especially valuable now—adding another vegetable to the southern Italian sauce won't seem unusual to your child at all.

In the United States, ketchup is one of the most common bridges between flavors during the preschool and elementary years—kids tend to

Feeding Baby Green Tip

Sweet Stuff After Two: The Rules

Adding a few sweetened foods in the diet can be good sometime after the second birthday, especially to teach children how to behave in a world of sweetness. As birthday parties begin, they will encounter more and more cakes and cookies and candy and ice cream—and they need to know some healthy ways to respond. Here are my suggestions:

- Eat sweets in moderation. One small piece of cake at a birthday occasionally is fine. One piece of cake for dessert every night is not!

- When possible, choose sweet foods that also have higher nutrient value—desserts based on fruits, dairy, or whole grain, rather than on processed white flour and fat. You might try banana bread or zucchini bread instead of a doughnut; low-fat frozen yogurt, ice cream, or sorbet rather than a cake. Perhaps with berries on top. Or berries in a tart.

- Use sweetness to help you enjoy good things you might not otherwise. A drop of honey and a sprinkle of cinnamon or cardamom mixed into plain yogurt and bananas can taste like a delicious pudding or ice cream if you haven't overloaded your taste buds with sugar.

put it on everything. Although jokes are still made about President Ronald Reagan's assertion that ketchup counts as a vegetable, the main ingredient in ketchup is tomatoes—which contain an important nutrient called lycopene, one of nature's most potent antioxidants, known to help prevent and heal cell damage. Foods rich in lycopene can lower cancer and heart disease risk. Tomatoes are, by far, the number one source of lycopene in the American diet, providing an estimated 80 percent of the lycopene consumed.[21] Unfortunately, many conventional brands include high fructose corn syrup and added chemicals. If you use ketchup, chose an organic one. Organic ketchup can average *57 percent more lycopene and double the antioxidants of conventional ketchup!*[22] They also tend to have a low sugar content and a simple, clean ingredient list—but do check the label to make

Feeding Baby Green Recipes

Veggie Dips

These Mediterranean-inspired veggie dips are great in Treasure Trays (see Chapter Eight) for your toddler, and as dips for lunch, dinner, or a casual party. They make new veggies welcome!

Baba Ganoush

1 large eggplant, about 1½ pounds

¾ teaspoon salt

2 cloves garlic

¼ cup lemon juice

2 tablespoons tahini

1 tablespoon extra virgin olive oil

½ teaspoon ground cumin, to taste

Kosher salt, to taste

1. Preheat the oven to 400 degrees F. Prick the eggplant with a fork, place it on a cookie sheet, and roast for about 40 minutes or until very soft inside. Allow to cool completely.
2. Scoop out the eggplant's pulp and process in a food processor with the remaining ingredients until it is almost pureed but still has some texture. Adjust seasoning to taste. Refrigerate until ready to use.

Serves 8 (Yield: 1½ cups)

NUTRITION FACTS (AMOUNT PER SERVING)

Calories: 53	Sodium: 76mg	Sugars: 1.54g
Total Fat: 3.46g	Total Carbs: 5.21g	Protein: 1.35g
Cholesterol: —	Dietary Fiber: 2.36g	

Tip:

*As soon as they are interested,
start teaching kids to understand food labels
and nutrition facts for themselves.*

Hummus

2 cups dried garbanzo beans

½ cup lemon juice (4 to 5 lemons)

½ teaspoon salt

⅓ to ½ cup water

⅓ cup extra virgin olive oil

½ cup tahini

1. Soak the dried garbanzo beans in a large bowl with 6 cups of water for at least 3 hours or overnight. Drain, transfer to a medium saucepan, and cover with cold water to at least 2 inches above the level of the beans. Bring to a boil, and then cook gently over medium heat and cook gently until *very* soft, about 45 minutes.
2. Drain the beans and pulse in a food processor with the lemon juice, salt, and ⅓ cup of water until very smooth. Add the olive oil and tahini, and process again until completely smooth and creamy. If the hummus is too thick, add a little more water.

Serves 12 (Yield 4 cups)

NUTRITION FACTS (AMOUNT PER SERVING)

Calories: 233	Sodium: 112mg	Sugars: 3.81g
Total Fat: 11.98g	Total Carbs: 23.71g	Protein: 8.25g
Cholesterol: —	Dietary Fiber: 6.77g	

sure. You can find the organic versions for about the same cost, and many kids (and adults) I know prefer the taste—even though it has half the sugar or less. Ketchup is still sweet, though, so use it sparingly.

Small amounts of ketchup could enable kids to enjoy many new foods, and just switching from conventional to organic ketchup could significantly increase the nutrients in America's diet and decrease conventional tomato farming methods. How simple! And you might want to think about switching to organic pizza and marinara sauce at the same time, if you don't make your own.

Along these same lines, scientists have given kids tastes of a particular dip enough times that it became familiar to them. Kids were much more likely to accept a new food—even a new chip—if it came with the familiar dip.[23] (See our "Veggie Dips" recipes.)

Repetition of tastes or smells remains a solid tool at this age. The "let's see" bite is a reasonable request that both expects something of your child and is responsive to his decision about whether to continue or not. Before long (though much longer now than at earlier ages), the new flavor can become not new at all. And it's still easier now than it will be later; kids tend to be more open to new flavors between ages two and four than between four and eight.[24]

I suggest expecting kids to remain at the table at least through the main course. Try to cultivate the habit of trying at least one bite of the foods you prepare for the family (but don't get into a battle over it). Keep portions of new foods small. Leave any refused foods within reach on the table, without comment. Always have at least one alternative on the table that your child will eat—but not necessarily a favorite (he may be more interested in trying your stir-fry if the alternative is a little boring). And be sure your child sees you naturally enjoying the refused foods, without making a show of it.

Engage with Aroma Kitchens full of good things cooking can smell great. And those lovely aromas pull kids in like magnets. Take advantage of your child's natural curiosity about food to give him even more to do in the kitchen. There are plenty of good cookbooks with simple, healthy recipes children can make (with your supervision). If you go shopping for ingredients together, and serve his dish to the whole family, your little chef will feel a priceless personal connection with good food.

You can also help him start an herb garden in small pots, outdoors or in the kitchen, in a sunny window. As he learns to smell the difference between basil, mint, rosemary, thyme, oregano, chives, and parsley, he's building a scent vocabulary that he'll never lose.

Engage with Sight You already know that just seeing real fruits and vegetables and healthy drinks in the home can increase kids' enjoyment of them. That's one of the reasons why we always have a bowl of appetizing fresh fruit on our counter at home. Having healthy foods and drinks available in a readily accessible form and in a place where kids know to look is predictive of how much they will eat.[25]

Nevertheless, preschoolers and school-age kids are increasingly influenced by what they see others eating outside the home. Watching a teacher enthusiastically enjoying a food makes kids much more likely to taste it and enjoy it—though this is less effective if the child is seated with peers who have a different attitude toward healthy food.[26]

One of the best ways to overcome the fear of new foods and to teach kids to like a new food when they are in school or preschool is for them to see other *kids* enjoying the food. It must taste good! Older kids are more powerful influences than peers, who are more powerful than younger kids.[27] Be on the alert for older kids, even just a bit older—in your extended family, in your neighborhood, on various teams, anywhere in your community—who could be good role models. Invite them or their families over. Create opportunities for your child to see them eating. Even one meal could be well worth the effort.

Engage with Sounds and Language Language is even more powerful for kids after the second birthday than it has ever been before. What is said about food can change how it is experienced. If your child hears a friend describe vegetables as "yucky," for example, this could influence him to refuse vegetables—even if he has been enjoying them for years. On the flip side, studies using functional MRI machines have shown that hearing positive things about food can make them actually taste better to the listener. The mind is very powerful in influencing how we experience and interpret the world.[28]

Do what you can to use your own words to encourage healthy food choices. Use words that express your honest enjoyment—describe the best parts of the taste, color, crispness, freshness, weight, and aroma. You can enhance the experience with an appreciative phrase. Be genuine. Enjoy.

Choose the Right Amount

We saw earlier that babies and toddlers can be remarkably good at naturally eating just the right amount of calories, as long as their hunger drives aren't tricked by giving them empty calories or sweetened beverages. The important way to achieve the right amounts at earlier ages was to choose healthy foods at reasonable time intervals, and to let the child decide how much to eat.

To a certain extent, all of this is still true: it's your preschooler or school-age child's job to decide how much to eat—though it may be even easier for them to be tricked into eating too much if they get processed, tasty, calorie rich, sweet, or salty foods. And be forewarned: there are now more factors that can trick them into eating too much.

As adults, we are unconsciously influenced by portion size. If we are offered popcorn, for instance, in two containers of different sizes, we will eat more from the larger container without even thinking about it. When researchers have looked for this same tendency in children, some have not found an impact of portion size on total amount consumed at age three, but it is clearly there by age five.[29] If you think your child is eating too little, try increasing the size of the plate. Too much? Try shrinking it.

This can be especially important when eating out—which today makes up so much of our food intake. Often restaurant meals serve portions that are about twice what anyone really needs. Unless you frequent the unusual restaurants that offer reasonable portion sizes, establish the habit of splitting a meal with your child or bringing home half of each of your meals as a later treat.

As a general rule of thumb, two- or three-year-old boys and girls need 1,000 calories a day. From ages four through eight, girls need 1,200 calories and boys need 1,400 calories.[30] Assume for the moment that a girl and boy each get two cups a day of one-percent milk, for a total of about 200 calories. Also assume two 100-calorie snacks a day (though some kids may do better with one snack or three). That would leave three 200-calorie meals a day for two- and three-year-olds, three 267-calorie meals a day for four- through eight-year-old girls, and three 333-calorie meals for boys.

By comparison, a small cheeseburger at Burger King has 330 calories, a small fries has 230, and a small soft drink has 140. This is a grand total of 700 calories[31]—and more than any of them should usually get for two meals put together. More than three meals for a three-year-old.

And what if you succumb to your child's new sweet tooth and add a small chocolate Oreo shake? That has 680 calories by itself, and the "small" meal would have 1,240 calories—more than an eight-year-old girl should get in an entire day even if she had nothing else at all. An extra forty calories a day may not seem like much, but that would be more than 14,000 calories a year—enough to make a healthy child unhealthy.

Feeding Baby Green Tip

Watching Your Child's Weight

The best way to tell if children are getting an amount of food over time that matches their metabolism, body type, and exercise level is to follow their growth curves. During the first two years, children have routine health visits every two to six months. After the second birthday, it may be only every year or even two.

I recommend weighing your children and checking their height at least every three months to see where they are on the growth curves. It's much easier to change course if caught early. If they are below the 5th percentile or above the 85th percentile in body mass index (BMI), or have changed significantly since the last time a health care provider checked them, be sure to report this to your health care provider.

That meal, by the way, would also have 780 milligrams of sodium in the cheeseburger, 380 milligrams of sodium in the small fries, and 480 milligrams in the small shake (yes, more than in the fries). This totals 1,640 milligrams, more than a three-year-old should get in an entire day ever. If you are "good" and ask for the fries with no added salt (only 240 milligrams of sodium), you would still be at 1,500 milligrams in a single meal.

And fat? An eight-year-old girl shouldn't have more than 300 calories of fat in a day. The cheeseburger has 144, the small fries 208, totaling 352. The small shake would add another 384, bringing the total calories from fat to over 700.

Does that mean you should count calories for your child? For a healthy child, growing well, I would not count calories at home. But I absolutely do recommend counting fast-food calories if you choose to go to fast-food or chain restaurants. The combination of saltiness, sweetness, rich calories, and excessive portion sizes could completely trick their bodies into eating too much (even if you order small sizes with no added salt). If the calories aren't on the menu, ask for a nutrition guide or look online.

Paradoxically, though, restricting access to forbidden foods can also trick kids into eating too many calories. When a tempting food is in sight but out of reach, once kids do get hold of it they tend to eat more than they would have otherwise. When five-year-old kids played in a room for twenty minutes with free access to food—except to some cookies in a transparent jar on the table—they tended to eat more cookies later when they did get hold of them than they would have if they had been allowed free access to the cookies all along.[32]

Usually, out of sight is out of mind. Taking charge of what's in the fridge, the pantry, and what's in the cupboards is helpful and powerful. Even so, too strictly forbidding foods out of sight can create an excessive longing for them.

I spoke recently with Gary Beauchamp, one of the brilliant pioneers into how taste preferences are influenced, starting even in the earliest weeks of pregnancy. He talked about limiting sweets versus outlawing them, how forbidding sweets can lead to bingeing. He related a story of a family that went to great extremes to protect their child from sweets. No candy, no desserts, no sugar. Sweets weren't ever brought in the house, so the child was never exposed—but one day he discovered some leftover chewing gum under a desk at school, and became a regular under-the-desk explorer, obsessed with sampling in this way as often as possible to get something sweet.

In getting kids to eat the right amount, the goal is neither to forbid nor to push, but to celebrate the great flavors of a variety of healthy, whole foods—to help your child learn not just to follow rules, but also to deeply enjoy great food.

Choose the Right Variety

Food jags—where kids want the same thing at every meal for weeks—are common in the preschool years. Your child may want nothing to eat but oat cereal O's and cheese. Don't worry, don't focus on it, and don't give in to every whim. It will stop eventually. It's unlikely he'll eat only O's forever!

If you see this starting to happen, have a few meals where that food isn't around at all—though perhaps there's something similar—another cereal, perhaps, or a few O's mixed in with a new food. Use other menu choices popular in your family to remind him of his taste for variety before a deep habit sets in, rather than just giving in to his whim.

I do recommend a chewable multivitamin and multimineral through-out these years to cover the bases, and keep everyone more relaxed. One nutrient I'm particularly concerned about is the omega-3 fat DHA. By age three, children should be averaging at least 150 milligrams a day. Many children, though, don't eat DHA rich foods such as fish. One analysis found typical three-year-olds only getting an average of 19 milligrams a day. If they don't eat fish, consider DHA eggs, or great-tasting DHA powder that you can sprinkle on their food or in their beverages. They probably won't notice any difference.

Customize Needs for Every Body

By the time kids reach ages four through eight, boys and girls have slightly different calorie and nutritional needs.

For girls the recommended daily variety is about 2 cups of nonfat organic milk (or the equivalent), 3 ounces of lean meat or beans, 1.5 cups of fruit, 1 cup of vegetables, and 4 ounces of whole grains. The milk and vegetable recommendations stay the same as at ages two to three. Whole grains, though, go up by 33 percent; fruit and meat or beans each go up by 50 percent.

For boys it's 2 cups of nonfat organic milk (or the equivalent), 4 ounces of lean meat or beans, 1.5 cups of fruit, 1.5 cups of vegetables, and 5 ounces of whole grains. Milk stays the same as at ages two to three. Fruits, vegetables, and meat or beans each go up by 50 percent. Whole grains go up by 67 percent.

Now that kids' brains are largely grown, they no longer need more fat than the rest of the family. Switching to nonfat dairy now is fine, especially if there are any concerns about too much fat or too many calories from other sources.

Continue to vary the veggies. Serve something green at every lunch and dinner, as well as a veggie of another color. Kids may be more likely to eat more, smaller portions of a variety of vegetables than a cup and a half of just one type.

Exercise!

Healthy kids age two to eight don't need to work out in a gym, but they do need a lot of active play to thrive. At minimum, they should get one hour a day of moderate to vigorous physical activity—and two hours a day is probably even better. Group activities such as soccer or dance class can be one great way to do this. Walking to or from school or other activities can be an added bonus. Lifting weights can even be good exercise in elementary school, if done gently and correctly—and if it's fun. We used to think this might be harmful to kids, but the evidence shows benefit, not harm.

Getting physical activity yourself will help you model better eating and a healthier lifestyle to your child. Consciously teach your child about energy-in and energy-out.

It's even better when you can be active *together*. Teach your child to swim and enjoy active play together in the water. Teach your child to ride a bike and take safe rides together—be sure wear your helmets! Find trails near your home and go for hikes together. Ski together, sled together, dance together, play ball in the park together. Make up games. Be active. Have fun.

Reap the Benefits of Green

When Frances Moore Lappé's *Diet for a Small Planet* exploded onto the scene in 1971, it started something of a revolution in the way America began to think: people started to make the connection between eating lower on the food chain, their own health, and the health of the planet.

Using the products of industrial agriculture to raise livestock is *very* expensive. Frances explained, "For every 16 pounds of grain and soy fed to beef cattle in the United States, we only get 1 pound back in meat on our plates."[33] If eaten directly, that much grain would provide eight times the protein of a pound of hamburger, with only three times the fat.

Other livestock, she calculated, are much more efficient: hogs take 6 pounds, turkeys take 4, and chickens take 3 pounds of grain and soy to produce 1 pound of meat or poultry on the table. It only takes 1 pound of grain to produce 1 pint of milk.

You could also measure the cost of grain-fed meat in its fossil fuel cost. Taking all of our livestock together (and excluding milk), the United States averaged 7 pounds of grain and soy to produce 1 pound of meat or poultry—enough grain to feed every man, woman, and child on the planet.

The math has changed some since Frances did her initial calculations, but the situation today is even worse. With the rise of meat consumption in China and much of the developing world, the wasteful calculus of too much grain-fed meat has become a major threat to the global environment.

As Michael Jacobson calculates in *Six Arguments for a Greener Diet*,[34] today we spend 181 million pounds of pesticides, 22 billion pounds of fertilizer, and 17 trillion gallons of irrigation water on our feed grains each year, which end up polluting our air, water, and soil—and depleting our previous heritage of topsoil and groundwater. More than 40 percent of our irrigated land grows feed for livestock. It takes 18,000 gallons of water to produce a pound of grain-fed beef. As if that weren't enough, 100 calories worth of grain-fed beef requires 1,600 calories of fossil fuels to produce (whereas 100 calories of plant foods require only 50 calories of fossil fuels). And 19 percent of methane, the greenhouse gas, is emitted by cattle.

You can be part of the solution by saying no to the feedlots, and choosing only beef that is grass fed and grass finished. You can help by choosing organic. You can help by choosing livestock that is more efficient than cattle. And of course, you can help by eating less meat, by enjoying meatless meals or meatless days, and by making meat a side dish rather than a main course.

∽

Epilogue
LEARNING TO LOVE GREAT FOOD

SINCE THE DAWN of time, parents have had a deep inner urge to give their babies the very best. Feeding our babies well is perhaps the deepest and most intimate of these instincts.

In the natural world, delicious food, bountiful nutrients, and environmental health have often gone hand in hand. The ripest, most colorful fruit often tastes the best, smells the best, has grown in the healthiest soil, and is loaded with the best nutrients. In the latter half of the twentieth century, these strands sometimes unraveled, with nutrients destroyed by overprocessing, artificial colors and sweeteners added like too much makeup to empty foods, and our climate, air, water, and soil tattered by industrial farming practices. It's left our appetites confused and our bodies less healthy.

The good news is that you are starting fresh and can weave these strands back together. The instinct is written deep within your genes. And the ease and availability of food that is delicious and healthful is increasing every day—and helping to nurture the planet that nourishes us.

And your baby will respond. Both experience and the latest research on the nutritional intelligence of children confirm that when children are exposed to this way of eating before they are born and in the first two years—long before their first lasting conscious memory forms—they take to it with gusto. Learning to love great food is a gift you long to give your child, a gift that you can give, and perhaps one of the greatest treasures you can pass on to your baby's generation and all those that follow.

When it comes to *Feeding Baby Green*, how you eat in your family is at least as important as the car you drive or the light bulbs you change. How we eat is the central rhythm of how we care for our bodies, our families, and our planet.

Biodiversity Checklist

IF YOU LIKE, try to eat from each category the indicated number of times. I've included a number of examples from around the world. Don't worry about trying to eat everything in any category. As always, be sure foods for babies and toddlers are an appropriate size and shape to prevent choking.

	Pregnancy	Nursing	Spoon Fed	Finger Foods	Fork & Spoon
1. **Mushrooms:** crimini mushroom, oyster mushroom, portobello mushroom, shiitake mushroom	○ ○ ○ ○ ○ ○ ○ ○ ○ ○ ○ ○	○ ○ ○ ○ ○ ○ ○ ○ ○ ○ ○ ○	○ ○ ○ ○ ○ ○ ○ ○ ○ ○ ○ ○	○ ○ ○ ○ ○ ○ ○ ○ ○ ○ ○ ○ ○ ○ ○ ○	○ ○ ○ ○ ○ ○ ○ ○ ○ ○ ○ ○
2. **Amaranths:** amaranth grain, beet (greens and root), buckwheat, Chinese spinach, quinoa, spinach, Swiss chard	○ ○ ○ ○ ○ ○ ○ ○ ○ ○ ○ ○	○ ○ ○ ○ ○ ○ ○ ○ ○ ○ ○ ○	○ ○ ○ ○ ○ ○ ○ ○ ○ ○ ○ ○	○ ○ ○ ○ ○ ○ ○ ○ ○ ○ ○ ○ ○ ○ ○ ○	○ ○ ○ ○ ○ ○ ○ ○ ○ ○ ○ ○
3. **Umbrellifers:** anise, arracacha, caraway, carrot, celery, chervil, cilantro, coriander, cumin, dill, fennel, lovage, parsley, parsnip	○ ○ ○ ○ ○ ○ ○ ○ ○ ○ ○ ○	○ ○ ○ ○ ○ ○ ○ ○ ○ ○ ○ ○	○ ○ ○ ○ ○ ○ ○ ○ ○ ○ ○ ○	○ ○ ○ ○ ○ ○ ○ ○ ○ ○ ○ ○ ○ ○ ○ ○	○ ○ ○ ○ ○ ○ ○ ○ ○ ○ ○ ○
4. **Cruciferous vegetables:** broccoli, cabbage, cauliflower, Chinese cabbage, collard greens, cress, horseradish, mustard, mustard greens, radish, rapeseed, turnip, turnip greens, watercress	○ ○ ○ ○ ○ ○ ○ ○ ○ ○ ○ ○	○ ○ ○ ○ ○ ○ ○ ○ ○ ○ ○ ○	○ ○ ○ ○ ○ ○ ○ ○ ○ ○ ○ ○	○ ○ ○ ○ ○ ○ ○ ○ ○ ○ ○ ○ ○ ○ ○ ○	○ ○ ○ ○ ○ ○ ○ ○ ○ ○ ○ ○
5. **Bromeliads:** pineapple	○ ○ ○	○ ○ ○	○ ○ ○	○ ○ ○ ○	○ ○ ○
6. **Composites:** artichoke, chicory, edible flowers, Jerusalem artichoke, lettuces, safflower, sunflower seeds, yacon	○ ○ ○ ○ ○ ○ ○ ○ ○ ○ ○ ○	○ ○ ○ ○ ○ ○ ○ ○ ○ ○ ○ ○	○ ○ ○ ○ ○ ○ ○ ○ ○ ○ ○ ○	○ ○ ○ ○ ○ ○ ○ ○ ○ ○ ○ ○ ○ ○ ○ ○	○ ○ ○ ○ ○ ○ ○ ○ ○ ○ ○ ○

	Pregnancy	Nursing	Spoon Fed	Finger Foods	Fork & Spoon
7. **Bindweeds:** sweet potato, water, spinach	○ ○ ○ ○ ○ ○ ○ ○ ○ ○ ○ ○	○ ○ ○ ○ ○ ○ ○ ○ ○ ○ ○ ○	○ ○ ○ ○ ○ ○ ○ ○ ○ ○ ○ ○	○ ○ ○ ○ ○ ○ ○ ○ ○ ○ ○ ○ ○ ○ ○ ○	○ ○ ○ ○ ○ ○ ○ ○ ○ ○ ○ ○
8. **Gourds:** cantaloupe, casaba, crenshaw, cucumber, honeydew, muskmelon (including many different varieties around the world), pumpkin (and other winter squashes), watermelon, zucchini (and other summer squashes)	○ ○ ○ ○ ○ ○ ○ ○ ○ ○ ○ ○	○ ○ ○ ○ ○ ○ ○ ○ ○ ○ ○ ○	○ ○ ○ ○ ○ ○ ○ ○ ○ ○ ○ ○	○ ○ ○ ○ ○ ○ ○ ○ ○ ○ ○ ○ ○ ○ ○ ○	○ ○ ○ ○ ○ ○ ○ ○ ○ ○ ○ ○
9. **Heath plants:** blueberry, cranberry, huckleberry	○ ○ ○ ○ ○ ○ ○ ○ ○ ○ ○ ○	○ ○ ○ ○ ○ ○ ○ ○ ○ ○ ○ ○	○ ○ ○ ○ ○ ○ ○ ○ ○ ○ ○ ○	○ ○ ○ ○ ○ ○ ○ ○ ○ ○ ○ ○ ○ ○ ○ ○	○ ○ ○ ○ ○ ○ ○ ○ ○ ○ ○ ○
10. **Legumes (peas or beans):** azuki beans, black beans, carob, chickpeas, dried peas, green peas, kidney beans, lentils, lupins, navy beans, peanuts, pinto beans, snap peas, snow peas, soybeans, tamarind	○ ○ ○ ○ ○ ○ ○ ○ ○ ○ ○ ○ ○ ○ ○ ○ ○ ○	○ ○ ○ ○ ○ ○ ○ ○ ○ ○ ○ ○ ○ ○ ○ ○ ○ ○	○ ○ ○ ○ ○ ○ ○ ○ ○ ○ ○ ○ ○ ○ ○ ○ ○ ○	○ ○	○ ○ ○ ○ ○ ○ ○ ○ ○ ○ ○ ○ ○ ○ ○ ○ ○ ○
11. **Lilies:** asparagus, chive, garlic, leeks, onion, shallots	○ ○ ○ ○ ○ ○ ○ ○ ○ ○ ○ ○	○ ○ ○ ○ ○ ○ ○ ○ ○ ○ ○ ○	○ ○ ○ ○ ○ ○ ○ ○ ○ ○ ○ ○	○ ○ ○ ○ ○ ○ ○ ○ ○ ○ ○ ○ ○ ○ ○ ○	○ ○ ○ ○ ○ ○ ○ ○ ○ ○ ○ ○
12. **Woody trees:** hundreds of species of bananas and plantains	○ ○ ○ ○ ○ ○ ○ ○ ○ ○ ○ ○	○ ○ ○ ○ ○ ○ ○ ○ ○ ○ ○ ○	○ ○ ○ ○ ○ ○ ○ ○ ○ ○ ○ ○	○ ○ ○ ○ ○ ○ ○ ○ ○ ○ ○ ○ ○ ○ ○ ○	○ ○ ○ ○ ○ ○ ○ ○ ○ ○ ○ ○
13. **Sesames:** benne, black sesame, gomashio, sesame oil, sesame potherb, sesame seeds, tahini	○ ○ ○ ○ ○ ○ ○ ○ ○ ○ ○ ○	○ ○ ○ ○ ○ ○ ○ ○ ○ ○ ○ ○	○ ○ ○ ○ ○ ○ ○ ○ ○ ○ ○ ○	○ ○ ○ ○ ○ ○ ○ ○ ○ ○ ○ ○ ○ ○ ○ ○	○ ○ ○ ○ ○ ○ ○ ○ ○ ○ ○ ○
14. **True grasses:** barley, brown rice, corn, millet, oats, rye, spelt, wheat	○ ○ ○ ○ ○ ○ ○ ○ ○ ○ ○ ○	○ ○ ○ ○ ○ ○ ○ ○ ○ ○ ○ ○	○ ○ ○ ○ ○ ○ ○ ○ ○ ○ ○ ○	○ ○ ○ ○ ○ ○ ○ ○ ○ ○ ○ ○ ○ ○ ○ ○	○ ○ ○ ○ ○ ○ ○ ○ ○ ○ ○ ○

	Pregnancy	Nursing	Spoon Fed	Finger Foods	Fork & Spoon
15. **Rosy plants:** almond, apple, apricot, blackberry, cherry, loquat, medlar, peach, pear, plum, quince, raspberry, strawberry	○ ○ ○ ○ ○ ○ ○ ○ ○ ○ ○ ○	○ ○ ○ ○ ○ ○ ○ ○ ○ ○ ○ ○	○ ○ ○ ○ ○ ○ ○ ○ ○ ○ ○ ○	○ ○ ○ ○ ○ ○ ○ ○ ○ ○ ○ ○ ○ ○ ○ ○	○ ○ ○ ○ ○ ○ ○ ○ ○ ○ ○ ○
16. **Citrus plants:** grapefruit, kumquat, lemon, lime, mandarin, orange, tangerine	○ ○ ○ ○ ○ ○ ○ ○ ○ ○ ○ ○	○ ○ ○ ○ ○ ○ ○ ○ ○ ○ ○ ○	○ ○ ○ ○ ○ ○ ○ ○ ○ ○ ○ ○	○ ○ ○ ○ ○ ○ ○ ○ ○ ○ ○ ○ ○ ○ ○ ○	○ ○ ○ ○ ○ ○ ○ ○ ○ ○ ○ ○
17. **Nightshades (potatoes):** chili powder, chipotle, eggplant, fingerling potato, green bell pepper, jalapeno, paprika, red bell pepper, red potato, russet potato, tomatillo, tomatoes, uchuva, yellow bell pepper, Yukon gold potato	○ ○ ○ ○ ○ ○ ○ ○ ○ ○ ○ ○	○ ○ ○ ○ ○ ○ ○ ○ ○ ○ ○ ○	○ ○ ○ ○ ○ ○ ○ ○ ○ ○ ○ ○	○ ○ ○ ○ ○ ○ ○ ○ ○ ○ ○ ○ ○ ○ ○ ○	○ ○ ○ ○ ○ ○ ○ ○ ○ ○ ○ ○
18. **Grapes:** currants, grapes, raisins	○ ○ ○ ○ ○ ○ ○ ○ ○ ○ ○ ○	○ ○ ○ ○ ○ ○ ○ ○ ○ ○ ○ ○	○ ○ ○ ○ ○ ○ ○ ○ ○ ○ ○ ○	○ ○ ○ ○ ○ ○ ○ ○ ○ ○ ○ ○ ○ ○ ○ ○	○ ○ ○ ○ ○ ○ ○ ○ ○ ○ ○ ○
19. **Laurels:** avocados, bay leaves, cassia, cinnamon, sassafras	○ ○ ○ ○ ○ ○ ○ ○ ○ ○ ○ ○	○ ○ ○ ○ ○ ○ ○ ○ ○ ○ ○ ○	○ ○ ○ ○ ○ ○ ○ ○ ○ ○ ○ ○	○ ○ ○ ○ ○ ○ ○ ○ ○ ○ ○ ○ ○ ○ ○ ○	○ ○ ○ ○ ○ ○ ○ ○ ○ ○ ○ ○
20. **Myrtles:** allspice, cloves, feijoa, guava	○ ○ ○ ○ ○ ○ ○ ○ ○ ○ ○ ○	○ ○ ○ ○ ○ ○ ○ ○ ○ ○ ○ ○	○ ○ ○ ○ ○ ○ ○ ○ ○ ○ ○ ○	○ ○ ○ ○ ○ ○ ○ ○ ○ ○ ○ ○ ○ ○ ○ ○	○ ○ ○ ○ ○ ○ ○ ○ ○ ○ ○ ○
21. **Loosestrifes:** pomegranate	○ ○ ○ ○ ○ ○ ○ ○ ○ ○ ○ ○	○ ○ ○ ○ ○ ○ ○ ○ ○ ○ ○ ○	○ ○ ○ ○ ○ ○ ○ ○ ○ ○ ○ ○	○ ○ ○ ○ ○ ○ ○ ○ ○ ○ ○ ○ ○ ○ ○ ○	○ ○ ○ ○ ○ ○ ○ ○ ○ ○ ○ ○

Notes

Introduction: Today's Greener World

1. Nestle, M. *Food Politics: How the Food Industry Influences Nutrition and Health,* Revised and Expanded edition. Berkeley: University of California Press, 2007, p. 187.

2. Committee on Progress in Preventing Childhood Obesity. *Progress in Preventing Childhood Obesity: How Do We Measure Up?* Food and Nutrition Board, Institute of Medicine, 2007.

3. De Ferranti, S. D., Gauvreau, K., Ludwig, D. S., Neufeld, E. J., Newburger, J. W., and Rifai, N. "Prevalence of the Metabolic Syndrome in American Adolescents: Findings from the Third National Health and Nutrition Examination Survey." *Circulation,* 2004, *110*: 2494–2497.

4. The Writing Group for the SEARCH for Diabetes in Youth Study Group. "Incidence of Diabetes in Youth in the United States." *JAMA,* 2007, *297*: 2716–2724.

5. Suboptimal levels of ten nutrients have been identified in children in federal government and Institute of Medicine reports: calcium, fiber, folic acid, iron, magnesium, omega-3 fatty acids, phosphorus, vitamin C, vitamin E, and zinc. Institute of Medicine, Food and Nutrition Board, Board of Health Promotion and Disease Prevention. *Preventing Childhood Obesity: Health in the Balance.* (2005); Institute of Medicine. *Food Marketing to Children and Youth: Threat or Opportunity?* (2006). Insufficient levels of an additional three nutrients (bringing the total to thirteen) have been reported by the American Heart Association and the American Academy of Pediatrics: potassium, vitamin A, and vitamin D. American Heart Association, et al. "Dietary Recommendations for Children and Adolescents." *Pediatrics,* 2006, *117*(2): 544–559.

6. Fox, M. K., Reidy, K., Novak, T., and Zieglar, P. "Sources of Energy and Nutrients in the Diets of Infants and Toddlers." *Journal of American Dietetic Association,* Jan. 2006, *106*(1S): 28–42; Fox, M. K., Pac, S., Devaney, B., Jankowski, L. "Feeding Infants and Toddlers Study: What Foods Are Infants and Toddlers Eating?" *Journal of the American Dietetic Association,* Jan. 2004, *104*(1S): 22–30.

7. Bailey, M. *Trillion Dollar Moms: Marketing to a New Generation of Mothers.* Fort Lauderdale, FL: BSM Media, 2006.

Chapter 1: The Journey Toward *Feeding Baby Green*

1. Bentley, A. "Inventing Baby Food: Gerber and the Discourse of Infancy in the United States." In W. Belasco and P. Scranton (eds.), *Food Nations: Selling Taste in Consumer Societies.* Hagley Perspectives on Business and Culture. New York: Routledge, 2002, pp. 92–112.
2. *Ladies' Home Journal,* Aug. 1933. In Bentley, "Inventing Baby Food," p 50.
3. "The Food History Timeline 1956 to 1960." www.foodreference.com/html/html/food-timeline-1956.html. Accessed July 5, 2008.
4. "The History of Pizza Hut." www.recipepizza.com/the_history_of_pizza_hut.htm. Accessed July 5, 2008.
5. "The Food History Timeline 1956 to 1960."
6. Ibid.
7. "A Billion for Spam." *Time,* Sept. 21, 1959.
8. *Ladies' Home Journal,* July 1933. In Bentley, "Inventing Baby Food."
9. "The Food History Timeline 1961 to 1965." www.foodreference.com/html/html/food-timeline-1961.html. Accessed July 5, 2008.
10. "The Food History Timeline 1971 to 1975." www.foodreference.com/html/html/food-timeline-1971.html. Accessed July 5, 2008.
11. CDC: DES Update Home. www.cdc.gov/des. Accessed November 2008.
12. Swan, S. H., Liu, F., Overstreet, J. W., Brazil, C., and Skakkebaek, N. E. "Semen Quality of Fertile US Males in Relation to their Mothers' Beef Consumption During Pregnancy." *Human Reproduction,* 2007, *22*: 1497–1502.
13. Barron, J. "New Concerns About What Babies Eat." *New York Times.* Mar. 12, 1986.
14. Burros, M. "Eating Well." *New York Times.* Feb. 21, 1996.
15. Ibid.
16. Center for Science in the Public Interest. "Gerber Escalates 'Campaign of Lies' with Full-Page Deceptive Newspaper Ads." *CSPI Press Release.* Feb. 23, 1996.

Chapter 2: What You Need to Know About Nutritional Intelligence Before You Begin

1. Centers for Disease Control and Prevention. "Physical Activity for Everyone." www.cdc.gov/physicalactivity/everyone/guidelines/pregnancy.html. Accessed Jan. 10, 2009.
2. American Heart Association. "Exercise (Physical Activity) and Children." www.americanheart.org/presenter.jhtml?identifier=4596.
3. Benbrook, C., Zhao, X., Yanez, J., Davies, N., and Andrews, P. "New Evidence of the Nutritional Superiority of Organic Foods." *The Organic Center,* Mar. 2008. See also Brandt, K., and Molgaard, J. P. "Organic Agriculture: Does It Enhance or Reduce the Nutritional Value of Plant Foods?" *Journal of the Science of Food and Agriculture,* 2001, *81*: 924–931; Magkos, F., Arvaniti, F., and Zampelas, A. "Organic Food: Nutritious Food or Food for Thought? A Review of the Evidence." *International Journal of Food Sciences and Nutrition,* 2003, *54*(5): 357–371; Williams, C. M. "Nutritional Quality of Organic Foods: Shades of Grey or Shades of Green?" *Proceedings of the Nutrition Society,* 2002, *61*: 19–24; and Worthington, V. "Nutritional Quality of Organic Versus Conventional Fruits, Vegetables, and Grains," *Journal of Alternative and Complementary Medicine,* 2001, *7*(2): 161–173.

4. American Heart Association, et al. "Dietary Recommendations for Children and Adolescents." *Pediatrics,* 2006, *117*(2): 544–559. In the AHA recommendations, "Milk listed is fat-free (except for children under the age of 2 years)."

5. Benbrook, C., et al., "New Evidence of the Nutritional Superiority of Organic Foods."

6. Benbrook, C. "Simplifying the Pesticide Risk Equation: The Organic Option." *The Organic Center,* Mar. 2008, pp. 1–49.

Chapter 3: Early Pregnancy and Before

1. U.C. Berkeley. "Adequate Folic Acid in the Diet May Be Important for Both Men and Women of Reproductive Age, New U.C. Berkeley/U.S.D.A. study suggests." *Press Release.* Feb. 26, 2001.

2. Wallock, L. M., Tamura Tsunenobu, T., Mayr, C. A., Johnston, K. E., Ames, B. N., and Jacob, R. A. "Low Seminal Plasma Folate Concentrations Are Associated with Low Sperm Density and Count in Male Smokers and Nonsmokers." *Fertility and Sterility,* 2001, *75*: 252–259.

3. Young, S. S., Eskenazi, B., Marchetti, F. M., Block, G., and Wyrobek, A. J. "The Association of Folate, Zinc and Antioxidant Intake with Sperm Aneuploidy in Healthy Non-Smoking Men." *Human Reproduction,* 2008, *23*: 1014–1022.

4. Matthews, F., Johnson, P. J., and Neil, A. "You Are What Your Mother Eats: Evidence for Maternal Preconception Diet Influencing Foetal Sex in Humans." *Proceedings B: Biological Sciences. Proceedings of the Royal Society,* 2008, DOI: 10.1098/rspb .2008.0105.

5. Borrelli, F., Capasso, R., Aviello, G., Pittler, M. H., and Izzo, A. A. "Effectiveness and Safety of Ginger in the Treatment of Pregnancy-Induced Nausea and Vomiting." *Obstetrics and Gynecology,* Apr. 2005, *105*(4): 849–856.

6. Kolble, N., et al. "Gustatory and Olfactory Perception in the First Trimester of Pregnancy." *European Journal of Obstetrics, Gynecology, and Reproductive Biology,* Dec. 2001, *99*: 179–83.

7. Pope, J. F., Skinner, D., and Carruth, B. R. "Cravings and Aversions of Pregnant Adolescents." *Journal of the American Dietetic Association.* 1992, *92*: 1479–1482; Wijewardene, K., et al. "Dietary Cravings and Aversions During Pregnancy." *Indian Journal of Public Health,*1994, *3*: 95–98.

8. Eberhardt, M., Lee, C., and Liu, R. H. "Antioxidant Activity of Fresh Apples." *Nature,* 2000, *405*: 903–904; Boyer, J., and Lui, R. H. "Apple Phytochemicals and Their Health Benefits." *Nutrition Journal,* 2004, *3*: 5; Tsao, R., Yang, R., Young, J. C., and Zhu, H. "Polyphenolic Profiles in Eight Apple Cultivars Using High-Performance Liquid Chromatography (HPLC)." *Journal of Agricultural and Food Chemistry,* Oct. 8, 2003, *51*(21): 6347–6353; Weibel, F. P., Bickel, R., Leuthold, S., and Alfoldi, T. "Are Organically Grown Apples Tastier and Healthier? A Comparative Field Study Using Conventional and Alternative Methods to Measure Fruit Quality." *ISHS Acta Horticulutrae 517,* 2000 (Part 7: Quality of Horticultural Products).

9. From the U.S. Department of Health and Human Services, www.atsdr.cdc.gov/ tfacts17.html#bookmark04. Accessed Jan. 1, 2009. "How might I be exposed to polychlorinated biphenyls (PCBs)? (1) Using old fluorescent lighting fixtures and electrical devices and appliances, such as television sets and refrigerators, that were

made 30 or more years ago. These items may leak small amounts of PCBs into the air when they get hot during operation, and could be a source of skin exposure; (2) Eating contaminated food. The main dietary sources of PCBs are fish (especially sportfish caught in contaminated lakes or rivers), meat, and dairy products; (3) Breathing air near hazardous waste sites and drinking contaminated well water; (4) In the workplace during repair and maintenance of PCB transformers; accidents, fires or spills involving transformers, fluorescent lights, and other old electrical devices; and disposal of PCB materials."

10. Bayol, S. A., Simbi, B. H., Bertrand, J.A.B., and Strickland, N. C. "Offspring from Mothers Fed a 'Junk Food' Diet in Pregnancy and Lactation Exhibit Exacerbated Adiposity Which Is More Pronounced in Females." *The Journal of Physiology*, 2008, DOI: 10.1113/jphysiol.2008.153817.

11. Gene expression was changed for IGF-1, IRS-1, VEGF-A, PPARγ, leptin, adiponectin, adipsin, LPL, Glut 1, and Glut 3.

12. Kligler, B., and Chaudhary, S. "Peppermint Oil." *American Family Physician*, 2007, *75*: 1027–1030.

13. Butte, N. F., Ellis, K. J., Wong, W. W., Hopkinson, J. M., and Smith, E. O. "Composition of Gestational Weight Gain Impacts Maternal Fat Retention and Infant Birth Weight." *American Journal of Obstetrics and Gynecology*, 2003, *189*: 1423–1432.

14. Parr, A., Mellon, F., Colquhoun, I., and Davies, H. "Dihydrocaffeoyl Polyamines (Kukoamine and Allies) in Potato (Solanum tuberosum) Tubers Detected During Metabolite Profiling." *Journal of Agricultural and Food Chemistry*, 2005, *53*(13): 5461–5466.

15. USDA Agricultural Research Service. "Phytochemical Profilers Investigate Potato Benefits." *Agricultural Research*, Sept. 2007, *55*.

16. Kramer, M. S., and Kakuma, R. "Maternal Dietary Antigen Avoidance During Pregnancy and/or Lactation for Preventing or Treating Atopic Disease in the Child." *Cochrane Database of Systematic Reviews*, 2006, *3*: CD000133.

17. American Academy of Pediatrics. "Food Sensitivity." In R. E. Kleinman (ed.), *Pediatric Nutrition Handbook*. (5th ed.) Elk Grove Village, IL: American Academy of Pediatrics, 2004: 593–607.

18. Lack, G., Fox, D., Northstone, K., and Golding, J. "Avon Longitudinal Study of Parents and Children Study Team. Factors Associated with the Development of Peanut Allergy in Childhood." *New England Journal of Medicine*, 2003, *348*: 977–985.

19. Smink, A., Ribas-Fito, N., Torrent, M., Mendez, M. A., Grimalt, J. O., and Sunyer, J. "Exposure to Hexachlorobenzene During Pregnancy Increases the Risk of Overweight in Children Aged 6 Years." *Acta Paediatrica*, Oct. 2008, *97*(10): 1465–1469.

20. Verhulst, S. L., Nelen, V., Hond, E. D., et al. "Intra-Uterine Exposure to Environmental Pollutants and Body Mass Index During the First Three Years of Life." *Environmental Health Perspectives*, 2009, *117*: 122–126; Newbold, R. R., Padilla-Banks, E., Snyder, R. J., et al. "Developmental Exposure to Endocrine Disruptors and the Obesity Epidemic." *Reproductive Toxicology*, 2007, *23*: 290–296; Lassiter, T. L., Ryde, I. T., MacKillop, E. A., et al. "Exposure of Neonatal Rats to Parathion Elicits Sex-Selective Reprogramming of Metabolism and Alters Response to High-Fat Diet in Adulthood." *Environmental Health Perspectives*, 2008, *116*: 1456–1462; and Lassiter, T. L., and Brimijoin, S.

"Rats Gain Excess Weight After Developmental Exposure to the Organophosphorothionate Pesticide, Chlorpyrifos." *Neurotoxicology and Teratology,* 2008, *30:* 125–130.

21. Benbrook, C. *Simplifying the Pesticide Risk Equation: The Organic Option,* 2008: 1–49; Benbrook, C., Zhao, X., Davies, N., and Andrews, P. "New Evidence Confirms the Nutritional Superiority of Plant-Based Organic Foods." *The Organic Center,* 2008: 1–53.

22. Ibid.

Chapter 4: Middle and Late Pregnancy

1. Ochsenbein-Kölble, N., von Mering, R., Zimmermann, R., and Hummel, T. "Changes in Gustatory Function During the Course of Pregnancy and Postpartum." *BJOG: An International Journal of Obstetrics & Gynaecology,* 2005, *112*(12): 1636–1640.

2. Duffy, V. B., Bartoshuk, L. M., Striegel-Moore, R., Rodin, J. "Taste Changes Across Pregnancy." *Annals of the New York Academy of Sciences,* Nov. 30, 1998, *855:* 805–809; Brown, J. E., and Toma, R. B. "Taste Changes During Pregnancy." *American Journal of Clinical Nutrition,* 1986, *43:* 414–418.

3. Pitkin, R., and Reynolds, W. A. "Fetal Ingestion and Metabolism of Amniotic Fluid Protein." *American Journal of Obstetrics and Gynecology,* Oct. 15, 1975, *123*(4): 356–363.

4. Mennella, J. A., Coren, P., Jagnow, M. S., and Beauchamp, G. K. "Prenatal and Postnatal Flavor Learning by Human Infants." *Pediatrics,* June 6, 2001, *107*(6): e88.

5. Mennella, J., Turnbull, B., Ziegler, P., and Martinez, H. "Infant Feeding Practices and Early Flavor Experiences in Mexican Infants: An Intra-Cultural Study." *Journal of the American Dietetic Association,* 2005, *105*(6): 908–915.

6. Arias, C., and Chotro, M. G. "Amniotic Fluid Can Act as an Appetitive Unconditioned Stimulus in Preweanling Rats. *Developmental Psychobiol*ogy, Mar. 2007, *49*(2): 139–149; Mennella, Turnbull, Ziegler, and Martinez, "Infant Feeding Practices."

7. Gidding, S. S., Dennison, B. A., Birch, L. L., Daniels, S. R., Gilman, M. W., Lichtenstein, A. H., Rattay, K. T., Steinberger, J., Stettler, N., and Van Horn, L. "Dietary Recommendations for Children and Adolescents." *Pediatrics,* 2006, *117*(2): 544–559.

8. Savage, J. S., Fisher, J. O., and Birch, L. L. "Parental Influence on Eating Behavior: Conception to Adolescence." *Journal of Law, Medicine, and Ethics,* Spring 2007, *35*(1): 22–34.

9. Skeen, J. T., and Thiessen, D. D. "The Scent of Gerbil Cuisine." *Physiology & Behavior,* July, 1977, *19*(1): 11–14.

10. Bagamboula, C. F., Uyttendaeleand, M., Debevere, J. "Inhibitory Effect of Thyme and Basil Essential Oils, Carvacrol, Thymol, Estragol, Linalool and P-Cymene Towards *Shigella sonnei* and *S. flexneri.*" *Food Microbiology,* Feb. 2004, *21*(1): 33–42; Elgayyar, M., Draughon, F. A., Golden, D. A., Mount, J. R. "Antimicrobial Activity of Essential Oils from Plants Against Selected Pathogenic and Saprophytic Microorganisms." *Journal of Food Protection,* July 2001, *64*(7): 1019–1024; Opalchenova, G., and Obreshkova, D. "Comparative Studies on the Activity of Basil—An Essential Oil from Ocimum basilicum L.—Against Multidrug Resistant Clinical Isolates of the Genera Staphylococcus, Enterococcus and Pseudomonas by Using Different Test Methods." *Journal of Microbiological Methods,* July 2003, *54*(1): 105–110; Orafidiya,

L. O., Oyedele, A. O., Shittu, A. O., and Elujoba, A. A. "The Formulation of an Effective Topical Antibacterial Product Containing Ocimum Gratissimum Leaf Essential Oil." *International Journal of Pharmaceutics*, Aug. 14, 2001, *224*(1–2): 177–183.

11. Anderson, R. A., Broadhurst, C. L., Polansky, M. M., Schmidt, W. F., Khan, A., Flanagan, V. P., Schoene, N. W., and Graves, D. J. "Isolation and Characterization of Polyphenol Type-A Polymers from Cinnamon with Insulin-like Biological Activity." *Journal of Agricultural and Food Chemistry*, 2004, *52*: 65–70; Broadhurst, C. L., Polansky, M. M., and Anderson, R. A. "Insulin-like Biological Activity of Culinary and Medicinal Plant Aqueous Extracts in Vitro." *Journal of Agricultural and Food Chemistry*, Mar. 2000, *48*(3): 849–852; Hlebowicz, J., Darwiche, G., Björgell, O., and Almér, L. O. "Effect of Cinnamon on Postprandial Blood Glucose, Gastric Emptying, and Satiety in Healthy Subjects." *American Journal of Clinical Nutrition*, June 2007, *85*(6): 1552–1556; Impari-Radosevich, J., Deas, S., Polansky, M. M., et al. "Regulation of PTP-1 and Insulin Receptor Kinase by Fractions from Cinnamon: Implications for Cinnamon Regulation of Insulin Signaling." *Hormone Research*, Sept. 1998, *50*(3): 177–182; Khan, A., Safdar, M., Ali Khan, M. M., Khattak, K. N., and Anderson, R. A. "Cinnamon Improves Glucose and Lipids of People with Type 2 Diabetes." *Diabetes Care*, Dec. 2003, *26*(12): 3215–3218; Qin, B., Nagasaki, M., Ren, M., Bajotto, G., Oshida, Y., Sato, Y. "Cinnamon Extract Prevents the Insulin Resistance Induced by a High-Fructose Diet." *Hormone and Metabolic Research*, Feb. 2004, *36*(2):119–125.

12. Zoladz, P., Raudenbush, B., and Lilley, S. "Cinnamon Perks Performance." Paper presented at the annual meeting of the Association for Chemoreception Sciences, held in Sarasota, Florida, Apr. 21–25, 2004.

13. Martinez-Tome, M., Jimenez, A. M., Ruggieri, S., et al. "Antioxidant Properties of Mediterranean Spices Compared with Common Food Additives." *Journal of Food Protection*, Sept. 2001, *64*(9): 1412–1419.

14. Thimmulappa, R. K., Mai, K. H., Srisuma, S., et al. "Identification of Nrf2-regulated Genes Induced by the Chemopreventive Agent Sulforaphane by Oligonucleotide Microarray." *Cancer Research*, Sept. 15, 2002, *62*(18): 5196–5203.

15. Lagouri, V., and Boskou, D. "Nutrient Antioxidants in Oregano." *International Journal of Food Sciences and Nutrition*, Nov. 1996, *47*(6): 493–497; Martinez-Tome, M., Jimenez, A. M., Ruggieri, S., et al. "Antioxidant Properties of Mediterranean Spices Compared with Common Food Additives." *Journal of Food Protection*, Sept. 2001, *64*(9): 1412–1419; Takacsova, M., Pribela, A., and Faktorova, M. "Study of the Antioxidative Effects of Thyme, Sage, Juniper and Oregano." *Nahrung/Food*, 1995, *39*(3): 241–243; Zheng, W., and Wang, S. Y. "Antioxidant Activity and Phenolic Compounds in Selected Herbs." *Journal of Agricultural and Food Chemistry*, 2002, *49*: 5165–5170.

16. Akgul, A., and Kivanc, M. "Inhibitory Effects of Selected Turkish Spices and Oregano Components on Some Foodborne Fungi." *International Journal of Food Microbiology* May 1988, *6*(3): 263–268; Lambert, R. J., Skandamis, P. N., Coote, P. J., and Nychas, G. J. "A Study of the Minimum Inhibitory Concentration and Mode of Action of Oregano Essential Oil, Thymol and Carvacrol." *Journal of Applied Microbiology*, Sept. 2001, *91*(3): 453–462.

17. Tildesley, N. T., Kennedy, D. O., Perry, E. K., Ballard, C. G., Savelev, S., Wesnes, K. A., and Scholey, A. B. "*Salvia lavandulaefolia* (Spanish Sage) Enhances Memory in

Healthy Young Volunteers." *Pharmacology, Biochemistry, and Behavior,* June 2003, *75*(3): 669–674.

18. Cosentino, S., Tuberoso, C. I., Pisano, B., et al. "In-Vitro Antimicrobial Activity and Chemical Composition of Sardinian Thymus Essential Oils." *Letters in Applied Microbiololgy,* Aug. 1999, *29*(2): 130–135; Rasooli, I., and Mirmostafa, S. A. "Bacterial Susceptibility to and Chemical Composition of Essential Oils from Thymus Kotschyanus and Thymus Persicus." *Journal of Agricultural and Food Chemistry,* Apr. 9, 2003, *51*(8): 2200–2205.

19. Balasubramanian, K. "Molecular Orbital Basis for Yellow Curry Spice Curcumin's Prevention of Alzheimer's Disease." *Journal of Agricultural and Food Chemistry,* 2006, *54*(10): 3512–3520; Dorai, T., Cao, Y. C., Dorai, B., et al. "Therapeutic Potential of Curcumin in Human Prostate Cancer. III. Curcumin Inhibits Proliferation, Induces Apoptosis, and Inhibits Angiogenesis of LNCaP Prostate Cancer Cells in Vivo." *Prostate,* June 1, 2001, *47*(4): 293–303; Egan, M. E., Pearson, M., Weiner, S. A., Rajendran, V., Rubin, D., Glockner-Pagel, J., Canny, S., Du, K., Lukacs, G. L., and Caplan, M. J. "Curcumin, a Major Constituent of Turmeric, Corrects Cystic Fibrosis Defects." *Science,* Apr. 23, 2004, *304*(5670): 600–602; Nagabhushan, M., and Bhide, S. V. "Curcumin as an Inhibitor of Cancer." *Journal of the American College of Nutrition,* Apr. 1992, *11*(2): 192–198; Nakamura, K., Yasunaga, Y., Segawa, T., et al. "Curcumin Down-Regulates AR Gene Expression and Activation in Prostate Cancer Cell Lines." *International Journal of Oncology,* Oct. 2002, *21*(4): 825–830; Shah, B. H., Nawaz, Z., Pertani, S. A., et al. "Inhibitory Effect of Curcumin, a Food Spice from Turmeric, on Platelet-Activating Factor and Arachidonic Acid-Mediated Platelet Aggregation Through Inhibition of Thromboxane Formation and Ca2+ Signa." *Biochemical Pharmacology,* Oct. 1, 1999, *58*(7): 1167–1167; Shishodia, S., Amin, H. M., Lai, R., and Aggarwal, B. B. "Curcumin (Diferuloylmethane) Inhibits Constitutive NF-Kappab Activation, Induces G1/S Arrest, Suppresses Proliferation, and Induces Apoptosis in Mantle Cell Lymphoma." *Biochemical Pharmacology,* Sept. 1, 2005, *70*(5): 700–713.

20. Herz, R. S., and Cupchik, G. C. "The Emotional Distinctiveness of Odor-Evoked Memories." *Chemical Senses,* 1995, *20*: 517–528; Herz, R. S. "Are Odors the Best Cues to Memory? A Cross-Modal Comparison of Associative Memory Stimulia." *Annals of the New York Academy of Sciences,* 1998, *885*(1): 670–674.

21. Herz, R. S., Eliassen, J., Beland, B., and Souza, T. "Neuroimaging Evidence for the Emotional Potency of Odor-Evoked Memory." *Neuropsychologia,* 2004, *42*(3): 371–378.

22. Schaal, B., Marlier, L., and Soussignan, R. "Human Fetuses Learn Odours from Their Pregnant Mother's Diet." *Chemical Senses,* 2000, *25*: 729–737.

23. Marlier, L., Schaal, B., Soussignan, R. "Bottle-Fed Neonates Prefer an Odor Experienced in Utero to an Odor Experienced Postnatally in the Feeding Context." *Developmental Psychobiology,* Sept. 1998, *33*(2): 133–145.

24. Bilko, A., Altbacker, V., and Hudson, R. "Transmission of Food Preference in the Rabbit: The Means of Information Transfer." *Physiology & Behavior,* Nov. 1994, *56*(5): 907–912; Schaal, Marlier, and Soussignan, "Human Fetuses Learn Odours."

25. Smotherman, W. P. "Odor Aversion Learning by the Rat Fetus." *Physiology & Behavior,* Nov. 1982, *29*(5): 769–771.

26. Stevens, J. C. "Detection of Very Complex Taste Mixtures." *Annals of the New York Academy of Sciences,* 1998, *855*(1): 831–833.

27. DeCasper, A. J., Lecanuet, J. P., Busnel, M. C., Granier-Deferre, C., and Mageais, R. "Fetal Reactions to Recurrent Newborn Speech." *Infant Behavior and Development,* 1994, *17*: 159–164; DeCasper, A. J., and Spence, M. J. "Auditory Mediated Behavior During the Newborn Period: A Cognitive View." In M.J.S. Weiss and P. R. Zelazo (eds.), *Newborn Attention: Biological Constraints and the Influence of Experience.* Norwood, NJ: Ablex, 1991.

28. Institute of Medicine. *Weight Gain During Pregnancy: Re-examining the Guidelines.* Washington, DC: National Academy Press, 2009.

29. Institute of Medicine. *Weight Gain During Pregnancy,* p. 107.

30. American Academy of Pediatrics. *Pediatric Nutrition Handbook.* (6th ed.) Elk Grove Village: American Academy of Pediatrics, 2009, p. 252.

31. Baskin-Robbins Nutrition Information: Sundaes, www.baskinrobbins.com/Nutrition/product.aspx?Category=Sundaes&id=SN012. Accessed Nov. 2008.

32. Zambrano, E., Bautista, C. J., Deás, M., Martínez-Samayoa, P. M., González-Zamorano, M., Ledesma, H., Morales, J., Larrea, F., and Nathanielsz, P. W. "A Low Maternal Protein Diet During Pregnancy and Lactation Has Sex- and Window of Exposure-Specific Effects on Offspring Growth and Food Intake, Glucose Metabolism and Serum Leptin in the Rat." *Journal of Physiology,* Feb. 15, 2006, *571*(Pt 1): 221–230.

33. Ettinger, A. S., Lamadrid-Figueroa, H., Tellez-Rojo, M. M., Mercado-Garcia, A., Peterson, K. E., Schwartz, J., Hu, H., and Hernandez-Avila, M. "Effect of Calcium Supplementation on Blood Lead Levels in Pregnancy: A Randomized Placebo-Controlled Trial." *Environmental Health Perspectives,* 2009, *117*(1): 26–31.

34. Williams, R. B., and Mills, C. F. "Battling Iron Deficiency Anaemia." *World Health Organization,* 2003, 35.

35. Kummeling, I., Thijs, C., Huber, M., van de Vijver, L. P., Snijders, B. E., Penders, J., Stelma, F., van Ree, R., van den Brandt, P. A., and Dagnelie, P.C. "Consumption of Organic Foods and the Risk of Atopic Disease During the First 2 Years of Life in the Netherlands." *British Journal of Nutrition,* Mar. 2008, *99*(3): 598–605; Rist, L., Mueller, A., Barthel, C., Snijders, B., Jansen, M., Simoes-Wust, A. P., Huber, M., Kummeling, I., von Mandach, U., Steinhart, H., and Thijs, C. "Influence of Organic Diet on the Amount of Conjugated Linoleic Acids in the Breast Milk of Lactating Women in the Netherlands." *British Journal of Nutrition,* 2007, *97*: 735–743.

36. Fetita, L. S."Consequences of Fetal Exposure to Maternal Diabetes in Offspring." *Journal of Clinical Endocrinology and Metabolism,* Oct. 1, 2006, *91*(10): 3718–3724.

37. Tepper, B. J., and Seldner, A. C. "Sweet Taste and Intake of Sweet Foods in Normal Pregnancy and Pregnancy Complicated by Gestational Diabetes Mellitus." *American Journal of Clinical Nutrition,* Aug. 1999, *70*(2): 277–284.

38. Egeland, G. M., Skjaevren, R., and Irgens, L. M. "Birth Characteristics of Women Who Develop Gestational Diabetes: Population-Based Study." *BMJ,* Sept. 2, 2000, *321*: 546–547.

39. Hunt, K. J., and Schuller, K. L. "The Increasing Prevalence of Diabetes in Pregnancy." *Obstetrics and Gynecology Clinics of North America.* June 1, 2007, *34*(2): 173–199.

40. Dabelea, D., Hanson, R. L., Lindsay R. S., Pettit, D. J., Imperatore, G., Gabit, M. M., Roumain, J., Bennett, P. H., and Knowler, W. C. "Intrauterine Exposure to Diabetes Conveys Risks for Type 2 Diabetes and Obesity: A Study of Discordant Sibships." *Diabetes,* 2000, *49*(12): 2208–2211.

41. Salbe, A. D. "Comparison of Plasma Insulin Levels After a Mixed-Meal Challenge in Children with and Without Intrauterine Exposure to Diabetes." *Journal of Clinical Endocrinology and Metabolism,* Feb. 1, 2007, *92*(2): 624–628.

42. Curhan, G. C., Willett, W. C., Rimm, E. B., Spiegelman, D., Ascherio, A. L., Stampfer, M. J. "Birth Weight and Adult Hypertension, Diabetes Mellitus, and Obesity in U.S. Men." *Circulation,* 1996, *94*: 3246–3250; Ravelli, A. C., van der Meulen, J. H., Michels, R. P., Osmond, C., Barker, D. J., Hales, C. N., and Bleker, O. P. "Glucose Tolerance in Adults After Prenatal Exposure to Famine." *Lancet,* 1998, *351*: 173–177.

43. Curhan, G. C., Willett, W. C., Rimm, E. B., Spiegelman, D., Ascherio, A. L., Stampfer, M. J. "Birth Weight and Adult Hypertension, Diabetes Mellitus, and Obesity in U.S. Men." *Circulation,* 1996, *94*: 3246–3250.

44. Gambling, L., Dunford, S., Wallace, D. I., Zuur, G., Solanky, N., Srai, S. K., and McArdle, H. J. "Iron Deficiency During Pregnancy Affects Postnatal Blood Pressure in the Rat." *Journal of Physiology,* Oct. 15, 2003, *552*(Pt 2): 603–610.

45. Bergel, E., and Belizan, J. "A Deficient Maternal Calcium Intake During Pregnancy Increases Blood Pressure of the Offspring in Adult Results." *British Journal of Obstetrics & Gynaecology,* 2002, *109*: 540–545.

46. Langley-Evans, S. C., and Jackson, A. A. "Increased Systolic Blood Pressure in Adult Rats Induced by Fetal Exposure to Maternal Low Protein Diets." *Clinical Science,* 1994, *86*: 217–222.

47. Hesse, V., Voigt, M., Sälzer, A., Steinberg, S., Friese, K., Keller, E., et al. "Alterations in Height, Weight, and Body Mass Index of Newborns, Children, and Young Adults in Eastern Germany After German Reunification." *Journal of Pediatrics,* 2003, *142*: 259–262.

48. Harder, T. "The Intrauterine Environmental Adipogenesis." *Journal of Pediatrics,* Apr. 1, 2004, *144*(4): 551–552.

49. Dabelea, et al., "Intrauterine Exposure to Diabetes."

50. CDC Growth Chart. "2 to 20 Years: Boys Body Mass Index-For-Age Percentiles." *Center for Disease Control,* Oct. 16, 2000.

51. Prentice, A. "Maternal Calcium Metabolism and Bone Mineral Status." *American Journal of Clinical Nutrition,* 2000, *71*(suppl): 1312S–1316S.

52. Carlson E., et al. "A Comparative Evaluation of Vegan, Vegetarian, and Omnivore Diets." *Journal of Plant Foods,* 1985, *6*: 89–100.

53. Bung, P., Artal, R., Khodiguian, N., and Kjos, S. "Exercise in Gestational Diabetes: An Optional Therapeutic Approach?" *Diabetes,* Dec. 1991, *40* (suppl 2): 182–185; Clapp, J. F. "The Effects of Maternal Exercise on Fetal Oxygenation and Feto-Placental Growth." *European Journal of Obstetrics & Gynecology and Reproductive Bioliology,* Sept. 22, 2003, *110* (suppl): S80–85; Da Costa, D., Rippen, N., Dritsa, M., and Ring, A. "Self-Reported Leisure-Time Physical Activity During Pregnancy and Relationship to Psychological Well-Being." *Journal of Psychosomatic Obstetrics*

and Gynaecology, June 2003, *24*(2): 111–119; Katz, V. L. "Exercise in Water During Pregnancy." *Clinical Obstetrics and Gynecology,* June 2003, *46*(2): 432–441; Mottola, M. F., and Campbell, M. K. "Activity Patterns During Pregnancy." *Canadian Journal of Applied Physiology,* Aug. 2003, *28*(4): 642–653; Ning, Y., Williams, M. A., Dempsey, J. C., Sorensen, T. K., Frederick, I. O., and Luthy, D. A. "Correlates of Recreational Physical Activity in Early Pregnancy." *Journal of Maternal-Fetal & Neonatal Medicine,* June 2003, *13*(6): 385–393; Orskou, J., Henriksen, T. B., Kesmodel, U., and Secher, N. J. "Maternal Characteristics and Lifestyle Factors and the Risk of Delivering High Birth Weight Infants." *Obstetrics & Gynecology,* July 2003, *102*(1): 115–120; Sorenson, T. K., Williams, M. A., Lee, I-M., Dashow, E. E., Thompson, M. L., and Luthy, D. A. "Recreational Physical Activity During Pregnancy and Risk of Preeclampsia." *Hypertension,* June 2003, *41*(6): 1273–1280.

54. American College of Obstetricians and Gynecologists. "Exercise During Pregnancy and the Postpartum Period." *Clinical Obstetrics and Gynecology,* June 2003, *46*(2): 496–499; Wolfe, L. A., and Davies, G. A. "Canadian Guidelines for Exercise in Pregnancy." *Clinical Obstetrics and Gynecology,* June 2003, *46*(2): 488–495.

55. Finamore, A., Roselli, M., Britti, S., Monastra, G., Ambra, R., Turrini, A., and Mengheri, E. "Intestinal and Peripheral Immune Response to MON810 Maize Ingestion in Weaning and Old Mice." *Journal of Agricultural and Food Chemistry,* published early online: http://pubs.ac.org, Nov. 16, 2008; Velimirov, A., et al. "Biological Effects of Transgenic Maize NK603xMON810 Fed in Long Term Reproduction Studies in Mice." *Forschungsberichte der Sektion IV.* Band 3/2008. Nov. 11, 2008.

56. McCann, D., et al. "Food Additives and Hyperactive Behaviour in 3-year-old and 8/9-year-old Children in the Community: A Randomised, Double-Blinded, Placebo-Controlled Trial." *Lancet Online* DOI:10.1016/S0140-6736(07)61306-3.

57. Jacobsen, M. F. "Petition to Ban the Use of Yellow 5 and Other Food Dyes, in the Interim to Require a Warning on Foods Containing These Dyes, to Correct the Information the Food and Drug Administration Gives to Consumers on the Impact of These Dyes on the Behavior of Some Children, and to Require Neurotoxicity Testing of New Food Additives and Food Colors." *Center for Science in the Public Interest.* June 3, 2008. http://cspinet.org/new/pdf/petition-food-dyes.pdf.

58. Ibid.

Chapter 5: Newborns

1. Wallman, J. A. "Minimal Vision Restriction Experiment: Preventing Chicks from Seeing Their Feet Affects Later Responses to Mealworms." *Developmental Psychobiology,* 1979, *12*: 391–397.

2. Masataka, N. "Effects of Experience with Live Insects on the Development of Fear of Snakes in Squirrel Monkeys (Saimiri sciureus)." *Animal Behaviour,* 1993, *46*: 741–746.

3. Field, T. M., Schanberg, S. M., Scafidi, F., Bauer, C. R., Vega-Lahr, N., Garcia, R., Nystrom, J., and Kuhn, C. M. "Tactile/Kinesthetic Stimulation Effects on Preterm Neonates." *Pediatrics,* May 1986, *77*(5): 654–658.

4. Schanberg, S. M., and Field, T. M. "Sensory Deprivation Stress and Supplemental Stimulation in the Rat Pup and Preterm Human Neonate." *Child Development,*

Dec. 1987, *58*(6): 1431–1447; Barnes, D. M. "Cells Without Growth Factors Commit Suicide." *Science,* Dec. 16, 1988, *242*(4885): 1510–1511.

5. Stettler, N., Stallings, V. A., Troxel, A. B., Zhao, J., Schinnar, R., Nelson, S. E., Ziegler, E. E., and Strom, B. L. "Weight Gain in the First Week of Life and Overweight in Adulthood." *Circulation,* Apr. 19, 2005, *111*: 1897–1903.

6. Abbott Laboratories. *Breastfeeding Data from the Mothers Survey.* Columbus, OH: Ross Products Division, Abbott Laboratories, 2004.

7. Ryan, A. S., Rush, D., Kreiger, F. W., and Lewandowski, G. E. "Recent Decline in Breast-Feeding Rates in the United States, 1984 Through 1989." *Pediatrics,* 1991, *88*: 719–727.

8. Schanler, R. J. "Suitability of Human Milk for Low-Birthweight Infants." *Clinics in Perinatology,* 1995, *22*: 207–222.

9. Goldman, A. S., Chheda, S., Keeney, S. E., Schmalsteig, F. C., and Schanler, R. J. "Immunologic Protection of the Premature Newborn by Human Milk." *Seminars in Perinatology,* 1994, *18*: 495–501.

10. Picciano, M. F. "Representative Values for Constituents of Human Milk." *Pediatric Clinics of North America,* 2001, *48*: 263–264.

11. Morteau, O., Gerard, C., Lu, B., Ghiran, S., Rits, M., Fujiwara, Y., Law, Y., Distelhorst, K., Nielsen, E. M., Hill, E. D., Kwan, R., Lazarus, N. H., Butcher, E. C., and Wilson, E. "An Indispensable Role for the Chemokine Receptor CCR10 in IgA Antibody-Secreting Cell Accumulation." *Journal of Immunology,* Nov. 1, 2008, *181*(9): 6309–6315.

12. American Academy of Pediatrics. *Pediatric Nutrition Handbook* (6th ed.), pp. 34–38.

13. Anderson, J. W., Johnstone, B. M., and Remley, D. T. "Breastfeeding and Cognitive Development: A Meta-Analysis." *American Journal of Clinical Nutrition,* 1999, *70*: 525–535.

14. La Leche League International. *The Breastfeeding Answer Book.* (3rd rev. ed.) Schaumberg, IL: La Leche League International, 2003.

15. The Human Milk Banking Association of North America. http://www.hmbana.org. Accessed Nov. 2008.

16. United Nations Children's Fund (UNICEF), Facts for Life, New York, 2002, Page 48. Available at: http://www.unicef.org/ffl/text.htm. Accessed Nov. 2008.

17. Winickoff, J. P., Friebely, J., Tanski, S. E., Sherrod, C., Matt, G. E., Hovell, M. F., and McMillen, R. C. "Beliefs About the Health Effects of 'Thirdhand' Smoke and Home Smoking Bans." *Pediatrics,* 2009, *123*: e74–e79.

18. U.S. Department of Health and Human Services. *The Health Consequences of Involuntary Exposure to Tobacco Smoke: A Report of the Surgeon General.* Washington, DC: USDHHS, 2006.

19. Zeiger, R. S., et al. "Soy Allergy in Infants and Children with IgE-Associated Cow's Milk Allergy." *Journal of Pediatrics,* 1999, *134*: 614–622.

Chapter 6: The First Months

1. Myers, K. P., and Sclafani, A. "Development of Learned Flavor Preferences." *Developmental Psychobiology,* 2006, 48: 380–388; Savage, J.O.F., and Birch, L. L. "Parental Influence on Eating Behavior." *Journal of Law, Medicine, and Ethics,* 2007, *35*(1): 22–34.

2. Bilko, A., et al. "Transmission of Food Preferences in the Rabbit: The Means of Information Transfer." *Physiology and Behavior,* 1994, *56*: 907–912.

3. Kuga, M., et al. "Changes in Gustatory Sense During Pregnancy." *Acta Otolaryngologica,* 2002, *546*(suppl): 146–153.

4. Ochsenbein-Kölble, N., von Mering, R., Zimmermann, R., and Hummel, T. "Changes in Gustatory Function During the Course of Pregnancy and Postpartum." *BJOG: An International Journal of Obstetrics & Gynaecology,* 2005, *112*(12): 1636–1640.

5. Mennella, J. A. "Mother's Milk: A Medium for Early Flavor Experiences." *Journal of Human Lactation,* Mar. 1, 1995, *11*(1): 39–45.

6. Sadock, B. J., and Sadock, V. A. *Kaplan & Sadock's Synopsis of Psychiatry.* (10th ed.) Philadelphia: Lippincott William & Wilkins, 2008, p.159.

7. Tsao, J.C.I., et al. "A Review of CAM for Procedural Pain in Infancy: Part II. Other Interventions." *Evidence-Based Complementary and Alternative Medicine (eCAM),* 2008, *5*(4): 399–407.

8. Hoffman, H. S. *Amorous Turkeys and Addicted Ducklings.* Concord, MA: Authors Cooperative, 1994.

9. Rawr, E. "Imprinting in Geese." *Scienceray.* Dec. 3, 2008. www.scienceray.com/Biology/Zoology/Imprinting-in-Geese.377565.

10. Wuensch, K. L. "Exposure to Onion Taste in Mother's Milk Leads to Enhanced Preference for Onion Diet Among Weanling Rats." *The Journal of General Psychology,* 1978, *99*: 163–167.

11. Mennella, J. A., Coren, P., Jagnow, M. S., and Beauchamp, G. K. "Prenatal and Postnatal Flavor Learning by Human Infants." *Pediatrics,* June 2001, *107*(6): e88.

12. Mennella, J. A., and Beauchamp, G. K. "Experience with a Flavor in Mother's Milk Modifies the Infant's Acceptance of Flavored Cereal." *Developmental Psychobiology* Nov. 1, 1999, *35*(3): 197–203.

13. Mennella, J. A. "Maternal Diet Alters the Sensory Qualities of Human Milk and the Nursling's Behavior." *Pediatrics,* Oct. 1, 1991, *88*(4): 737–744.

14. Mennella, J. A. "The Effects of Repeated Exposure to Garlic-Flavored Milk on the Nursling's Behavior." *Pediatric Research,* Dec. 1, 1993, *34*(6): 805–808.

15. Hausner, H., et al. "Differential Transfer of Dietary Flavour Compounds into Human Breast Milk." *Physiology and Behavior,* 2008, *95*: 118–124.

16. Mennella, J. A., and Beauchamp, G. K. "The Human Infants' Response to Vanilla Flavors in Mother's Milk and Formula." *Infant Behavior and Development,* 1996, *19*: 13–19.

17. Sullivan, S. A., and Birch, L. L. "Infant Dietary Experience and Acceptance of Solid Foods." *Pediatrics,* 1994, *93*: 271–277.

18. Mennella, J. A. "Early Flavor Experiences: Research Update." *Nutrition Reviews,* July 1, 1998, *56*(7): 205–211.

19. Mennella, J. A., and Beauchamp, G. K. "Flavor Experiences During Formula Feeding Are Related to Preferences During Childhood." *Early Human Development,* July 1, 2002, *68*(2): 71–82.

20. Mennella, J. A., Kennedy, J. M., and Beauchamp, G. K. "Vegetable Acceptance by Infants: Effects of Formula Flavors." *Early Human Development,* 2006, *82*: 463–468.

21. Liem, D. G. "Sweet and Sour Preferences During Childhood: Role of Early Experiences." *Developmental Psychobiology,* Dec. 1, 2002, *41*(4): 388–395.

22. Hines, P. J. "The Invisible Bouquet." *Science,* Feb. 2006, *311*(5762): 803.

23. Goff, S. A., and Klee, H. J. "Plant Volatile Compounds: Sensory Cues for Health and Nutritional Value?" *Science,* 2006, *311*: 815–819.

24. Mennella, J. A. "Infants' Exploration of Scented Toys: Effects of Prior Experiences." *Chemical Senses,* Feb. 1, 1998, *23*(1): 11–17.

25. Stettler, N., Stallings, V. A., Troxel, A. B., Zhao, J., Schinnar, R., Nelson, S. E., Ziegler, E. E., and Strom, B. L. "Weight Gain in the First Week of Life and Overweight in Adulthood." *Circulation,* Apr. 19, 2005, *111*: 1897–1903.

26. Gordon, C. M., Feldman, H. A., Sinclair, L., Williams, A. L., Kleinman, P. K., Perez-Rossello, J., and Cox, J. E. "Prevalence of Vitamin D Deficiency Among Healthy Infants and Toddlers." *Archives of Pediatrics and Adolescent Medicine,* 2008, *162*: 505–512.

27. Misra, M., et al. "Vitamin D Deficiency in Children and Its Management: Review of Current Knowledge and Recommendations." *Pediatrics,* 2008, *122*: 398–417.

28. Simmons, R. "Developmental Origins of Adult Metabolic Disease." *Endocrinology & Metabolism Clinics of North America,* 2006, *35*: 193–204.

29. Greer, F. R., Sicherer, S. H., and Burks, A.W., and and the Committee on Nutrition and Section on Allergy and Immunology. "Effects of Early Nutritional Interventions on the Development of Atopic Disease in Infants and Children: The Role of Maternal Dietary Restriction, Breastfeeding, Timing of Introduction of Complementary Foods, and Hydrolyzed Formulas." *Pediatrics,* 2008, *121*: 183–191.

30. Kummeling, I., Thijs, C., Huber, M., van de Vijver, L. P., Snijders, B. E., Penders, J., Stelma, F., van Ree, R., van den Brandt, P. A., and Dagnelie, P. C. "Consumption of Organic Foods and the Risk of Atopic Disease During the First 2 Years of Life in the Netherlands." *British Journal of Nutrition,* Mar. 2008, *99*(3): 598–605.

31. Savage, J.O.F., and Birch, L. L. "Parental Influence on Eating Behavior." *Journal of Law, Medicine, and Ethics,* 2007, *35*(1): 22–34.

32. Zambrano, E., Bautista, C. J., Deás, M., Martínez-Samayoa, P. M., González-Zamorano, M., Ledesma, H., Morales, J., Larrea, F., and Nathanielsz, P. W. "A Low Maternal Protein Diet During Pregnancy and Lactation Has Sex- and Window of Exposure-Specific Effects on Offspring Growth and Food Intake, Glucose Metabolism and Serum Leptin in the Rat." *Journal of Physiology,* Feb. 15, 2006, *571*(Pt 1): 221–230.

33. McIntosh, M., and Miller, C. "A Diet Containing Food Rich in Soluble and Insoluble Fiber Improves Glycemic Control and Reduces Hyperlipidemia Among Patients with Type 2 Diabetes Mellitus." *Nutrition Reviews,* Feb. 2001, *59*(2): 52–55; Pittaway, J. K., Ahuja, K. D., Cehun, M., Chronopoulos, A., Robertson, I. K., Nestel, P. J., and Ball, M. J. "Dietary Supplementation with Chickpeas for at Least 5 Weeks Results in Small but Significant Reductions in Serum Total and Low-Density Lipoprotein Cholesterols in Adult Women and Men." *Annals of Nutrition & Metabolism,* Dec. 21, 2006, *50*(6): 512–518.

34. Edenharder, R., Keller, G., Platt, K. L., and Unger, K. K. "Isolation and Characterization of Structurally Novel Antimutagenic Flavonoids from Spinach (Spinacia oleracea)." *Journal of Agricultural and Food Chemistry,* June 2001, *49*(6): 2767–2773; Gates, M. A., Tworoger, S. S., Hecht, J. L., De Vivo, I., Rosner, B., and Hankinson, S. E. "A Prospective Study of Dietary Flavonoid Intake and Incidence of Epithelial Ovarian Cancer." *International Journal of Cancer,* Nov. 15, 2007, *121*(10): 2225–2232; He, T., Huang, C. Y., Chen, H., Hou, Y. H. "Effects of Spinach Powder

Fat-Soluble Extract on Proliferation of Human Gastric Adenocarcinoma Cells." *Biomedical and Environmental Sciences,* Dec. 1999, *12*(4): 247–252; Longnecker, M. P., Newcomb, P. A., Mittendorf, R., et al. "Intake of Carrots, Spinach, and Supplements Containing Vitamin A in Relation to Risk of Breast Cancer." *Cancer Epidemiology, Biomarkers, and Prevention,* Nov. 1997, *6*(11): 887–889; Nyska, A., Lomnitski, L., Spalding, J., et al. "Topical and Oral Administration of the Natural Water-Soluble Antioxidant from Spinach Reduces the Multiplicity of Papillomas in the Tg.AC Mouse Model." *Toxicology Letters,* May 31, 2001, *122*(1): 33–34.

35. Joseph, J. A., Shukitt-Hale, B., Denisova, N. A, et al. "Reversals of Age-Related Declines in Neuronal Signal Transduction, Cognitive, and Motor Behavioral Deficits with Blueberry, Spinach, or Strawberry Dietary Supplementation." *Journal of Neuroscience,* Sept. 15, 1999, *19*(18): 8114–8121; Morris, M. C., Evans, D. A., Tangney, C. C., Bienias, J. L., and Wilson, R. S. "Associations of Vegetable and Fruit Consumption with Age-Related Cognitive Change." *Neurology,* Oct. 24, 2006, *67*(8): 1370–1376; Wang, Y., Chang, C. F., Chou, J., Chen, H. L., Deng, X., Harvey, B. K., Cadet, J. L., and Bickford, P. C. "Dietary Supplementation with Blueberries, Spinach, or Spirulina Reduces Ischemic Brain Damage." *Experimental Neurology,* May 2005, *193*(1): 75–84.

36. Gumy, C., Chandsawangbhuwana, C., Dzyakanchuk, A. A., Kratschmar, D. V., Baker, M. E., and Odermatt, A. 2008. "Dibutyltin Disrupts Glucocorticoid Receptor Function and Impairs Glucocorticoid-Induced Suppression of Cytokine Production." PLoS ONE doi:10.1371/journal.pone.0003545.

37. Edginton, A. and Ritter, L. 2008. "Predicting Plasma Concentrations of Bisphenol A in Young Children (< Two Years) Following Typical Feeding Schedules Using a Physiologically-Based Toxicokinetic Model." *Environmental Health Perspectives* doi:10.1289/ehp.0800073.

Chapter 7: Starting Solids

1. Next Stop Bangkok. www.nextstopbangkok.com/information/thai_food/. Accessed Dec. 30, 2008.

2. The Rice Association. www.riceassociation.org.uk/factsandfigures.htm. Accessed November 1, 2008.

3. Mennella, J. A. "Mothers' Milk Enhances the Acceptance of Cereal During Weaning." *Pediatric Research,* Feb. 1, 1997, *41*(2): 188–192.

4. Gilbertson, T. A. "Role of the Taste System in Ingestive Behavior: Studies in NaCl and Fatty Acid Transduction." *Annals of the New York Academy of Sciences,* Nov. 30, 1998, *855*: 860–867.

5. Stewart, R. E., DeSimone, J. A., and Hill, D. L. "New Perspectives in Gustatory Physiology: Transduction, Development, and Plasticity." *American Journal of Physiology,* 1997, *272*: C1–26.

6. Beauchamp, G. K., Cowart, B. J., Mennella, J. A., and Marsh, R. R. "Infant Salt Taste: Developmental, Methodological, and Contextual Factors," *Developmental Psychobiology,* 1994, *27*(6): 353–365.

7. Birch, L. L. "Development of Food Preferences," *Annual Review of Nutrition,* 1999, *19*: 41–62.

8. Cowart, B. J. "Development of Taste Perception in Humans: Sensitivity and Preference Throughout the Life Span," *Psychological Bulletin*, 1981, *90*(1): 43–73.

9. Carruth, B. R., Ziegler, P., Gordon, A., and Barr, S. I. "Prevalence of Picky Eaters Among Infants and Toddlers and Their Caregiver's Decisions About Offering a Food," *Journal of the American Dietetic Association*, 2004, *104*: S57–S64.

10. Maier, A., Chabanet, C., Schaal, B., Issanchou, S., Leathwood, P. "Effects of Repeated Exposure on Acceptance of Initially Disliked Vegetables in 7-Month Old Infants." *Food Quality & Preference*, 2007, *18*: 1023–1032.

11. Van den Bree, M.B.M., Eaves, L. J., and Dwyer, J. T. "Genetic and Environmental Influences on Eating Patterns of Twins Aged >50 Y." *American Journal of Clinical Nutrition*, 1999, *70*: 456–465; Krondl, M., Coleman, P., Wade, J., and Milner, J. "A Twin Study Examining the Genetic Influence on Food Selection." *Human Nutrition, Applied Nutrition*, 1983, *37*A: 189–198.

12. Fabsitz, R. R., Garrison, R. J., Feinleib, M., and Hjortland, M. "A Twin Analysis of Dietary Intake: Evidence for a Need to Control for Possible Environmental Differences in MZ and DZ Twins," *Behavior Genetics, 8*, 1978: 15–25; Rozin, P., and Millman, L. "Family Environment, Not Heredity, Accounts for Family Resemblances in Food Preferences and Attitudes: A Twin Study." *Appetite*, 1987, *8*: 125–134.

13. Hikami, K., Hasegawa, Y., and Matsuzawa, T. "Social Transmission of Food Preference in Japanese Monkeys (*Macaca fuscata*) After Mere Exposure or Aversion Training." *Journal of Comparative Psychology*, 1990, *104*: 233–237.

14. Galef, B. G., and Whiskin, E. E. "Socially Transmitted Food Preferences Can Be Used to Study Long-Term Memory in Rats." *Learning & Behavior*, 2003, *31*: 160–164.

15. Birch, L. L., Shoba, B. C., Pirok, E., and Steinberg, L. "What Kind of Exposure Reduces Children's Food Neophobia? Looking vs. Tasting?" *Appetite*, 1987, *9*: 171–178.

16. Mason, S. J., Harris, G., and Blissett, J. "Tube Feeding in Infancy: Implications for the Development of Normal Eating and Drinking Skills." *Dysphagia*, 2005, *20*: 46–61.

17. Blossfield, I., Collins, A., Kiely, M., and Delahunty, C. "Texture Preferences of 12-Month-Old Infants and the Role of Early Experiences." *Food Quality and Preference*, 2007, *18*: 396–404. A study showing that the intake of textured food in the first year is determined mainly by prior experience.

18. Leathwood, P., and Maier, A. "Early Influences on Taste Preferences." *Nestlé Nutrition Workshop Series: Pediatric Program*, 2005, *56*: 127–141; Maier, A. "Influence des pratiques d'allaitement et de sevrage sur l'acceptation de flaveurs nouvelles chez le jeune enfant: variabilité intra- et inter-régionale." Thèse de Doctorat de l'Université de Bourgogne, 2007; Maier, A. S., Chabanet, C. S., Issanchou, S., Leathwood, P., and Schaal, B. "Breastfeeding and Experience with a Variety of Vegetables Increases Acceptance of New Flavors by Infants at Weaning." *Chemical Senses*, 2006, *31*: E5.

19. Shelov, S. P., ed. *Your Baby's First Year*. (2nd ed.) American Academy of Pediatrics. New York: Bantam Books, 2005, p. 275.

20. Breen, F. M., et al. "Heritability of Food Preferences in Children." *Physiology and Behavior*, 2006, *88*: 443–447.

21. Du Toit, G., et al. "Early Consumption of Peanuts in Infancy Is Associated with a Low Prevalence of Peanut Allergy." *Journal of Allergy and Clinical Immunology*, 2008, *122*: 984–991.

22. Shelov, S. P. *Your Baby's First Year,* p. 277.

23. Greer, F. R., et al. "Infant Methemoglobinemia: The Role of Dietary Nitrate in Food and Water." *Pediatrics,* 2005, *116*: 784–786.

24. Keating, J. P., Lell, M. E., Strauss, A. W., Zarkowsky, H., and Smith, G. E. "Infantile Methemoglobinemia Caused by Carrot Juice." *New England Journal of Medicine,* 1973, *288*: 824–826.

25. Sanchez-Echaniz, J., Benito-Fernandez, J., and Mintegui-Raso, S. "Methemoglobinemia and Consumption of Vegetables in Infants." *Pediatrics,* 2001, *107*: 1024–1028; Hack, W. W., Douwes, A. C., and Veerman, A. J. "Spinach: A Source of Nitrite Poisoning in Young Children." [in Dutch] *Nederlands Tijdschrift voor Geneeskunde,* 1983, *127*: 1428–1431; Faivre, J., Faivre, M., Klepping, C., and Roche, L. "Methemoglobinemias Caused by Ingestion of Nitrites and Nitrates." [in French]. *Annales de la Nutrition et de l'Alimentation,* 1976, *30*: 831–838; Ritter, R., and Schulze, U. "Methemoglobinemia in an Infant Following Nitrite Poisoning by a Dinner of Kohlrabi." [in German]. *Deutsch Krankenpflegez,* 1971, *24*: 233–235.

26. Dusdieker, L. B., et al. "Nitrate in Baby Foods: Adding to the Nitrate Mosaic." *Archives of Pediatrics and Adolescent Medicine,* 1994, *148*: 490–494.

27. Greer et al., "Infant Methemoglobinemia."

28. Fox, M. K., Pac, S., Devaney, B., and Jankowski, L. "Feeding Infants and Toddlers Study: What Foods Are Infants and Toddlers Eating?" *Journal of the American Dietetic Association,* 2004, *104*: s22–30.

29. Dandelski, J. R. *Marine Dead Zones: Understanding the Problem.* Congressional Research Service. Report for Congress 1998. "Hypoxia, the Gulf of Mexico's Summertime Foe." *Watermark.* Sept. 2004, *26*: 3–5; Berman, J. R., Arrigo, K. R., and Matson, P. A. "Agricultural Runoff Fuels Large Phytoplankton Blooms in Vulnerable Areas of the Ocean." *Nature,* 2005, *434*: 211–214.

30. Davis, D., Epp, M. D., and Riordan, H. D. "Changes in USDA Food Composition Data for 43 Garden Crops, 1950 to 1999." *Journal of the American College of Nutrition,* 2004, *23*(6): 669–682.

31. Benbrook, C., Zhao, X., Yanez, J., Davies, N., and Andrews, P. "New Evidence of the Nutritional Superiority of Organic Foods." *The Organic Center,* Mar. 2008. See also Brandt, K., and Molgaard, J. P. "Organic Agriculture: Does It Enhance or Reduce the Nutritional Value of Plant Foods?" *Journal of the Science of Food and Agriculture,* 2001, *81*: 924–931; Magkos, F., Arvaniti, F., and Zampelas, A. "Organic Food: Nutritious Food or Food for Thought? A Review of the Evidence." *International Journal of Food Sciences and Nutrition,* 2003, *54*(5): 357–371; Williams, C. M. "Nutritional Quality of Organic Foods: Shades of Grey or Shades of Green?" *Proceedings of the Nutrition Society,* 2002, *61*: 19–24; Worthington, V. "Nutritional Quality of Organic Versus Conventional Fruits, Vegetables, and Grains," *Journal of Alternative and Complementary Medicine,* 2001, *7*(2): 161–173.

Chapter 8: Becoming a Toddler

1. Fox, M. K., Pac, S., Devaney, B., and Jankowski, L. "Feeding Infants and Toddlers Study: What Foods Are Infants and Toddlers Eating?" *Journal of the American Dietetic Association,* 2004, *104*: S22–30.

2. Ibid.

3. Benton, D. "Role of Parents in the Determination of the Food Preferences of Children and the Development of Obesity." *International Journal of Obesity,* 2004, *28*: 858–869.

4. Ibid.

5. Prescott, J., Soo, J., Campbell, H., and Roberts, C. "Responses of PROP Taster Groups to Variations in Sensory Qualities Within Foods and Beverages." *Physiology and Behavior,* 2004, *82*: 459–469.

6. Keller, K. L., and Tepper, B. J. "Inherited Taste Sensitivity to 6-n-propylthiouracil in Diet and Body Weight in Children." *Obesity Research,* 2004, *12*: 904–912.

7. Visalberghi, E., and Addessi, E. "Seeing Group Members Eating a Familiar Food Enhances the Acceptance of Novel Foods in Capuchin Monkeys." *Animal Behavior,* 2000, *60*: 69–76.

8. Galef, B. G., and Kennett, D. J. "Different Mechanisms for Social Transmission of Diet Preference in Rat Pups of Different Ages." *Developmental Psychobiology,* 1987, *20*: 209–215; Galef, B. G., and Whiskin, E. E. "Social Influences on the Amount of Food Eaten by Norway Rats." *Appetite,* 2000, *34*: 327–332; Hikami, K., Hasegawa, Y., and Matsuzawa, T. "Social Transmission of Food Preferences in Japanese Monkeys (*Macaca fuscata*) After Mere Exposure or Aversion Training." *Journal of Comparative Psychology,* 1990, *104*: 233–237.

9. Wyrwicka, W. "Social Effects on Development of Food Preferences." *Acta Neurobiologiae Experimentalis,* 1993, *53*: 485–493.

10. Carruth, B. R., Ziegler, P. J., Gordon, A., and Barr, S. I. "Prevalence of Picky Eaters Among Infants and Toddlers and the Caregivers' Decisions About Offering a New Food." *Journal of the American Dietetic Association,* 2004, *104*: s57–64.

11. Food and Nutrition Board, Institute of Medicine, National Academies. "Dietary Reference Intakes (DRIs): Recommended Intakes for Individuals, Macronutrients." 2002.

12. Food and Nutrition Board, Institute of Medicine, National Academies. "Dietary Reference Intakes (DRIs): Recommended Intakes for Individuals, Elements." 2004.

13. U.S. Department of Agriculture, Agricultural Research Service. USDA National Nutrient Database for Standard Reference. SR21 dataset, 2008, Nutrient Data Laboratory Homepage, www.ars.usda.gov/ba/bhnrc/ndl.

14. American Academy of Pediatrics. "The Use and Misuse of Fruit Juice in Pediatrics." *Pediatrics,* 2007, *119*: 405.

15. Zeedyk, M. S. "What's Life in a Baby Buggy Like? The Impact of Buggy Orientation on Parent-Infant Interaction and Infant Stress." *The National Literacy Trust,* Nov. 2008, 1–35.

16. Morris, C. E., and Sands, D. C. "The Breeder's Dilemma—Yield or Nutrition?" *Nature Biotechnology,* 2006, *9*: 1078–1080.

17. Dantas, G., et al. "Bacteria Subsisting on Antibiotics." *Science,* 2008, *320*: 100.

18. Rule, A. M., Evans, S. L., and Silbergeld, E. K. "Food Animal Transport: A Potential Source of Community Exposure to Health Hazards from Industrial Farming (CAFOs)." *Journal of Infection and Public Health,* 2008, *1*: 33–39.

Chapter 9: Toddlers

1. National Center for Health Statistics. *Clinical Growth Charts, Set 1. Data Table of Weight-for-Age Charts.* May 30, 2000.
2. Roberts, S. B., and Heyman, M. B. *Feeding Your Child for Lifelong Health.* New York: Bantam Books, 1999, p. 163.
3. Skinner, J. D., Zieglar, P., Pac, S., and Devaney, B. "Meal and Snack Patterns of Infants and Toddlers." *Journal of the American Dietetic Association,* 2004, *104*: S65–70.
4. Nicklaus, S. "Development of Food Variety in Children." *Appetite,* 2009, *52*: 253–255.
5. American Heart Association, et al. "Dietary Recommendations for Children and Adolescents." *Pediatrics,* 2006, *117*(2): 544–559.
6. U.S. Department of Agriculture, Agricultural Research Service. USDA National Nutrient Database for Standard Reference, SR21 dataset, 2008, Nutrient Data Laboratory Homepage, www.ars.usda.gov/ba/bhnrc/ndl.
7. American Heart Association, et al. "Dietary Recommendations for Children and Adolescents." *Pediatrics,* 2006, *117*(2): 544–559.
8. Roberts and Heyman, *Feeding Your Child for Lifelong Health,* p. 178.
9. Bateman, B., Warner, J. O., Hutchinson, E., Dean, T., Rowlandson, P., Gant, C., Grundy, J., Fitzgerald, C., and Stevenson, J. "The Effects of a Double-Blind, Placebo-Controlled, Artificial Food Colourings and Benzoate Preservative Challenge on Hyperactivity in a General Population Sample of Preschool Children." Archives of Diseases in Childhood, 2004, *89*: 506–511.

Chapter 10: A Glimpse Ahead

1. Questions used in the Rhee study (note 3) include "How often do you expect your child to (1) sit or play quietly (or refrain from interrupting) while adults are having a conversation? (2) Be agreeable about an unexpected change in plans? (3) Accept a new babysitter or caregiver without complaint? (4) Be patient when trying to do something difficult? (5) Go to bed without a hassle? (6) Refrain from interrupting when you are on the telephone? (7) Show self-control when disappointed? (8) Stay in bed once put to bed? (9) Be on 'best behavior' when you are in public (church, store, bus, or train)? (10) Wait his or her turn without fussing? (11) Control anger outbursts (eg, no kicking, biting, and scratching)?"
2. Patrick. H., Nicklas, T. A., Hughes, S. O., and Morales, M. "The Benefits of Authoritative Feeding Style: Caregiver Feeding Styles and Children's Food Consumption Patterns." *Appetite,* 2005, *44*: 243–249.
3. Rhee, K. E., Lumeng, J. C., Appugliese, D. P., Kaciroti, N., and Bradley, R. H. "Parenting Styles and Overweight Status in First Grade," *Pediatrics,* 2006, *117*(6): 2047–2054.
4. Linn, S., and Novosat, C. L. "Calories for Sale: Food Marketing to Children in the Twenty-First Century." *The Annals of the American Academy of Political and Social Science,* 2008, *615*: 133–155.
5. Institute of Medicine Committee on Food Marketing and the Diets of Children and Youth. *Food Marketing to Children and Youth: Threat or Opportunity?* Washington, DC: The National Academies Press, 2006.

6. Eggerton, J. "Food-Marketing Debate Heats Up; Congress to Join FCC and FTC in Pressing for Action." *Broadcasting & Cable,* May 21, 2007. www.broadcastingcable .com/article/CA6444875.html. Accessed Dec 15, 2008.

7. Harrison, K. H., and Marske, A. L. "Nutritional Content of Foods Advertised During the Television Programs Children Watch Most." *American Journal of Public Health,* 2005, *9*: 1568–1574.

8. Robinson, T. N., Borzekowski, D.L.G., Matheson, D., and Kraemer, H. C. "Effects of Fast Food Branding on Young Children's Taste Preferences." *Archives of Pediatrics & Adolescent Medicine,* 2007, *161*: 792–797.

9. Borzekowski, D.L.G., and Robinson, T. N. "The 30-Second Effect: An Experiment Revealing the Impact of Television Commercials on Food Preferences of Preschoolers." *Journal of the American Dietetic Association,* 2001, *101*(1): 42–46.

10. Robinson, T. N., Saphir, M. N., Kraemer, H. C., Varady, A., and Haydel, K. F. "Effects of Reducing Television Viewing on Children's Requests for Toys: A Randomized Controlled Trial." *Journal of Developmental & Behavioral Pediatrics,* 2001, *22*(3): 179–184.

11. Linn and Novosat, "Calories for Sale," pp. 133–155.

12. Lugaila, T. "A Child's Day: 2000 (Selected Indicators of Child Well-Being)," in *Current Population Reports: U.S. Census Bureau,* 2003: 70–89.

13. U.S. Census Bureau, *Survey of Income and Program Participation, Who's Minding the Kids? Child Care Arrangements,* Spring 1999.

14. Nielsen, S. J., Siega-Riz, A. M., and and Popkin, B. M. "Trends in Energy Intake in U.S. Between 1977 and 1996: Similar Shifts Seen Across Age Groups." *Obesity Research,* 2002, *5*: 370–378.

15. U.S. Bureau of Labor Statistics, *Consumer Expenditures in 2003* (U.S. Department of Labor, 2003): at Table 6: Composition of Consumer Unit: Average Annual Expenditures and Characteristics, Consumer Expenditure Survey, 2003.

16. Council of Economic Advisors. "Teens and Their Parents in the 21st Century: An Examination of the Trends in Teen Behavior and the Role of Parental Involvement." 2000. Available at: http://clinton3.nara.gov/WH/EOP/CEA/html/Teens_Paper_Final. pdf. Accessed Dec. 7, 2008; Fonseca, H., Ireland, M., and Resnick, M. D. "Familial Correlates of Extreme Weight Control Behaviors Among Adolescents." *International Journal of Eating Disorders,* 2002, *32*: 441–448; Gillman, M. W., Rifas-Shiman, S. L., Frazier, A. L., et al. "Family Dinner and Diet Quality Among Older Children." *Archives of Family Medicine,* 2000, *9*: 235–240; Kandel, D. B., and Davies, M. "Epidemiology of Depressive Mood in Adolescents: An Empirical Study." *Archives of General Psychiatry,* 1982, *39*: 1205–1212; Kingon, Y. S., and O'Sullivan, A. L. "The Family as a Protective Asset in Adolescent Development." *Journal of Holistic Nursing,* 2001, *19*: 102–121; Koivisto Hursti, U. K. "Factors Influencing Children's Food Choice." *Annals of Medicine,* 1999, *31*(Sup. 1): 26–32; Neumark-Sztainer, D., Hannan, P. J., Story, M., Croll, J., and Perry, C. J. "Family Meal Patterns." *Journal of the American Dietetic Association,* 2003, *103*: 317–322; Neumark-Sztainer, D., Story, M., Ackard, D., Moe, J., and Perry, C. J. "Family Meals Among Adolescents: Findings from a Pilot Study." *Journal of Nutrition Education,* 2000, *32*: 335–340; Neumark-Sztainer, D., Story, M., Ackard, D., Moe, J., and Perry, C. J. "The 'Family Meal': Views of

Adolescents." *Journal of Nutrition Education,* 2000, *32*: 329–334; Neumark-Sztainer, D., Story, M., Hannan, P. J., and Moe, J. "Overweight Status and Eating Patterns Among Adolescents." *American Journal of Public Health,* 2002, *92*: 844–851; Neumark-Sztainer, D., Story, M., Hannan, P. J., Perry, C. L., and Irving, L. M. "Weight-Related Concerns and Behaviors Among Overweight and Nonoverweight Adolescents." *Archives of Pediatrics & Adolescent Medicine,* 2002, *156*: 171–178; Neumark-Sztainer, D., Wall, M., Story, M., and Fulkerson, J. "Are Family Meal Patterns Associated with Disordered Eating Behaviors Among Adolescents?" *Journal of Adolescent Health,* forthcoming; Neumark-Sztainer, D., Wall, M., Story, M., and Perry, C. J. "Correlates of Unhealthy Weight Control Behaviors Among Adolescents." *Health Psychology,* 2003, *22*: 88–98; Resnick, M. D., Bearman, P. S., Blum, R. W., et al. "Protecting Adolescents from Harm." *JAMA,* 1997, *278*: 823–832; Resnick, M. D., Harris, L. J., and Blum, R. W. "The Impact of Caring and Connectedness on Adolescent Health and Well-Being." *Journal of Paediatric Child Health,* 1993, *29*: 1–9; Videon, T. M., and Manning, C. K. "Influences on Adolescent Eating Patterns: The Importance of Family Meals." *Journal of Adolescent Health,* 2003, *32*: 365–373.

17. Borowsky, I. W., Ireland, M., Resnick, M. D. "Adolescent Suicide Attempts: Risks and Protectors." *Pediatrics,* 2001, *107*: 485–493.

18. Coon, K. A. "Relationships Between Use of Television During Meals and Children's Food Consumption Patterns." *Pediatrics,* 2001, *107*(1): E7.

19. Pereira, M. A., Kartasjov, A. I., Ebbeling, C. B., Van Horn, L., Slattery, M. L., Jacobs, D. R., and Ludwig, D. S. "Fast-Food Habits, Weight Gain, and Insulin Resistance (The CARDIA Study): 15-Year Prospective Analysis." *Lancet,* 2005, *365*: 36–42.

20. Pliner, P. "Cognitive Schemas: How We Can Use Them to Improve Children's Acceptance of Diverse and Unfamiliar Foods?" *British Journal of Nutrition,* 2008, *99*: S2–6.

21. American Dietetic Association. "Nutrition Fact Sheet: Lycopene—An Antioxidant for Good Health." www.eatright.org/cps/rde/xchg/SID-5303FFEA-A120B9BE/ada/hs.xsl/nutrition_5328_ENU_HTML.htm. Accessed Feb. 13, 2007; USDA Food and Nutrition Information Center. "Antioxidants, Phytochemicals and Functional Foods." Sept. 11, 2006. http://fnic.nal.usda.gov/. Accessed Feb. 13, 2007; Nutrition Data. "Nutrient Search Tool for the USDA's National Nutrient Database for Standard Reference." www.nutritiondata.com. Accessed Feb. 5, 2007. In a search of foods highest in lycopene, 38 out of the first 40 on the list were tomato products. Only watermelon and guava also made it into the top 40. The next important non-tomato-based sources are pink grapefruit at number 60 and red bell peppers at 91. Tomato sauce has over 50 times more lycopene per calorie than a red pepper. Catsup has 15 times more lycopene per calorie than a red pepper (and more than 50 times more lycopene per ounce). According to the USDA Food Consumption (Per Capita) Data System, www.ers.usda.gov/Data/FoodConsumption/, accessed Mar. 3, 2006, Americans on average eat only 13 pounds per year of watermelon, 7 pounds per year of all bell peppers (not just red bell peppers), and 7.9 pounds per year of all grapefruit (not just pink grapefruit). Per capita guava consumption is not available.

22. Ishida, B. K., and Chapman, M. H. "A Comparison of the Carotenoid Content and Total Antioxidant Activity in Catsup from Several Commercial Sources in the United States." *Journal of Agricultural and Food Chemistry,* Dec. 29, 2004, *52*(26).

23. Pliner, P., and Stallberg-White, C. "Pass the Ketchup Please; Familiar Flavours Increase Children's Willingness to Taste Novel Foods." *Appetite,* 2000, *34*: 95–103.

24. Skinner, J., Carruth, B. R., Bounds, W., and Ziegler P. J. "Children's Food Preferences: A Longitudinal Analysis." *Journal of the American Dietetic Association,* 2002, *102*(11): 1638–1647.

25. Cullen, K. W., Baranowski, T., Owens, E., Marsh, T., Rittenberry, L., and de Moor, C. "Availability, Accessibility, and Preferences for Fruit, 100% Fruit Juice, and Vegetables Influence Children's Dietary Behavior." *Health Education and Behavior,* 2003, *30*(5): 615–626; Hearn, M., Baranowski, T., Baranowski, J., Doyle, C., Smith, M., Lin, L. S., and Resnicow, K. "Environmental Influences on Dietary Behavior Among Children: Availability and Accessibility of Fruits and Vegetables Enable Consumption." *Journal of Health Education,* 1998, *29*(1): 26–32.

26. Hendy, H. M. "Effectiveness of Trained Peer Models to Encourage Food Acceptance in Preschool Children." *Appetite,* 2002, *39*: 217–225.

27. Birch, L. L. "Effect of Peer Models' Food Model Choices and Eating Behaviours on Preschoolers' Food Preferences." *Child Development,* 1980, *51*: 489–496.

28. Plassmann, H., O'Doherty, J., Shiv, B., and Rangel, A. "Marketing Actions Can Modulate Neural Representations of Experienced Pleasantness." *Proceedings of the National Academy of Sciences of the United States of America (PNAS),* 2008, *105*: 1050–1054.

29. Rolls, R. J., Engell, D., and Birch, L. L. "Serving Portion Size Influences 5-Year-Old but Not 3-Year-Old Children's Food Intakes." *Journal of the American Dietetic Association,* 2000, *100*(2): 232–234; Fisher, J. O., Rolls, R. J., and Birch, L. L. "Children's Bite Size and Intake of an Entree Are Greater with Large Portions Than with Age-Appropriate or Self-Selected Portions." *American Journal of Clinical Nutrition,* 2003, *77*(5): 1164–1170.

30. American Heart Association, et al. "Dietary Recommendations for Children and Adolescents." *Pediatrics,* 2006, *117*(2): 544–559.

31. Burger King. "U.S. Nutritional Information. Core Menu Items." Jan. 2008. www.bk.com/Nutrition/PDFs/brochure.pdf. Accessed Jan. 4, 2009.

32. Fisher, J. O., and Birch, L. L. "Restricting Access to a Palatable Food Affects Children's Behavioral Response, Food Selection and Intake." *American Journal of Clinical Nutrition,* 1999, *69*: 1264–1272.

33. Lappé, F. M. *Diet for a Small Planet, 20th Anniversary Edition.* New York: Ballantine Books, 1991. I'm also honored to have a copy of the original manuscript she submitted to her publisher. Thanks, Frankie!

34. Jacobson, M. F. *Six Arguments for a Greener Diet.* Washington, DC: Citizens for Science in the Public Interest, 2006.

The Author

A FATHER OF four, Alan Greene, M.D., F.A.A.P., has devoted himself to answering parents' questions about their children's health, combining science, practical wisdom, empathy, and a deep respect for parents, children, and the environment.

Dr. Greene is a graduate of Princeton University and the University of California at San Francisco. He entered primary care pediatrics in 1993, and is currently a clinical professor of pediatrics at Stanford University School of Medicine, attending pediatrician at Packard Children's Hospital, and a senior fellow at the University of California San Francisco Center for the Health Professions.

Dr. Greene is the author of *Raising Baby Green*, winner of the Nautilus Gold Medal for Best Parenting Book of the Year, and *From First Kicks to First Steps*. In 1995, he launched DrGreene.com, cited by the AMA as the "pioneer physician Web site" on the Internet. He has received the distinction of being one of "America's Top Doctors" for the past six years and was named the Children's Health Hero of the Internet by Intel.

Index

Page references followed by *p* indicate a photograph.